ACCOMMODATIONS
IN HIGHER EDUCATION UNDER THE
AMERICANS WITH DISABILITIES ACT (ADA)

Accommodations in Higher Education under the Americans with Disabilities Act (ADA)

A No-Nonsense Guide
for Clinicians, Educators, Administrators, and Lawyers

Edited by

Michael Gordon, PhD
Shelby Keiser, MS

Foreword by Alta Lapoint

GSI Publications
DeWitt, NY

and

The Guilford Press
New York   London

© 1998 GSI Publications
P.O. Box 746, DeWitt, NY 13214
Copublished with The Guilford Press
A Division of Guilford Publications, Inc.
72 Spring Street, New York, NY 10012

Printed in the United States of America

This book is printed on acid-free paper.

Last digit is print number: 9 8 7 6 5 4 3 2 1

Library of Congress Cataloging-in-Publication Data

Accommodations in higher education under the Americans with
    Disabilities Act (ADA) : a no-nonsense guide for clinicians,
    educators, administrators, and lawyers / edited by Michael
    Gordon, Shelby Keiser.
        p.   cm.
    Includes bibliographical references and index.
    ISBN 1-57230-359-X (hard)
    1. Disability evaluation—United States.   2. Handicapped college
students—Legal status, laws, etc.—United States.   I. Gordon, Michael,
PhD.   II. Keiser, Shelby.
RA1055.5.A28   1998
362.4´046—dc21   98-13963
                                                              CIP

To my parents, Ruth and Joseph Gordon,
for the gifts of life, love,
and a penchant for asking questions
                    —M.G.

To my family, for their love and support
                    —S.K.

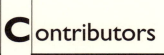Contributors

David A. Damari, OD, FCOVD, is an assistant professor at Southern College of Optometry in Memphis, TN. He teaches classes in Strabismus and Amblyopia, Vision Therapy, and Pediatric Visual Examination. He is an attending clinician at the Eye Institute of Southern College of Optometry and an examiner for the International Examination and Certification Board of the College of Optometrists in Vision Development.

James G. Frierson, MBA, JD, is an attorney and professor in the College of Business at East Tennessee State University in Johnson City. He is the author of over 150 articles and books, including the *Employer's Guide to the Americans with Disabilities Act* and *Preventing Employment Lawsuits: An Employer's Guide to Hiring, Discipline and Discharge.* He also contributed to the leading legal treatise on the ADA, *Disability Discrimination in Employment Law.*

Michael Gordon, PhD, is a professor of psychiatry and Director of the ADHD Program at SUNY Health Science Center in Syracuse, NY. Dr. Gordon is author of *How to Operate an ADHD Clinic or Subspecialty Practice* (GSI Publications, 1995) as well as numerous other books and articles about externalizing disorders. He is also developer of a test of attention and self-control that is used internationally.

Shelby Keiser, MS, is manager of the Office of Test Accommodations at the National Board of Medical Examiners. She is a member of the AHEAD Ad Hoc Committee on Documentation of Learning Disabilities and the Consortium on Documentation of ADHD. A former director of the Disabled Student Service Office at Harcum College in Bryn Mawr, PA, Ms. Keiser has served as a consultant in the diagnosis and remediation of reading and learning disabilities.

Barbara J. Lorry, PhD, is director of psychotherapy services at the Child Study Institute of Bryn Mawr College, Bryn Mawr, PA. Certified in psychology, school psychology, and as a reading specialist, Dr. Lorry teaches, consults, and conducts a private clinical practice in Bryn Mawr, PA.

Joan M. McGuire, PhD, is an associate professor in the Educational Psychology Department at the University of Connecticut, Director of the University Program for College Students with Learning Disabilities, and codirector of the Postsecondary Education Disability Unit. She is a coauthor of *Promoting Postsecondary Education for Students with Learning Disabilities: A Handbook for Practitioners* (Pro-Ed, 1993).

Kevin R. Murphy PhD, is an assistant professor of psychiatry and chief of the Adult Attention-Deficit Hyperactivity Disorder Clinic at the University of Massachusetts Medical Center in Worcester, MA. Dr. Murphy is a member of the Professional Advisory Board of CH.A.D.D. and has authored several articles and book chapters on adult ADHD. He has coauthored (with Suzanne LeVert) a book entitled *Out of the Fog: Treatment Options and Coping Strategies for Adult Attention Deficit Disorder* (Hyperion, 1995).

Edward Schweizer, MD, is an associate professor in the Department of Psychiatry at the University of Pennsylvania School of Medicine, Philadelphia, and Director of the Mood and Anxiety Disorders Research Unit.

Stanley F. Wainapel, MD, is clinical director of the Department of Rehabilitation Medicine at the Montefiore Medical Center and associate professor of clinical rehabilitation medicine at Albert Einstein College of Medicine, Bronx, NY. He has served as former president of the American Society of handicapped physicians and has published articles relating to physical disability among physicians.

Lauren Wylonis, MD, is currently chief resident in the Department of Psychiatry at the University of Pennsylvania School of Medicine in Philadelphia, PA. She will shortly be beginning a Forensic Psychiatry Fellowship at Case Western Reserve in Cleveland, Ohio.

Acknowledgments

From the outset, we have been intensely aware that the subject of accommodations is an unusually sensitive one, because it involves bedrock issues of decency, fairness, and money. It has therefore been of utmost importance to us that we approach this topic with as much accuracy and balance as we could possibly muster.

Toward that end we have relied heavily upon input not only from our contributors, but also from a large contingent of other professionals from many disciplines. They include Drs. Russell Barkley, Marla Brassard, Deborah Harmon Hines, Charles Cunningham, Dawn Flanagan, Sam Goldstein, Wendy Gordon, Synnove Heggoy, Martin Irwin, Howard Kane, George Litchford, Prakash Masand, Maria Nahmias, and Laura Rothstein. We also had outstanding help from Anna Brackett, Joan Fisher, David Fram, Lisa MacLachlan, Bob Matloff, Jon Reynolds, Jack Robertson, Louise Russell, and Seymour Weingarten.

We especially thank Drs. Jerry Golden and Larry Lewandowski for services that soared far beyond the call of normal duty and collegiality. We very much appreciate their boundless wisdom, support, and friendship.

Finally, we would like to acknowledge the expertise and cooperativeness of our contributors. They were good sports about our editorial intrusions and unreasonable expectations around deadlines. It was a pleasure collaborating with them.

MICHAEL GORDON, PhD
SHELBY KEISER, MS

F oreword

I dare say that I cherish the protections afforded by the Americans with Disabilities Act (ADA; 1990, PL 101-336) more than most. My appreciation is both personal and professional. Because I am physically disabled, I have benefited directly from all the many improvements in accessibility stipulated by the law. In fact, every time I approach a door in a public building, I have reason to be thankful for this legislation: A bout with polio left me with little use of my arms, thereby making it impossible for me to manipulate a round door knob. Because the ADA mandates automatic entryways and handicap-friendly handles, it has literally opened doors for me that would have otherwise remained shut.

The ADA and its legal predecessors have helped me in ways that extend well beyond improved access to public buildings. When I was first able to work, I was turned down for exactly 22 jobs as a receptionist, a position for which I was well qualified. What obviously deterred prospective employers was that I would have to use my feet to accomplish certain tasks. It was not until I became associated with a program sponsored by the Office of Vocational Rehabilitation that I could gain employment. That program was a direct result of the Rehabilitation Act of 1973, a legal forerunner of the ADA.

All of these antidiscrimination laws have assured me that I will not be hindered because of disabilities that are irrelevant to my job performance. While I would never look to the law to provide me with an excuse if I underperform, I can wake up every morning knowing that I am protected from discrimination simply because I have disabilities. This knowledge has allowed me to pursue a career that not long ago would have stretched well beyond my reach.

My experience with antidiscrimination laws is not simply as a "protected individual." For 18 years I have been deeply immersed in working with others who have disabilities. As best I can determine, I was the first person in the country to be hired full-time by a major employer to oversee disability services. My role as Coordinator of Disabilities Services means that I become involved whenever a disabled student, employee, patient, or visitor demonstrates a need for accommodations. If, for example, a deaf person is admitted to our medical school, I work with all involved to assess the student's needs and to ensure that the accommodations are properly designed and implemented. I also place employees, some with devastating disabilities, in positions that better allow their talents to flourish.

I could literally fill the pages of this book with true accounts of people who, without the ADA and the kinds of services I provide, would never have had the opportunity to become productive citizens. On any given day, I can walk down the halls of our medical center and point to dozens of disabled individuals who have become valued and, in some cases, beloved members of our student body, faculty, and hospital staff.

For example, our institution currently trains a young woman who is legally blind. She was the first severely visually handicapped medical student ever admitted to our school. Thanks to video microscopes, readers, faculty who consented to prepare materials in large type, the concerted efforts of counselors and aides, and her own inestimable talents, this student continues in an extended program.

Another former student of ours, although hearing impaired, had no problems during the first 2 years of training when most of his days were spent in classrooms or laboratories. In fact, no one was aware of his disability because he did not bring it to our attention and was faring well in our programs.

By the third year's initiation into clinical work, however, complaints from instructors and attendings began to mount. Concerns were voiced that he was inattentive during rounds and that his ability to use a stethoscope was severely limited. The situation deteriorated to the point that the student's medical career was in jeopardy. Fortunately he disclosed to our dean in charge of ADA compliance that he was unable to hear when standing (or running) in the bustle of a medical ward. He also could not make out heart sounds using standard equipment. To help accommodate him, the medical school purchased an amplified stethoscope and worked with the student to make better use of his hearing aids. We are all proud that he is now a fully functioning and successful physician.

With all my personal and professional involvement with the ADA, am I a diehard, unquestioning fan of this legislation? For the most part, I have been an on-site witness to its benefits. This law and the attitude toward disabilities it conveys have made a difference for many, many individuals. But I have also come to appreciate how laws, even laws as right-minded as the ADA, can have unintended effects. Let me give you one example: I recently worked with an employee who not long ago graduated from college with a degree in the biological sciences. Because of certain disabilities, he had been granted a full platter of accommodations by the college. These primarily involved unlimited time for taking tests and for completing lab work. Unfortunately, the demands of work life in the "real world" rarely allow for extra time, especially in a medical center where speed is often of the essence. Despite his college degree and our best efforts, this employee was absolutely unable to perform his laboratory duties at a reasonable pace. In my opinion, the generous accommodations he received during his training masked his fundamental inability to meet the requirements of most jobs in his field. In a sense, he had been overaccommodated and undercounseled. Judging from how devastated he was by his work experience, I wish that he had received (or perhaps listened to) advice earlier in his training about suitable careers.

The ADA is intended to help people who, with reasonable accommodations, are able to meet job demands. It is not a guarantee that every disabled person can work at any job he or she chooses, even if no amount of accommodations would allow for success. Sometimes, in our zeal to overcome disabilities, we set the stage for failure by placing ourselves or our clients in circumstances that are ultimately untenable. Goals that are set unrealistically high are just as dangerous as goals that are set too low. I hope we all learn to strive for the most that is possible, rather than for what may be desirable but unattainable.

Like many of my colleagues who coordinate ADA activities, I have also become deeply concerned about the number of individuals who demand accommodations even though their claims of disability are questionable. I would never want to deny someone with legitimate disabilities a chance to receive reasonable accommodations. However, the entire process is diminished when a law designed to protect the rights of the disabled is distorted by those with an oversized sense of entitlement.

One virtue of the book you're about to read is that it thoughtfully and fairly addresses the process by which clinicians, universities, and employers must come to terms with ADA mandates. The authors are neither exuberant cheerleaders nor jaded skeptics about this law or its ramifications. What comes across instead is their willingness to provide an honest and practical guide for all of us who are struggling with this pivotal and wide-reaching legislation.

ALTA LAPOINT
Coordinator of Disability Services, University of Massachusetts Medical Center
Member, Governor's Committee on the Employment of People with Disabilities
Member, Business Leadership Network of the President's Committee on the Employment of People with Disabilities

Preface

On a warm day in late July and flanked by a bipartisan throng, President George Bush signed the Americans with Disabilities Act of 1990 (ADA; PL 101-336) into law. For people with disabilities, this event has a significance not unlike what the Civil Rights Act of 1965 has for other minorities. Both were hard-fought pieces of legislation with similar aims: to guarantee rights to those of our citizens who are too often denied them. The two laws are regarded, and justifiably so, as towering landmarks in our country's efforts to eradicate discrimination and to promote equal opportunity.

Even though most of us know the ADA simply as "that law requiring wheelchair ramps and handicapped parking spaces," its impact extends far beyond inclined walkways and blue symbols on pavement. From the moment of its enactment, the ADA has had an extraordinary impact on the fabric of our society. It has forced powerful changes in the way our country hires and fires employees, designs buildings, and develops transportation systems. It also has sparked an explosion of litigation that has clogged our court system with remarkable numbers of antidiscrimination cases.

A lesser-known but increasingly visible consequence of the ADA concerns the pressures it has brought to bear on institutions of higher learning and on professional testing organizations. Because the law mandates that these entities are responsible for providing accommodations to disabled individuals, institutions across the country have been scrambling to comply. They have had to develop protocols for verifying that an individual indeed suffers from a disability. They also have been forced to determine what represents fair and reasonable accommodations for each potential form of impairment. This process has been complicated because the ADA and its attendant regulations and legal rulings have not been especially helpful in providing guidance. In fact, years after the actual implementation of the law in 1992, efforts to conform with its mandates are still clouded by ambiguity.

For these institutions, the ADA has meant more than simply developing methods for helping disabled individuals. More pressing is the sheer number of students and examinees who are seeking accommodations under the law. For example, the number of examinees petitioning for test accommodations on the New York State Bar examination has skyrocketed over the past 4 years. The situation is much the same at colleges and universities in every state. As an example, Cornell University has seen an almost three-fold rise in the number of students claiming a disability over the past 5 years. As one college administrator put it, "What was once a rare and simple process has become a monumental administrative enterprise."

The vast majority of ADA claims in higher education are based not on physical disabilities, but on learning and psychiatric disorders. In fact, while the proportions vary somewhat from setting to setting, physical disabilities usually represent only about one quarter of the claims. The rest are comprised of individuals who feel they suffer from what the ADA describes as "substantial limitation" in the ability to learn.

Regardless of what one might feel about the ADA as a piece of legislation, there can be no argument that it has been good business not only for lawyers, but also for clinicians and consultants of every stripe. Each student seeking accommodations consults a physician, psychologist, or other clinician to establish documentation of a disability. When that documentation is submitted to the academic institution or testing organization, they in turn may hire consultants to review the materials and to advise them whether accommodations should be granted. If an applicant disagrees with the determination, he or she will sometimes bring suit against the institution who, once again, will be forced to hire lawyers and expert witnesses. Even when the process is nonlitigious, it still requires all colleges, universities, and testing organizations to develop and finance a bureaucracy whose function is to oversee ADA-related activities.

While most lawyers have been keenly aware of the ADA and all its ramifications from the outset, most clinicians and administrators are just beginning to see its large footprint appear on the office floor. To be fair, it has only been within the past several years that sizeable numbers of students and examinees have sought ADA-style accommodations. Nonetheless, the pressure is now on for all of us who deal with students and examinees to understand the law in full.

This book is designed to bring clinicians and educators up to speed on the ADA's requirements for the preparation and review of disabilities documentation. It turns out that the law calls for standards of documentation that are different from what most of us typically confront. The conceptual underpinnings of those requirements are also at odds with many of the ideas that more commonly form the basis for determining diagnostic status and treatment recommendations. Our goal for the first chapter is to outline the overarching concepts of the law as it pertains to preparing and reviewing documentation. In each of the subsequent chapters, our contributors provide specific recommendations for conducting evaluations, writing reports, and interpreting information submitted for the major psychiatric, learning, and physical disorders that are frequently the basis for claims.

We want to emphasize as clearly as we possibly can that this book is about the *process* of identifying and accommodating disabilities under the ADA. It is not an effort to grind any particular ideological axe, to launch an attack on the law itself, or to raise questions about the legitimacy of these various disorders. As far as any of us are concerned, individuals with bona fide disabilities are entitled to and should receive reasonable accommodations if they are otherwise qualified. Period. All of the contributors in one way or another have a history of advocating for individuals with disabilities. We sincerely do not intend any of our comments to cast doubt on the fundamental importance of eradicating discrimination against those with genuine disabilities.

At the same time, we see it as critical that the process be kept as fair as possible for all the parties involved. Ultimately, no one is well served by a system that becomes arbitrary or chaotic. Maintaining a level of fairness is no easy task because of two inescapable realities: (1) the laws and regulations themselves are so open to interpretation, and (2) the diagnostic criteria for most disorders are anything but pristinely clear. Whenever the rules of a game are ambiguous, tussles over their application will inevitably ensue.

The players in this particular event also have agendas that are bound to collide. The disabilities community understandably wants to protect the rights of its constituents to reasonable accommodations. Many have fought hard to win that right for themselves, for their clients, and for disabled individuals generally. We have learned through repeated experience that disabilities advocates become nervous when we even discuss diagnostic standards. Although they may agree intellectually with the need for firm criteria, they fear that such standards can be misused to deny accommodations. We get the same sort of reaction from some educators who, by dint of their position, are more concerned about facilitating educational success than about verifying diagnostic decision trees.

Advocates are not the only ones who can become jittery when the topic of the ADA is broached. Many testing organizations and university officials fear that overly lax standards will dilute the integrity of their testing process, degree requirements, and overall academic mission. They worry aloud about criteria that might make it too easy for people who may not be truly disabled to gain accommodations. They also want to protect students who do not have disabilities from a form of reverse discrimination.

The ADA's implementation, then, involves a classic balancing of rights, in this case the right of the disabled to gain equal access and the right of educational/testing organizations to maintain academic integrity and freedom. When procedures for that implementation are examined, both sides manifest a kind of "slippery slope panic disorder," a fear that any tightening or loosening of the process, even when sensible, will set off a cascade of undesirable consequences. We approach this book with the intent of wending our way through the middle of the intersection at which those interests cross. We endeavor to offer a reasoned approach to this law, one that takes into account both its intent to level the playing field, but also its inherent safeguards against the field becoming tilted.

MICHAEL GORDON, PhD
SHELBY KEISER, MS

Contents

Contents

ESSENTIAL CONCEPTS/ ADMINISTRATIVE CONSIDERATIONS

1 | Underpinnings

Michael Gordon, PhD
Shelby Keiser, MS

INTRODUCTION

In this chapter we discuss the essential concepts that drive the provision of accommodations in higher education and professional testing. These principles form the basis for all of the chapters that follow. Indeed, what changes over the course of this book is simply the administrative function or clinical disorder to which they are applied.

Most of these concepts are straightforward and embody the epitome of common sense. Others may represent a departure from how you have traditionally viewed the process by which disabilities are identified and treated. At every turn we will attempt to provide a solid rationale for taking that alternate route.

Because our goal is not to provide a treatise on the Americans with Disabilities Act (ADA; 1990, PL 101-336), we will dispense with a full discussion of its historical roots, its place within the matrix of disability law, or its interpretation by courts and regulatory agencies. In the Resources section of this book, you will find references that provide this sort of information. Instead, we will state the proverbial bottom lines that, from our perspective, should hold sway when making ADA-related decisions.

One quick comment before we present these principles: Throughout this chapter we will make statements like, "According to the ADA . . . " or "The ADA dictates that . . ." While is some instances it will be clear that we are referring solely to the original act passed by Congress, in most cases we more accurately mean, "According to the ADA, its associated regulations, and the thrust of legal opinion." Repeating this phrase in every instance becomes unwieldy. Therefore, we generally use "ADA" as a catchword not only for the law itself, but also for its various interpretations by governmental and judicial agencies.

THE PRINCIPLES

- **Principle 1: The ADA is a civil rights act, not an entitlement program.**

Most of us who are involved in the assessment of disabilities/disorders have as our reference point the special education laws that have developed over the past 20 years. The most recent incarnation of these laws is called the Individuals with Disabilities Education Act (IDEA; 1975, PL 101-476). It represents an expansion and revision of the well-known Public Law 94-142 (the Education for All Handicapped Children Act of 1975), which legislated funding for special educational services in the "least restrictive environment."

Both of these laws entitle children with disabilities to a free and appropriate education that allows for achievement. While eligibility criteria for services vary from state to state, the basic concept is that poorly achieving children are entitled to remedial services that correct or circumvent deficiencies. Therefore, within this educational framework, funding is mandated that identifies children with significant problems and provides them with appropriate services that facilitate successful learning.

The Americans with Disabilities Act evolved from an entirely different tradition. It emerged from a series of workplace antidiscrimination laws and court rulings that trace their origins to the Civil Rights Act of 1964. That landmark legislation, of course, was designed to protect the rights of all citizens, regardless of race, color, or creed. Since that time, protections have been extended to ensure the rights of women, older Americans, and (with the passage of Section 504 of the Rehabilitation Act of 1973 [PL 93-112] and the Americans with Disabilities Act of 1990 [PL 101-336]) to individuals with disabilities. All of these laws were intended to eradicate discrimination against certain "protected" groups. In each case, Congress endeavored to level the playing field so that everyone had the same access and opportunity, unhindered by prejudice.

Clinicians who evaluate students requesting ADA-type accommodations must therefore understand that the concepts that form the nucleus of these antidiscrimination laws are fundamentally different from those at the heart of special education mandates. The educational model seeks to foster successful learning in students at the elementary and secondary levels. It reflects society's decision to provide services for poorly achieving children so that they might enjoy more positive outcomes.

In contrast, the antidiscrimination model is outcome-neutral. The ADA does not dictate that a student must pass every course or examination. The individual who contends, "Because I am learning disabled, you (the institution or test organization) must set conditions that allow me to pass" misreads the intent of the law and the thrust of the ensuing regulations.

The ADA guarantees that individuals who are otherwise qualified for jobs or educational programs will not be denied access simply because they have a disability. For example, it ensures that an individual with paraplegia, who is otherwise qualified to process insurance claims, has physical access to the office building where he works. His disability, because it does not affect his ability to perform the essential functions of the job, should not stand in the way of his employment.

By the same token, accommodations should not give that person an advantage over other employees for long-term hiring, promotions, or other job-related benefits. The intent of the law, again, was to level the playing field, not to tilt it. And, without a doubt, it was *not* designed to guarantee that the disabled individual find success on the job or during educational training. It is an outcome-neutral law that simply ensures that an individual with a disability will not be prevented from competing with others as long as he or she meets the same qualifications.

Many students, advocates, educators, and clinicians are confused about these fundamental differences between special education and antidiscrimination laws. If one does not understand those distinctions, for example, it becomes hard to fathom why a student who qualified for accommodations in secondary school may not be qualified under the ADA in college. It also can cause upset because ADA-compliance administrators must focus more on whether students have equal opportunity rather than on optimizing academic success.

What clinicians and educators must always keep in mind, then, is that the ADA is a civil rights act, not an entitlement program. No funding was mandated for remedial services, nor was it Congress's stated intent to ensure that everyone reach every goal. Unlike the education laws, the ADA was designed to ensure that individuals with a disability have access to places of learning and work. Its goal is to guarantee that individuals with legitimate disabilities are not discriminated against or denied equal access to the same programs, services and facilities available to others.

- **Principle 2: To be protected by the ADA, an individual must be disabled relative to the general population.**

The Americans with Disabilities Act was crafted to protect the rights of individuals who qualify as "disabled." The law defines disability as follows:

> The term disability means, with respect to an individual, a physical or mental impairment that substantially limits one or more of the major life activities of such individual, a record of such an impairment; or being regarded as having such an impairment.

Like many laws passed by Congress, the actual meaning of many key phrases is left wide open to interpretation. What constitutes a "physical or mental impairment" or a "major life activity"? Is taking an examination a "major life activity"? Are weaknesses in written expression a handicap for someone in a program that requires little writing? And, even more importantly, how impaired does an individual have to be to meet the standard of a "substantial limitation?" Is someone "substantially" limited if he can't read as quickly as classmates in a professional school? Can a former high school valedictorian claim to be substantially limited because she expected to get A's in college but graduated with a B– average? Can a right-handed individual consider himself disabled if he's missing three fingers on his left hand?

The federal agencies charged with writing regulations based on the ADA's definition of disability have provided guidance for such determinations. To begin with, the regulations and ensuing case law have established that limitations of "major life activities" include learning and mental disorders. In guidelines published by the Equal Employment Opportunity Commission (EEOC), "major life activities" are defined as "functions such as caring for oneself, performing manual tasks, walking, seeing, hearing, speaking, breathing, learning, and working." The "learning and working" functions are the basis for considering individuals with learning disabilities, attention deficit disorders, and various other psychiatric disorders to be qualified as disabled under the law.

For clinicians and administrators, the most important clarifications have defined what constitutes "substantial limitation." These explanations are crucial because determinations of disability under the ADA ultimately turn on assessments of severity, not necessarily on the precise classification of the disorder itself. For example, many individuals experience periods of deep sadness during the course of their lives. At what point does sadness become a depression serious enough to warrant consideration as a disability? Without some reasonable standard against which impairment can be judged, the process can quickly become a diagnostic free-for-all in which individuals with relatively minor skill weakness or emotional upsets are deemed disabled under the law and entitled to accommodations.

Understanding the regulatory guidelines for defining "substantial limitation" is central to grasping how characterizations of disability under this legal framework can differ from special education procedures and psychiatric diagnosis. According to these regulations, one judges limitations compared to what is common *to most people* in the population. To quote EEOC language, "An individual is not substantially limited in a major life activity if the limitation does not amount to a significant restriction when *compared with the abilities of the average person* [italics added]." The regulations from the Department of Justice make a similar clarification.

The regulations illustrate this principle by stating that "an individual who had once been able to walk at an extraordinary speed would not be substantially limited in the major life activity of walking if, as a result of a physical impairment, he or she were only able to walk at an average speed, or even at moderately below average speed." This statutory language was intended to ensure that the ADA covered serious disabilities and not those that were minor or trivial.

Establishing the general population as the norm against which to judge impairment has profound implications for determinations of disabilities in postsecondary education. Perhaps its import is best highlighted with an example (loosely adapted from an actual case): James S. is a dental student who had successfully completed 2 years of dental school. Along with his classmates, he took the first of a series of board examinations that are required for graduation and, ultimately, for licensure. To his dismay, he failed the exam. Undaunted, he studied even harder, but, upon the next administration, he still did not pass. At this point, the dean's office notified him that he would be placed on suspension until he successfully completed the exam.

To explore his options, James met with the dean, who in turn suggested that he make an appointment with a psychologist specializing in learning disabilities. After taking a brief history, the clinician administered a series of psychological and educational tests to determine if James had a learning disability.

The results indicated that James had an IQ in the superior range and generally strong abilities across the board. The one exception came in a measure of reading speed, which put him in the average to low-average range. The specialist concluded that James was learning disabled in reading because of the discrepancy between his overall IQ and the measure of reading speed. He then suggested that James petition the organization that administers the board exam for special accommodations under the ADA. Specifically, the report recommended that James receive twice the allotted time to complete the exam.

After reviewing the documentation, the testing organization determined that, according to the ADA definition of disability, James was not disabled. His request for accommodations was therefore denied. In his letter, the administrator indicated that, while the testing did demonstrate an isolated fall-off in an important skill, it was only a relative weakness that did not have a significant impact on James's overall functioning or ability to learn. In fact, his scores in reading speed still fell within a range that, in ADA terms, was "typical of the average person."

By setting "average abilities of most persons" as the standard, the federal regulatory agencies adopted a benchmark that again departs from the educational tradition represented by PL 94-142 and IDEA. For determining learning disabilities in elementary and secondary school students, most states allow discrepancies between aptitude and achievement to serve as the basis for establishing eligibility. If our dental student were still in sixth grade and experienced failure, he likely could qualify for services because his achievement in one area significantly departed from his overall level of intellectual functioning. While IDEA still requires evidence of impairment, it does allow states leeway in setting standards based on relative weaknesses. But for ADA-type determinations, the government has indicated that deficits must be judged relative to the average level of performance within the general population.

Judging comparisons against what is typical of "most people" may also unlink clinical diagnoses from ADA-related designations. While psychiatric diagnoses require "clinically significant impairment," that determination is very much left open to the clinician's discretion. In moderate to severe cases of a disorder, "clinically significant impairment" (the DSM-IV language) and "substantial limitation relative to the general population" (ADA-regulatory language) may overlap, and thus amount to the same declaration of abnormality.

But clinicians also may render a diagnosis (and perhaps dispense treatment) even if a patient does not meet all the established criteria for the pervasiveness, chronicity, or severity of the core symptoms. Practitioners may decide to treat these milder or subclinical variants of a disorder because they sense that the patient suffers sufficiently to warrant some intervention. It becomes a decision left to the judgment of doctor and patient. However, while it may be wholly justified to identify and treat symptoms that fall in the margins between normality and abnormality, it may also be inappropriate to declare that they rise to the level of impairment required by the ADA. Theoretically, a patient could be treated for a disorder, but still not qualify as disabled under the law.

Is it fair to use the average person as a standard for determinations of abnormality? A full answer to this thorny question falls well beyond the scope of this book. But we will comment just enough to pique your interest in the many issues that arise in this arena: Some argue that establishing the "average person standard" essentially precludes most students in higher education from being granted accommodations for learning and attentional disorders. After all, how likely is it that someone could gain entry into a competitive college or graduate/professional school if certain key skills fell in the lower reaches of the normal curve? Not very. Almost by definition, individuals who are accepted to college are high functioning relative to the general population.

Some therefore contend that a person should be declared disabled on the basis of weaknesses that are either relative to his or her overall functioning or to peers at the same educational level. In this way, more subtle forms of disorders can serve as justification for providing accommodations. Using standards that are relative to one's own mosaic of abilities or to an educational cohort, our mythical dental student would qualify for accommodations. Even though all his abilities were at least average, compared to classmates in dental school, he would be impaired.

On the opposite side of the fence are those who see the "average person standard" as the only sensible one to adopt in disabilities determinations. They point out that, if deficits can be determined relativistically, you are as disabled as the company you keep. For instance, if someone with average math skills decided to enter a program in nuclear physics, he could conceivably be declared "disabled" because his math skills would likely fall far below what was typical of most students in that program. Advocates for the more conservative stance assert that the law was not intended to guarantee that people succeed in programs even if their skills might not be best suited to those particular educational demands. These advocates worry aloud that such a broad definition of disability could encompass much of the population. The concern is that the ADA will transform from an antidiscrimination law to one that seeks to ensure academic and occupational success without regard to performance standards and essential job functions.

More liberal definitions of impairment may also risk trivializing the entire notion of disability, especially for learning and psychiatric disorders. If Robert has thoroughly normal abilities but claims to have a disability simply because he wants to graduate from a program that requires certain superior skills, is that fair? Can someone be disabled even if all of their cognitive abilities are at least average?

Consider the following analogy: Sam asks his physician to sign a document declaring him disabled so he can obtain a handicapped parking sticker. Sam justifies that claim because he is an average thrower, but a spectacularly fast runner. His argument is that the discrepancy between those abilities represents a physical disability. We assume that most physicians would not buy this argument. But, in many ways, this is the same logic some clinicians use to justify a determination of a learning disability for someone with at least average abilities.

The ultimate fear, of course, is that skepticism will mount to such a degree that people with serious disorders will have their rights curtailed. Associated with this concern is that time, money, and energies will be devoted to higher functioning individuals like Robert, to the detriment of those with more profound disabilities.

Regardless of one's view of its fairness, the "average person" comparison appears to be the yardstick against which impairment is being judged. You will find that authors of subsequent chapters keep returning to this concept because it underlies the basis for defining impairment for the full range of disorders.

Before moving on to the next principle, we want to address an issue that routinely emerges in debates over the ADA. When many encounter the law's relatively stringent criteria for disability, they ask some version of the following questions: "Why should we be so concerned about enforcing these strict criteria? Doesn't a good and decent society help all of its citizens maximize their potential? Why do ADA administrators want to deny help to people who might benefit from it?"

We do not think anyone would question the benefits of social and educational policies that allowed all individuals to fulfill their potential. It just turns out that this legislation was not designed to pursue that particular ideal. Also, as we point out throughout this book, there are worthy objectives that compete with individual prerogatives: protection of public safety and the rights of those who do not seek accommodations. We also wonder whether declaring someone disabled is always the best method for ensuring that a student receives an appropriate education.

- **Principle 3: Successful compensation belies substantial impairment.**

Clinicians who advocate for the provision of accommodations to a generally high functioning student have to contend with this question: If Susan is so impaired by a learning disability that she requires a note taker and extra time on examinations for professional school, how was she able to graduate from high school at the top of her class and then from college with a B average (without ever requiring accommodations)? Typically, the evaluator accounts for high functioning by claiming that the student was only successful because of hard work or high intelligence. The practitioner will write something to this effect: "Susan was able to adjust because she was so motivated to achieve and worked much harder than her classmates. Now that she is in graduate school, she requires accommodations because the work is becoming so demanding."

We generally assume that "substantial impairment" means that an individual is currently significantly restricted in the ability to function relative to others *despite* reasonable attempts at compensation. What characterizes true disability is that efforts at compensation go far beyond what most of us endure in daily life. Furthermore, compensatory efforts are often unsuccessful in allowing for normal functioning. We are not entirely sure that having to work hard is, by itself, sufficient evidence of a disability. Indeed, most if not all of us have had to struggle in school and at our vocations in those areas that we find more daunting.

What often becomes a judgment call in disability determinations for learning and psychiatric disorders concerns this notion of "reasonable attempts at compensation." At what point do efforts at compensation travel beyond the struggles most of us endure to keep our jobs and run our lives? Is striving to overcome weakness in certain skills a sign of disability? Might it not be an indication that sometimes educational mastery requires unusually hard work? If someone stumbles in a post-secondary program, is it possible that the failure points more to the need for career counseling than for disabilities accommodations? Usually, claims of disability in well-compensated individuals are only convincing if the individual pays an enormous price for being able to compensate.

We should also point out that someone who performs well enough *without special accommodations* to gain admission to a postgraduate program is likely not disabled in ADA terms even if he begins to encounter failure. Why? Because someone who achieves well enough to reach this high level of education is already functioning better than most people. It is therefore likely that such an individual would not meet the "substantial limitation relative to the general population" standard we discussed in Principle 2.

Another question arises when evaluating someone for a disability: "If a person with a legitimate and well-documented disability has generally been able to compensate successfully, is he or she still disabled and entitled to accommodation?" Let's say that Sally meets all accepted criteria for severe myopia. Without her contact lenses, the world is but a blur of images. But with corrective lenses, her vision is at least average. Is she disabled? What if Jerry suffered from a severe anxiety disorder but now, thanks to psychotropic medication and counseling, he consistently fares well? Is he still disabled?

You will read in the following chapters that, generally, clinicians are required to demonstrate that the patient is *functionally impaired under current circumstances*. Even though Sally meets criteria for a clinical diagnosis of myopia, the successful correction of that eye disorder means that she may not require accommodations. An individual can suffer from a disability but not need accommodations in certain circumstances. In Jerry's case, too, if his anxiety disorder remains in check over time with the help of psychiatric treatment, he may not require accommodations, even though he may still meet diagnostic criteria.

- **Principle 4: The process of qualifying an individual as disabled under the ADA requires current, detailed, and professional documentation.**

Many educational institutions and testing organizations have written policies that dictate general requirements for documentation. Although we have not conducted a formal survey of such policies, our impression is that they commonly involve three elements. First, most institutions stipulate that the documentation not be more than 3 or 4 years old. The requirement that the documentation be up to date reflects the need to establish current impairment. The impact of symptoms for any particular disorder can vary over time and depend upon current circumstances.

The second component of most policies requires that evaluations be conducted by a qualified professional. Who qualifies as a professional depends on the nature of the disorder and standards for training in that particular field. The general expectation is that people conducting evaluations have terminal degrees in their profession and are fully trained in differential diagnosis. Finally, documentation policies usually stipulate that the professional use procedures that conform with prevailing standards of practice. For psychiatric and learning disorders, these standards involve, at a minimum, diagnostic criteria established by the DSM-IV (American Psychiatric Association, 1994).

Regardless of what any particular policy requires, they almost all expect that the student/examinee provide documentation sufficient to allow for careful administrative review. Our experience is that some clinicians are uncomfortable about being asked to justify their diagnoses and recommendations. They feel that their clinical conclusions alone should be adequate. It is not uncommon for requests for accommodations to be scrawled on prescription pads. Few institutions will accept a simple statement confirming the diagnosis and accommodations request.

What professionals must take to heart is that the ADA determinations are quasi-legal enterprises that have meaningful consequences for all involved. They can affect grades, licensure, academic requirements, testing procedures, and employment policies. Designations of disability can also cost an institution or society at large considerable sums of money.

For these reasons, judges have supported the institution's right to review the merits of each individual case in detail. Indeed, we can find nothing that entitles accommodations on demand without credible supporting evidence. In this regard, ADA determinations follow in the same tradition as applications for Workers' Compensation and the Social Security Insurance program.

- **Principle 5: Institutions are required to provide accommodations only to those individuals who meet the essential functions of a job or educational program.**

The ADA was intended to protect individuals who were "otherwise qualified" to perform the "essential functions" of a job. In essence, the law says that you cannot discriminate against someone who is capable of working, simply because of non-job-related hindrances imposed by the disability. Congress wanted to protect an individual with a disability from being considered unqualified because of the inability to perform marginal or incidental job functions. The illustration we used in Principle 1 involved an insurance claims adjuster with paraplegia who was perfectly able to handle the job as long as he could gain access to the office building. If the employer can make reasonable accommodations that do not cause the company undue hardship, that employee's needs must be addressed.

But the flip side of the "otherwise qualified" and "essential functions" language also holds sway. An employer or institution is not required to accommodate individuals who, for whatever reason, are unable to perform essential job-related tasks. A common example offered is that of a blind person who wants to become a bus driver. Clearly, someone without vision is unable to perform the essential functions inherent in being a bus driver. No type or amount of accommodation would enable such a person to operate the vehicle safely.

You will find that the "otherwise qualified" language colors decisions made by clinicians and administrators alike. Here's a typical scenario: James, the dental student in our example from Principle 2, has a classmate, Carol. Unlike James, Carol has experienced academic difficulties far more serious than simply failing the dental board exam. She could not pass many of the basic science courses during the first

2 years. Her clinical supervisors also expressed concern about her lack of competence in performing certain important procedures.

Carol put forth so much effort to succeed that she became depressed, anxious, and had trouble concentrating. In desperation, she consulted a local psychologist who administered psychological testing, the results of which indicated that her IQ fell in the low-average range. Almost all of her skills tested far below what is typical of dental students and some even dipped below the abilities of the average American. Nonetheless, the psychologist recommended to the dental school that the student be accorded accommodations under the ADA.

Is the dental school obligated to provide accommodations? To be honest, we're not entirely sure what a judge would rule. Our sense is that the school could make the argument that Carol was not qualified to perform the essential functions associated with being a dental student. And how could they accommodate to such skill limitations? The school could further contend that Carol would be far better off seeking a career more suited to her abilities.

These cases of individuals who may not be qualified for jobs or educational programs (but who still request accommodations) are terribly complicated both on legal and interpersonal grounds. Much of the difficulty swirls around balances between the individual's rights to employment or education and the rights of others to be safe and well served. While it may be proper to afford someone like Carol all possible opportunities to graduate, is it not also fair to protect future patients from a dentist or doctor who may not be competent?

To take this matter further: Should a policeman with an impulse control disorder be allowed to carry a gun? What should be done about an air traffic controller with severe attention deficits? Or a postal worker with an explosive personality? Or a teacher who is often severely paranoid or delusional? We certainly do not have the answers to these questions because they ultimately hinge on individual circumstances. But the ADA will increasingly force employers, institutions, and judges to balance the rights of the disabled with those of coworkers, colleagues, and potential clients.

- **Principle 6: Accommodations should only address the interactions between functional impairments and task demands.**

Accommodations are generally viewed as assistive devices or adaptations that serve to ease the impact of the disability on a particular activity. For example, ramps and curb cuts are common accommodations for individuals who use wheelchairs. These architectural alterations allow access to buildings and other areas. For people with learning disabilities, use of a word processor and spell checker are accommodations that can ease the effect of impaired expressive language skills or written communication.

If a clinician determines that an individual is indeed qualified as disabled under the ADA, the next step is to identify reasonable accommodations. Those accommodations must be justified based upon two considerations: (1) the specific nature of the person's functional impairment, and (2) the educational or testing environment in which that individual will be functioning. The evaluator must provide a rationale for any recommended accommodations and must explain how those adjustments or technical aids would cancel or ease the impact of the impairment on the task in question.

Accommodations are task-specific and are meant to eliminate or reduce the impact of the impairment on a particular activity. Thus, an individual who must dictate test answers because of a limitation in his ability to write would not need accommodations for oral examinations. Likewise, an individual who requires a ramp to access a building because of limited ability to walk would not need additional time to complete cognitive tasks, such as assignments or examinations. In essence, there must be a demonstrated match between the disability and the task requirements.

Our point here is that assignment of a diagnostic label does not mean that the individual is automatically entitled to accommodations. The clinician must identify the specific functional limitations and recommend effective accommodations to ease those limitations as they might emerge in a particular testing or academic situation. For example, someone with multiple sclerosis might be unable to write or type fluently. In a lecture class, the reasonable accommodation might be the provision of a note taker. In a testing situation, a sensible accommodation might be to allow the student to speak into a tape recorder. If the test happened to require marking a scanning form, perhaps the accommodation would be to permit the student to write the answers in a test booklet so that a proctor could transfer them to the form at the end of the test. But if the test were an oral examination, the student would clearly not require accommodations because his or her limitations involve writing, not speaking or listening.

Sometimes students request accommodations that are simply not in keeping with the nature of the functional impairment. To give an example: Roger submits documentation to a licensing organization that he suffers from irritable bowel syndrome. He makes two requests for accommodations. First, he wants to be seated near the restroom because he may need to use it often during the course of the day. The test organization has no problem granting this request. But Roger also wants double the allotted time to take the examination. Here the ADA administrator balks. What are the functional impairments associated with irritable bowel syndrome that would require extra time to work on the test? While off-the-clock breaks may be justified, it is hard to provide a rationale for extended time working on the test itself. Accommodations must flow logically from a specific assessment both of the disability and of the task demands.

Another key concept in justifying accommodations relates back to the outcome neutrality of these antidiscrimination laws. Under Section 504 and ADA, the explanation that someone "would benefit from" a particular accommodation is not sufficient. As we have repeatedly indicated, the intent of the law is not to guarantee success in a particular program or endeavor. This stance is eloquently described in an opinion by the Office of Civil Rights in the *Golden Gate University (CA)* case (9NDLR 182) on July 10, 1996. In this instance, a student asserted the right to accommodations so that he could achieve a certain grade:

> [The student] appears to be of the misapprehension that the duty to provide academic adjustments includes a responsibility to provide such adjustments until a certain outcome is achieved, e.g., a grade of A. This is not what was contemplated by the OCR regulations. The objective is to create equal opportunity, not equal outcomes. Tests are modified to achieve greater validity not higher grades. Indeed, the regulation implementing Section 504 explicitly states that services provided by recipients, "to be equally effective, are not required to produce the identical result or level of achievement for disabled and nondisabled persons, but must afford disabled persons equal opportunity to obtain the same result, to gain the same benefit, or to reach the same level of achievement."

The focus of an accommodation request should therefore *not* be on what would help the individual pass the exam or have greater success meeting course requirements. The orientation instead should be toward accommodations that would correct or circumvent functional impairments that might otherwise preclude a fair opportunity to take a course or sit for an examination.

To return to the example of the student with multiple sclerosis: Let's say she was granted the accommodation of taking her comprehensive examinations for graduate school using a scribe for recording answers. This accommodation was deemed wholly reasonable because her disorder led to a functional impairment in writing that could be fairly accommodated through dictation.

It turns out that, even with accommodations, she failed the examination and then petitioned the graduate school for both a scribe *and* extra time on the next administration. She based her claim on the fact that she failed the exam initially because she did not have enough time. She writes in the application, "Having a scribe was not enough to help me pass the test. Now I need extra time so I have more time to think about my answers." We would imagine that the ADA officer would have trouble with this approach. The law does not mandate that accommodations should be applied until success is achieved. If the applicant could prove that dictating the answers took too much time, perhaps the request or some other reasonable accommodation would be granted. Otherwise, her application would likely be denied.

Before leaving this principle, we want to draw an important distinction between legal and informal accommodations in academic settings: We assume that institutions in the business of educating students want them to learn. Some students, of course, are able to master the material without special assistance, while others, for whatever reason, require a more tailored education. Indeed, ADA or no ADA, many programs have for years gone out of their way to provide any reasonable help necessary to facilitate academic progress. We would guess that the same can be said for many executives who, laws aside, find it both humane and profitable to help employees with special needs become more productive. Institutions are free to aid their students and employees as much as they wish, even to an extent far beyond the dictates of legal mandates.

Academic institutions will, of course, vary in the standards they set to determine who does and does not qualify for informal accommodations. For example, some institutions may concentrate on providing their students with marketable workplace skills as opposed to directing them toward graduate-level education. With a mission geared more toward employability, these colleges may place greater focus on a successful learning outcome and find it appropriate to provide remedial and other assistance as necessary to foster their goals. However, other postsecondary programs and testing organizations may have mandates that justify setting different criteria for accommodations.

This distinction is important because the history of past accommodations often weighs heavily in new requests for accommodations, especially for learning disabilities and ADHD. That an individual has received accommodations in the past may serve as evidence of long-standing impairment. It also may suggest what would be reasonable accommodations for the current circumstances. For example, a high school student unable to read may have always required materials to be read on an audiotape. That same accommodation may make sense when he goes to college. Problems can arise, however, when prior accommodations were based on looser criteria or within different educational contexts. For this reason, some students are surprised when accommodations that were quickly granted for one program are not provided in another.

IN CLOSING . . .

To understand the ADA, many of us have to think about impairment in ways that are foreign and perhaps uncomfortable. The law essentially requires us to unlink many concepts that we normally intertwine. Clinicians, for example, are apt to equate a diagnosis with a disability. For ADA determinations, however, those two terms are not synonymous. Similarly, special educators typically view a diagnostic label as a means of securing services so that youngsters can achieve to the fullest. Again, the ADA forces a contrasting consideration of disability that can easily lead to different results. The challenge to all of us, the contributors to this book very much included, is to adjust to this antidiscrimination framework in a manner that is consistent and equitable.

REFERENCES

American Psychiatric Association. (1994). *Diagnostic and statistical manual of mental disorders* (4th ed.). Washington, DC: Author.

2 | Educational Accommodations: A University Administrator's View

Joan McGuire, PhD

INTRODUCTION

Students with disabilities are enrolling in postsecondary educational settings more than ever before. According to recent data gathered by the American Council on Education (Henderson, 1995), the segment of the college population with disabilities that has witnessed the most growth involves those with learning disabilities (LD). In 1988, 15.3% of full-time college freshmen with disabilities indicated a learning disability. By 1994, that figure had more than doubled to 32.2% of incoming freshmen with disabilities. Further swelling the ranks of students seeking accommodations has been a surge in those who indicate attention-deficit/hyperactivity disorder (ADHD).

This chapter familiarizes the reader with the role of the postsecondary disability service administrator in assuring equitable treatment of students with disabilities. Because LD, ADHD, and other psychiatric disabilities now predominate the pool of students who seek accommodations, I will focus much of my discussion on them. These "invisible" disorders also pose special challenges for the administrator trying to determine if accommodations are reasonable and fair.

ROLES OF A DISABILITY SERVICE ADMINISTRATOR

The disability service administrator (DSA) wears many different professional hats. Individuals in this role must possess skills and knowledge in the areas of administration, direct service, consultation/collaboration, and institutional awareness. They must also engage in professional development activities if they are to keep abreast of the critical issues in the field (Madaus, 1998). In a survey of DSAs conducted in 1993 by the Association on Higher Education and Disability (AHEAD), approximately one quarter (26.1%) of the respondents (*n* = 897) indicated their primary role was as administrator, followed by service director (20.7%), service provider (15.9%), counselor (12.7%), or LD specialist (8.8%).

The DSA interacts with students on a regular basis. Whether in the initial intake interview or as part of an ongoing supportive relationship, the disability service administrator occupies a pivotal role in ensuring equal access within the context of reasonable accommodations. On any given day, the administrator of an office for disability services encounters a remarkable range of situations that require attention. Here is a sampling of events that might confront an administrator during the course of a normal week:

- A student requests a sign language interpreter and note takers because of a profound hearing loss.
- A student who self-identifies with a learning disability one week prior to final exams seeks extended test time.
- A student files a complaint regarding physical accessibility to a campus building.
- A student with a bipolar disorder wants to apply for clinical placement in a local hospital.
- A student with ADHD wants a reduced course load and testing accommodations on the basis of a note from her pediatrician.
- A student with LD wants the same accommodations he received in high school (i.e., oral essay exams, no foreign language, and no penalty for misspelled words in writing assignments) when the documentation substantiating his request is shaky at best (Korbel & Lucia, 1996).

The DSA is often the only professional on campus with direct responsiblity for overseeing day-to-day operations of the office that is the "clearinghouse" for disability-related services. While the campus might also employ an ADA (American with Disabilities Act; 1990, PL 101-336) compliance officer and perhaps a counselor who offers personal and academic advice, most daily decisions rest with the DSA.

The "essential functions" of the job of a disability service administrator are manifold. These include:

- Determining a student's eligibility for protection under the ADA.
- Analyzing documentation to ensure that it reasonably supports the claim of disability.
- Deciding the nature of a reasonable accommodation on a case-by-case basis.
- Developing institutional policies and procedures.

Some decisions are relatively easy because of the nature of the disability. Physical disabilities are often simpler to verify and the accommodations are more obvious. However, even in this arena complexities arise. For example, although a wheelchair user must be assured physical access to an institution's programs and services, the ADA does not require every existing facility to be fully accessible (Harris, Horn, & McCarthy, 1994).

Other decisions are less clear and, in fact, often cross into controversial areas. We live in an era of expanded awareness among consumers about the rights of persons with disabilities. Many professionals are quick to provide consumers with a diagnosis, especially LD and ADHD. Often the documentation is inadequate or contains conclusions that are poorly justified.

The job of the DSA is further complicated because many consumers and professionals view disability as an entitlement. They frequently request a laundry list of accommodations, many of which bear no relationship to the stated disability. The disability service administrator is often in the position of having to educate students and their evaluators about the fundamental assumptions underlying the ADA.

Because institutions of higher education have the obligation to maintain their academic standards, another role of a DSA is to provide technical assistance to faculty and administration. That assistance can cover many areas: educating them about the requirements of the law, helping academic programs formulate technical standards for participation, and guiding the process by which eligible students are afforded reasonable accommodations.

Sometimes this assistance is relatively simple to offer because legal precedents have been established. For example, in the Supreme

Court's only opinion to date regarding the construct "otherwise quali-fied," it was determined that a university does have the right to main-tain standards. In the case of *Southeastern Community College v. Davis* (1979), a student with a hearing impairment was denied admission to a nurses' training program because her hearing disability precluded her participation in the normal clinical training program and care for patients. The court upheld the college's position, maintaining that the law does not impose a requirement to lower or to effect substan-tial modifications of standards to accommodate a student with a dis-ability.

In other instances, however, disability service administrators have little to guide them in their role as a technical assistant and accommo-dation decision maker. For example, consider a student whose learn-ing disability includes a slow rate of processing information (a fre-quent manifestation of a learning disability). What are the implica-tions for him when it comes to choosing a job for which he wants to prepare academically? How about the student with problems in writ-ten expression? To what degree is competency in writing an essential element of a course or program? Governmental regulations and case law are often of little help in making decisions about real-life situa-tions.

As institutions move into delineating technical standards across programs of study, disability service administrators will become in-creasingly involved in collaborating with faculty and administration. Most institutions are now just beginning to grapple with ADA issues and have far to travel before effective systems are in place. In many ways, the DSA will become pivotal in helping academic institutions assure that qualified students with disabilities have equal program-matic access without compromising a program's integrity.

The multidimensional roles of a disability service administrator are reflected by the many fields of training from which they come. Results of the surveys by AHEAD (1995) and Madaus (1996) were consistent in finding the following areas of training (rank-ordered according to largest percentage of respondents indicating their edu-cational preparation in this field): counseling, other (e.g., social work, law), special education, education (elementary, secondary, higher), and rehabilitation counseling. Given the diversity of backgrounds among DSAs, it seems a foregone conclusion that ongoing profes-sional training is critical if they are to ethically and fairly discharge the duties of their positions.

THE NOTION OF EQUILIBRIUM

Guiding the many roles of the disability service administrator are the regulations for Section 504 of the Rehabilitation Act of 1973 as well as those for Titles II and III of the ADA. As the authors in Chapter 1 make clear, the ADA is a civil rights statute that promises protection from discrimination on the basis of a disability. Determining reasonable accommodations becomes a delicate dance: the institution's rights and responsibilities must be weighed alongside those of the individual with a disability. Although there are some differences in the requirements for the three provisions (i.e., Section 504, Title II, and Title III), in general the same principles apply.

Many students enrolling in college as well as their parents mistakenly assume that the special education services they received in high school, as delineated in an individualized education program (IEP), will follow them into a postsecondary setting. Unlike the Individuals with Disabilities Education Act (IDEA), a revision of the Education for All Handicapped Children Act of 1975, neither Section 504 nor the ADA require colleges and universities to identify disabilities or provide remedial or tutorial services. The IDEA is an entitlement statute that assures eligible elementary and secondary students a free, appropriate, public education in the least restrictive environment. The ADA is a civil rights statute, requiring postsecondary institutions to guarantee nondiscriminatory treatment and equal access to programs and services.

DSAs are charged with determining if an individual is eligible for the protections inherent in the statutes. This responsibility requires a careful, case-by-case analysis that addresses two fundamental questions: Is this student an "individual with a disability," and, if so, does he or she qualify as someone who is otherwise qualified to carry out the duties of the program? In some settings, the "qualified" standard is less relevant. For example, in some community colleges that have open-enrollment admissions policies, anyone with a high school diploma or General Education Development (GED) diploma is typically "qualified" to enroll. In settings with more stringent admissions standards, students with disabilities must demonstrate their qualifications, whether those include academic performance in high school or on other college and standardized test scores (e.g., SATs). Again, postsecondary institutions are not obligated to alter their standards because a student has a disability.

The DSA's role, then, is to guide the search for an equilibrium between an individual's right to accommodations and the institution's right to maintain the integrity of its programs. This quest involves many thorny issues, such as the following:

- What role should the DSA assume when a student with a documented learning disability in written expression seeks entrance to a teacher preparation program that requires a minimum level of competency in writing skills?
- Will a student with ADHD who graduated from high school as the valedictorian and received no accommodations meet the definition of eligibility as a student with a disability in a postsecondary setting?
- What documentation of a learning disability is required to verify a student's eligibility for the accommodations of oral testing and a notetaker?
- Is it a reasonable accommodation for a student with a psychological disability to be permitted a medical withdrawal because of disruptive behavior in the classroom and the dormitory?

THE PROCESS OF DETERMINING ELIGIBILITY

Determining whether an individual has a disability which substantially limits one or more major life functions is usually the most challenging task that confronts the DSA. As noted in Title II of the ADA Technical Assistance Manual (U.S. Department of Justice, 1992), determination of a disability requires a rigorous process.

Although neither the ADA nor Section 504 require postsecondary settings to develop written policies and procedures covering disabilities services (Tucker & Goldstein, 1992), it is nevertheless best practice to formulate them. It is especially worthwhile because the Office for Civil Rights routinely requests such information when it investigates complaints. Colleges and universities are in a far better position to address difficult situations (and perhaps also to avoid them) when policies and procedures have been thoughtfully and carefully developed.

A number of areas should be addressed when developing written policies and procedures (see McGuire & Brinckerhoff, 1997). These include:

- Issues of confidentiality.
- What students must supply by way of documentation.
- Documentation review procedures.
- Course substitutions.
- Assurances of nondiscriminatory treatment.
- Grievance procedures.
- Faculty responsibilities for implementing accommodations.

Once the policies and procedures have been approved, it is important to make sure that they are widely disseminated. They should be published in all campus materials (e.g., course catalog, Web page) with explicit information about how to contact the DSA. All notices should include the DSA's name, campus address, and telephone number.

Once a student has self-identified, an institution has the right to require documentation of the disability. The responsibility for providing comprehensive and current documentation from qualified professionals, as well as the expenses involved, rests with the student.

Many institutions, including the University of Connecticut, have established written guidelines for documentation of a learning disability. In 1995, AHEAD created an Ad Hoc Committee and charged it with developing LD guidelines for distribution on a national level (AHEAD, 1996). These guidelines are presented in Appendix I.

Some advocates argue that a history of a learning disability is sufficient to justify current accommodations even if the student had been declassified prior to high school. An example: Eve was diagnosed with a learning disability in second grade and received special education services through eighth grade. By this point her skills had improved and she was deemed no longer in need of services. Now in college, she has requested accommodations and claims that no further documentation is required because the law states that individuals who have a *record* of a physical or mental impairment are covered. In other words, she feels that her prior diagnosis should be sufficient to trigger accommodations.

Her position, however, is not in keeping with the intent of the law. By this "record of impairment" language, the ADA is saying, in essence, that individuals cannot be discriminated against because they once were diagnosed with a disorder. For example, an employer cannot deny someone a job just because he once showed symptoms of manic depressive illness.

The "record of impairment" language was not intended to suggest that a diagnosis, once assigned, necessarily guarantees lifelong accommodations. The student has to supply evidence that the symptoms currently cause substantial impairment. For instance, while learning disabilities are permanent, they often manifest themselves differently across the age span in different contexts. Students who were once labelled as LD must update their documentation to demonstrate that, indeed, there is a current and substantial limitation to learning.

Most people define "disabilities" or "disabling conditions" broadly. For example, poverty or lack of education may impose real limitations on an individual's opportunities. Likewise, being only 5 feet tall may prove to be an insurmountable barrier to an individual whose ambition is to play professional basketball. Some might loosely characterize these conditions as "disabilities" because of the discrepancy between aspirations and actual abilities.

To rise to a level of disability under the ADA, however, a disability must impose substantial limitations on an individual's major life activities. Determining when an impairment results in a substantial limitation, in some cases, is obvious. For example, a student with a traumatic brain injury may experience substantial limitations in the major life functions of self-care, learning, and working.

In other cases, the judgment of substantial impairment is more complex because the claim of disability is based on relative, intra-individual discrepancies. Does a student of average intellectual ability have a learning disability if he performs 1.2 standard deviations from the mean on one subtest of the Woodcock–Johnson Psychoeducational Battery—Revised: Tests of Achievement (1989)?

Many students seek accommodations on the basis of a learning disability because of discrepancies between IQ and achievement or because of relative discrepancies among subtest scores. Yet the literature is replete with evidence that the notion of discrepancy, especially in adults, is fraught with statistical and technical problems (Brackett & McPherson, 1996; Feagano & McKinney, 1991; Gregg, Hoy, & Gay, 1996; Siegel, 1990).

Case law both in the employment and educational realms has sharpened the definition of what constitutes substantial impairment. An impairment substantially interferes with the accomplishment "of a major life activity when the individual's important life activities are restricted as to the conditions, manner, or duration under which they can be performed in comparison to most people" (U.S. Department of Justice, 1992). In the area of employment, "Judges are recognizing that you have to comply with the statutory definition. Often, someone has a condition that in some way affects them but doesn't rise to a disability under the law" (Gephart, 1997).

Establishing written guidelines for documentation is essential because they can be used as a benchmark against which a student's documentation is compared. Using the University of Connecticut's guidelines (McGuire, Anderson, & Shaw, 1997; see Appendix 2.1) as a model, an administrator might employ a decision-making approach in working with a student around the matter of reasonable accommodations.

The question is often raised about the suitability of a student's high school IEP or individualized transition program (ITP) as documentation for college-level accommodations. Although these records may verify that a student was eligible for special education services in high school, they may not delineate the nature and severity of the disability for postsecondary settings. Also, by college or graduate school, students are likely to have been afforded a wide range of accommodations, many of which would not necessarily be relevant to their current postsecondary program.

One problem that confronts the DSA is that there is no standard set of accommodations that make sense for any given disability. This is especially the case for the nonphysical disorders. Consider the following recommendations for students with LD gleaned from high school IEPs (McGuire, 1997):

- Extra time for written work.
- Extra time for tests.
- No spelling penalty.
- Selective seating.
- Tape recorder.
- Reduced homework.
- Availability of teacher notes.
- Retaking those parts of a test that require reteaching in the special education classroom.
- Clarifying directions and questions for assignments, quizzes, tests, and the like, when the student does not appear to understand.

Many of these accommodations would help all students, whether or not they have a disability. Furthermore, little research is available to demonstrate a scientific basis for establishing that specific accommodations are effective.

Scott (1994) has suggested a sequential process in deciding upon reasonable accommodations. After determining that the documentation does indeed support the existence of a disability and current impairment, the next step is to verify that the student is qualified to meet the academic and technical standards of a course or program with or without accommodation. To determine whether an accommodation is reasonable, Scott (1990) advised consideration of the essential components of the program or course. Analysis of the outcome variables that are unequivocally required of all participants is recommended. These include skills and competencies in the field as well as requirements for licensing or professional accreditation.

Before determining what, if any, accommodations are appropriate, the DSA must determine if the student meets the essential qualifications of the educational program. These accommodations are not intended to help unqualified individuals handle a job or training experience. Instead, they should enable an otherwise qualified individual to have an equal opportunity to participate.

When considering the construct of "reasonable accommodation," Scott (1990) suggests three possible types of accommodations:

- Aternative instructional methods (e.g., supplementing lectures with advance organizers or overhead transparencies).
- Auxiliary aids (e.g., taped texts, volunteer notetakers).
- Alternative methods of evaluation (e.g., oral vs. written testing, process and product assessment).

The precise nature of an accommodation for any particular student depends on the nature of the disability and the demands of the educational program. Decisions about what constitute reasonable accommodations are most difficult if the documentation of disability is itself questionable or incomplete. With reliable and valid documentation, the process of determining which accommodations are reasonable is greatly simplified. Unfortunately, the documentation that students submit is too often insufficient to allow for clear decisions.

In those cases where documentation is problematic, the DSA should establish procedures for an independent, blind review by one or more *qualified* professionals. The student must give signed consent for this review. The University of Connecticut is utilizing such an approach according to these procedures.

Figure 2.1 illustrates this process by means of a flowchart, which is reviewed jointly by the DSA and the student. If a student's documentation is found to be insufficient by the Documentation Review Team, he or she is apprised of grievance procedures. First, we explain to the student options for seeking another review of the documentation by a broader based, University-wide Academic Accommodation Review Panel. Second, formal grievance procedures are explained.

In addition to information about appeals, we give students whose documentation has been deemed insufficient a series of questions about the materials they submitted. These questions highlight areas in which the evaluation may have been incomplete or of questionable validity. Students, in turn, can present these questions to the evaluator(s) for elaboration and/or clarification.

To date, not one evaluator has submitted a response to such questions, presumably because the issues raised by our reviewers were legitimate and fair. When students cannot provide responses to our questions, they pursue other non-ADA-level support services, such as from the Writing Center or Math Center, that are widely available on our campus. The important lesson here is that providing students clear feedback about the reasons their requests were denied goes a long way in stemming appeals and formal grievance actions.

For DSAs who do not have access to qualified professionals who can conduct impartial and informed documentation reviews, it may be prudent to consider alternatives. One option is to hire outside consultants who have expertise in one or more of the disability categories. Unfortunately, university administrators often balk at the considerable expense involved in retaining a cadre of qualified professionals.

The DSA must often remind the administrator of the potentially heavy costs to the university if the documentation review process is not handled with utmost care. The institution stands at risk if evaluations are reviewed only by the DSA, most of whom do not have extensive training in the area of assessment. A plaintiff's attorney could legitimately question a process in which complicated clinical issues were judged by individuals without the appropriate credentials and technical expertise.

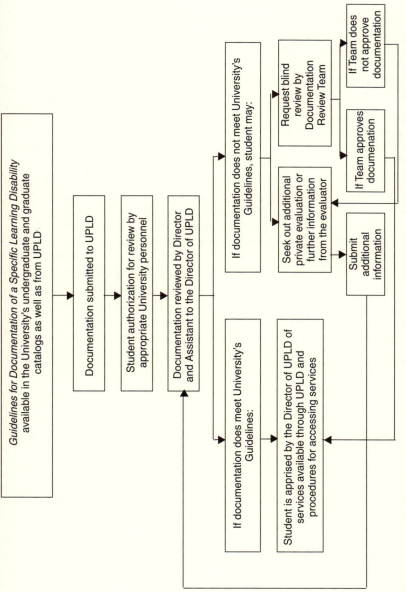

FIGURE 2.1. Documentaion review process for college students with learning disabilities at the University of Connecticut. From McGuire (1996). Copyright 1996 by the University Program for College Students with Learning Disabilities, University of Connecticut, Storrs, CT. Reprinted by permission in *Accommodations in Higher Education under the Americans with Disabilities Act (ADA)*, edited by Michael Gordon and Shelby Keiser. Permission to photocopy this figure is granted to purchasers of *Accommodations in Higher Education* for personal use only (see copyright page for details).

REVIEWING EVALUATIONS

The documentation that students submit when they seek accommodations often contains a series of psychological test reports and clinical reports written by mental health professionals. These reports vary greatly in their sophistication, relevance, and credibility. Hintze and Passarello (1997), drawing upon the work of Nezu and Nezu (1993), cautioned administrators to be alert regarding common errors in clinical reasoning that may be reflected in assessment and documentation reports, particularly in the area of learning disabilities. These include the following:

- Attributing learning problems to the readily available LD label without engaging in a process of ruling out alternative explanations for academic difficulties (e.g., frequent family moves during elementary and secondary school years that may have resulted in a lack of instruction in certain subject-related topics).
- Identifying a disability on the basis of one telltale sign (for example, a deficient achievement test score) at the exclusion of other possible explanations or contradictory features.
- Basing decisions on initial impressions (e.g., records that indicate diagnosis of LD in early elementary school), while discounting other information, even if it disagrees with initial impressions.

Sample Report

To illustrate the challenges facing DSAs in the area of documentation of a learning disability, a very typical case is presented, followed by a series of questions one might raise in the review process. This particular example is used because it illustrates the dilemmas faced by administrators in dealing with students with a history of a learning disability.

Name: John Jones   **Age**: 19
Date seen: 11/7, 11/15/95   **Date of birth**: 6/15/76

Evaluation Procedures

Interview

Wechsler Adult Intelligence Scale—Revised (WAIS-R)
Woodcock–Johnson Psychoeducational Battery—Revised: Tests of Achievement, Standard Battery

Reason for Referral

John and his parents requested a psychoeducational evaluation to determine factors contributing to academic difficulties and to help verify his eligibility for academic support services on the basis of a learning disability.

Background Information and Behavioral Observations

As a second grader, John was identified as needing support services because of lagging academic achievement in reading and basic math. John's mother provided records of a psychological evaluation conducted in 1983, including the Wechsler Intelligence Scale for Children—Revised (WISC-R), which indicated average ability but deficient visual–perceptual and visual–motor integration skills. By the end of fourth grade, he had progressed considerably and services were discontinued. The WISC-R was readministered in March and April 1986, yielding a Verbal IQ of 124, a Performance IQ of 117, and a Full Scale IQ of 123 (in the superior range). Subtest scores ranged from average to highly superior, indicating no areas of absolute deficiency, but the presence of relative weaknesses in a bright individual. In marked contrast were results on the Bender Visual Motor Gestalt Test and the Developmental Test of Visual–Motor Integration (VMI), which were considerably below average and consistent with the presence of a visual learning disability. The Kaufman Test of Educational Achievement reflected generally average academic mastery, not on a par with his intellectual aptitude, yet not so disparate as to meet the educational system's definition of a learning disability.

John reports that he has generally earned A's and B's, with C's in math in his high school courses. As a first semester student at Freedom University, he anticipated having to work harder and studied conscientiously, but earned failing or near failing test scores in both math and plant science. He states that although he can recall definitions, he has had difficulty understanding test questions in math and has had trouble integrating and applying information in his biology course.

During the two evaluation sessions, John appeared well groomed and poised. He maintained good eye contact and spoke in a pleasant, soft voice. He approached the testing situation in a cooperative, conscientious manner. When uncertain of verbal responses, he tended to answer with a questioning inflection, but was willing to venture a guess. Results of the evaluation appear to be an accurate reflection of John's current intellectual and academic functioning.

Test Results

Wechsler Adult Intelligence Scale—Revised (WAIS-R)

Verbal subtests	Scaled	Age-norm	Performance subtests	Scaled	Age-norm
Information	7	9	Picture Completion	11	12
Digit Span	13	14	Picture Arrangement	9	10
Vocabulary	10	12	Block Design	10	11
Arithmetic	11	13	Object Assembly	12	13
Comprehension	14	16	Digit Symbol	9	9
Similarities	12	14			

Verbal IQ: 116   Performance IQ: 103   Full Scale IQ: 112

Woodcock–Johnson Psychoeducational Battery—Revised: Tests of Achievement (Grade-Level Norms)

	Standard battery subtests		
	Grade equivalent	Scaled score	Percentile
Letter-Word Identification	16.8	113	81
Passage Comprehension	16.9+	122	93
Calculation	16.9+	115	84
Applied Problems	13.8	105	64
Dictation	8.9	91	26
Writing Samples	16.9+	126	96
Science	14.4	113	80
Social Studies	12.4	101	54
Humanities	7.5	96	40

	Standard battery clusters		
	Grade equivalent	Scaled score	Percentile
Broad Reading	16.9	117	88
Broad Mathematics	16.3	111	77
Broad Written Language	13.0	103	58
Broad Knowledge	11.2	98	44
Skills	13.1	104	60

On the WAIS-R, John obtained a Verbal IQ of 116 (in the high average range), a Performance IQ of 103 (in the average range), and a composite Full Scale IQ score of 112 (in the high average range). The difference between Verbal and Performance IQ scores is not statistically significant, but is consistent with somewhat greater verbal than visual–spatial skills. Although current

IQ scores are somewhat lower than those obtained on the WISC-R in 1986, particularly in the Performance area, they are not statistically significant. Subtest scores ranged from average to highly superior, indicating significant variability among specific cognitive skills, including absolute strengths and relative weaknesses.

John displayed particular ability in verbal, social, and abstract reasoning, and attention to short-term recall of rote verbal information. His knowledge of word meanings, verbal attention and concentration, numerical reasoning, short-term recall of auditorily or visually presented information, and ability to synthesize visual–spatial information were all above average. Areas of relative weakness included his fund of general knowledge, understanding of cause–effect and temporal relationships, visual sequencing, ability to analyze visual–spatial information, and visual–motor processing speed, all of which are average but considerably below the level of his strongest cognitive skills. When faced with a novel, multistep problem to be solved using visual abstract reasoning, visual sequencing, and/or visual–motor speed, John will likely have considerably more difficulty than when verbal reasoning and expression are required. Under these circumstances, his performance is likely to be less immediately successful than is true for the average student at Freedom University.

On the Woodcock–Johnson Psychoeducational Battery—Revised: Tests of Achievement (standard battery, scored on the basis of grade-level norms), John's scores ranged from average to superior for an individual at the 12.2 grade level. Skills range from the 7.5 grade level to 16.9+. Areas of particularly well-developed skill include reading comprehension, reading recognition, fluent written expression, and mathematical calculation, which is consistent with the verbal reasoning aptitude observed on the WAIS-R. As compared with other college freshmen, John was weak in his knowledge of the humanities and spelling and other writing mechanics. All other areas were at the level expected in light of his educational level and intellectual aptitude. There was, however, a disparity between his verbal fluency and comprehension, which are excellent, and several applied skills, all of which may have a bearing on current academic functioning.

John appears to be more adept at arithmetic calculations than at solving applied mathematical "word problems," which involve analyzing a situation in order to identify the relevant information and steps necessary to arrive at an answer, in addition to performing calculations correctly. In the process of solving such problems, he tended to write down each step, including many that would usually be automatic and unnecessary for a well-prepared college student. For example, when asked the number of inches in a certain fraction of a yard, John first had to calculate in writing the number of inches in a yard, based on 12" to a foot. To calculate 10% of an amount, he relied on paper and pencil instead of figuring out in his head. Several applied math items were missed because John could not recall the approach or formula necessary.

Another area of specific relative weakness is his somewhat spotty range of general factual information, particularly given his bright verbal ability. Early struggles with learning disabilities may have contributed to some "missing pieces" in his prior knowledge base. Focus on specific areas of interest and less attention to other domains (such as geography, social sciences, and the humanities) may account for unevenness in more advanced knowledge. It is possible that gaps in factual knowledge may at times create problems when John is faced with college level work, which presupposes a foundation of basic general knowledge. He may find that he has to learn a higher percentage of factual material to master course objectives than some others who have a greater store of knowledge through prior courses or general exposure.

John displayed strong word decoding and recognition ability, but had more trouble on a dictation task which involved active recall of correct spelling and punctuation. Results of the Writing Samples test revealed mechanical weaknesses, yet reflected strength in written expression of ideas, as is consistent with John's excellent verbal reasoning. John's spelling errors reflected an adequate grasp of phonics, but comparative weakness in visual recall necessary for correct spelling of more difficult words. Such a pattern is not surprising given a history of visual learning difficulties.

Conclusions and Recommendations

John possesses bright overall intellectual ability with specific cognitive skills and academic skills ranging from average to superior. Verbal reasoning and expression are particularly strong, with relative deficits in his fund of general knowledge and in areas vulnerable to the effects of visual learning difficulties, as one would expect given the earlier diagnosis of a visual learning disability. Over the intervening years, John has performed well in school and evidently developed some compensatory skills which have allowed him to function at an average or better level for the most part. The discrepancy between John's intellectual ability and achievement levels is less pronounced than it was when he was in early elementary grades. Nevertheless, unevenness in abilities and acquired knowledge may at times impede learning and performance at the more challenging college level, especially if the specific skills emphasized in a given course are those in which he is average (and thus somewhat below the level of most university students). The feelings of frustration and discouragement that undoubtedly exist may further undermine his efforts unless he can utilize strategies and resources to capitalize on his strengths and minimize the impact of relative deficits.

On the basis of test findings, the following recommendations are offered.

1. Given his history of a visual learning disability, John would benefit from being permitted extended time to complete tests and in-class assignments.

2. Given John's relative weakness in applied mathematics, one would expect that courses that involve mathematical operations for problem solving (as is true in some science courses) would be more challenging. When choosing a major as well as courses, John should consider this.

3. John is likely to have relative difficulty when asked to analyze abstract visual information, which may possibly be interfering with absorption of material or test questions presented in the form of formulas and diagrams and other such visually oriented formats. Translating visually presented information into verbal form is likely to enhance his absorption and comprehension of it. In addition, he may perform better if visually oriented tasks are concrete rather than highly abstract. Thus, hands on, practical problems may well be easier for him than those that are both visual and abstract.

4. Using audiotapes of lectures in addition to notes may be helpful, particularly if lecture content emphasizes explanation of visually oriented material such as diagrams and formulas.

5. Writing assignments should, ideally, be completed using a computer word processing program including spelling and grammar check features. Continued development of writing mechanics skills will profit from the use of spell and grammar checks, but John should attempt to proofread and correct any errors himself before using these aids.

6. When asked to absorb information visually and execute a visually oriented task, John is likely to learn and perform best if allowed extra time to work at his own pace.

7. John is encouraged to seek out any university learning support services for which he may be eligible.

A Review of the LD Report

Here are the kinds of questions a reviewer might raise about the preceding report. As you will see, not all of them represent criticisms of the conclusions. Many of the comments simply indicate a need for further clarification:

Reason for Referral

- In this section, the evaluator indicates that the testing was requested "to help verify his eligibility for academic support services on the basis of a learning disability." This sort of language makes an administrator worry that the professional assumed from the outset that John is eligible for LD support services. Is the evaluator offering to advocate when his role should be as an impartial diagnostician?

Background Information

- Prior testing showed "no areas of absolute deficiency, but the presence of relative weaknesses in a bright individual." Does the evaluator consider such discrepancies an indication of disability?
- How was the presence of a visual learning disability confirmed? Is a "visual learning disability" a legitimate diagnostic entity?
- Are the Bender and the VMI suitably normed for a 19-year-old? Do they measure similar constructs?

Test Results

- Choice of scores: Why were age-norm scores selected for the WAIS-R while grade-level norms were used for the Woodcock–Johnson?
- The evaluator does not seem to explore the possibility that certain low scores on the Woodcock–Johnson might have been due to past educational experiences, such as minimal exposure to certain subject matter

Test Interpretation

- Can the psychologist provide evidence that statistical differences translate to actual clinical or educational impairment?
- What is meant by "absolute strengths and relative weaknesses?" Why are relative weaknesses relevant to determinations of disability?
- If one considers that the mean of John's Verbal subtest scaled scores is 11.2, the mean of the Performance subtests scaled scores is 10.2, and the standard deviation for subtest scores is ±3, is the use of descriptors such as "significant variability" and "is apt to have considerably more difficulty" warranted?
- What is a "grade equivalency score of 7.5?" Why isn't a standard score reported?

- Is a disparity between verbal fluency and comprehension and several applied skills (e.g., dictation) evidence of a substantial limitation to learning?
- Are "gaps in factual knowledge" synonymous with a learning disability?
- What is meant by "a history of visual learning difficulties?"

Conclusions and Recommendations

- If John has developed "some compensatory skills which have allowed him to function at an average or better level for the most part," where is the evidence of a substantial limitation in current learning?
- How does "unevenness in abilities and acquired knowledge . . . imped(ing) his learning and performance at the more challenging college level, especially if the specific skills emphasized in a given course are those in which he is average (and thus somewhat below the level of most university students)" meet the parameters of a learning disability? Is the evaluator saying that John should be considered disabled even if his abilities fall within a normal range? Does the psychologist perhaps not understand the standard of the "average person?"
- Does "the impact of relative deficits" qualify John for protections under the ADA?
- Wouldn't the recommendations for using audiotapes and computer software be beneficial for many students?
- Is extended time warranted because of a learning disability? How would it alleviate this student's problems?
- Are there "learning support services" that John could access to assist him with his "relative weaknesses?"

IN CLOSING . . .

Because issues of eligibility, equal access, and reasonable accommodations are so complex, it behooves us all to collaborate in ensuring nondiscriminatory but sensible treatment of students with disabilities. Keeping the process fair is no easy task and requires students, clinicians, administrators, and faculty to work together in a spirit of cooperation. We have found it important to avoid entering into adversarial relationships with all the many parties involved. At the same time, we struggle to uphold reasonable standards and strict compliance with the law. Protecting the integrity of the entire process ultimately benefits student and university alike.

Appendix 2.1

UNIVERSITY OF CONNECTICUT GUIDELINES FOR DOCUMENTATION OF A SPECIFIC LEARNING DISABILITY*

Students who are seeking support services from the University of Connecticut Program for College Students with Learning Disabilities (UPLD) on the basis of a diagnosed specific learning disability are required to submit documentation to verify eligibility under Section 504 of the Rehabilitation Act of 1973 and the Americans with Disabilities Act of 1990. Protection under these civil rights statutes is based upon documentation of a learning disability that *currently substantially limits* some major life activity including learning.

The following guidelines are provided in the interest of assuring that documentation is appropriate to verify eligibility *and* support requests for reasonable accommodations, academic adjustments, and/or auxiliary aids on the basis of a learning disability that substantially limits one or more major life activities. The Director of UPLD is available to consult with diagnosticians regarding any of these guidelines.

1. Testing *must* be comprehensive. It is not acceptable to administer only one test for the purpose of diagnosis. Minimally, domains to be addressed must include (but not be limited to):

*From McGuire, Anderson, and Shaw (1997). Copyright 1996 by the University Program for College Students with Learning Disabilities, University of Connecticut, Storrs, CT. Reprinted by permission in *Accommodations in Higher Education under the Americans with Disabilities Act (ADA)*, edited by Michael Gordon and Shelby Keiser. Permission to photocopy this appendix is granted to purchasers of *Accommodations in Higher Education* for personal use only (see copyright page for details).

a. *Aptitude*. The Wechsler Adult Intelligence Scales (WAIS-R or WAIS-III) with subtest scores is the preferred instrument. The Woodcock–Johnson Psychoeducational Battery—Revised: Tests of Cognitive Ability *or* the Stanford–Binet Intelligence Scale: Fourth Edition is acceptable.

b. *Achievement*. Current levels of functioning in reading, mathematics, and written language are required. Acceptable instruments include the Woodcock–Johnson Psychoeducational Battery—Revised: Tests of Achievement; Wechsler Individual Achievement Test (WIAT); Stanford Test of Academic Skills (TASK); Scholastic Abilities Test for Adults (SATA); or specific achievement tests such as the Test of Written Language—2 (TOWL-2), Woodcock Reading Mastery Tests—Revised, or the Stanford Diagnostic Mathematics Test. The Wide Range Achievement Test —Revised or III (WRAT-R or III) are NOT comprehensive measures of achievement and therefore are not suitable.

c. *Information processing*. Specific areas of information processing (e.g., short- and long-term memory; sequential memory; auditory and visual perception/processing; processing speed) must be assessed. Information from subtests on the WAIS-R or WAIS-III, the Woodcock–Johnson Tests of Cognitive Ability, *or* the Detroit Tests of Learning Aptitude–Adult, *as well as* other instruments relevant to the presenting learning problem(s) may be used to address these areas.

This is not intended to be an exhaustive list or to restrict assessment in other pertinent and helpful areas such as vocational interests and aptitudes.

2. Testing must be *current*. In most cases, this means testing that has been conducted *within the past 3 years*. Because the provision of all reasonable accommodations and services is based upon assessment of the current impact of the student's disabilities on his or her academic performance, it is in a student's best interest to provide recent and appropriate documentation.

3. There must be *clear and specific* evidence and identification of a learning disability. Individual "learning styles" and "learning differences" in and of themselves do not constitute a learning disability.

4. *Actual test scores* must be provided. Standard scores are required; percentiles and grade equivalents are *not* acceptable unless standard scores are also included. This is important since certain University policies and procedures (e.g., petitioning for permission to substitute courses) require actual data to substantiate eligibility.

5. Professionals conducting assessment and rendering diagnoses of learn-

ing disabilities *must* be qualified to do so. Trained, certified and/or licensed school psychologists, neuropsychologists, clinical psychologists, learning disabilities specialists, and other professionals with training and experience relevant to adults and their evaluation are typically involved in the process of assessment. Experience in working with an adult population is *essential*.

6. Tests used to document eligibility must be technically sound (i.e., statistically reliable and valid) and standardized for use with an adult population.

7. Diagnostic reports must include the names, titles, and professional credentials (e.g., licensed psychologist) of the evaluators as well as the date(s) of testing. *All reports must be typed.*

8. A written summary of or background information about the student's relevant educational, medical, and family histories that relate to the learning disability must be included.

9. Any recommendation for an accommodation should be based on objective evidence of a *substantial limitation* to learning, supported by specific test results or clinical observations.

10. A description of any accommodation and/or auxiliary aid that has been used at the secondary or postsecondary level should be discussed. Include information about the specific conditions under which the accommodation was used (e.g., standardized testing, final exams) and whether or not it benefited the student. If no accommodations have been previously provided, a detailed explanation as to why none has been used and the rationale for the student's currently needing accommodation(s) must be provided.

All documentation is confidential.

Appendix 2.2

UNIVERSITY OF CONNECTICUT
DOCUMENTATION REVIEW PROCESS

The University of Connecticut provides services for students with specific learning disabilities through the Program for College Students with Learning Disabilities (UPLD). To access these services, students are responsible for providing current documentation that meets the University's *Guidelines for Documentation of a Specific Learning Disability*. These procedures are followed to determine eligibility for services including reasonable accommodations once documentation is provided to UPLD by a student:

1. The student is assured confidentiality by signing UPLD Student Authorization Form A (Release of Information to Authorized University of Connecticut Personnel).
2. Documentation is reviewed by the Director of UPLD and the Assistant to the Director of UPLD.
3. If the documentation meets the University's *Guidelines*, the Director will contact the student to discuss program services including accommodations. The student will indicate which level of service on the UPLD Continuum of Services she or he wishes to access.
4. If there are questions about the acceptability of a student's documentation, the Director will indicate this to the student, and advise that the documentation should be reviewed by the Documentation Review Team.
5. The Documentation Review Team consists of at least two faculty with expertise in the area of learning disabilities and assessment, advanced graduate student(s) in the Department of Educational Psychology, and additional professionals (e.g., faculty with expertise in a specific area) as appropriate.
6. The Documentation Review Team conducts a blind review of the documentation and communicates its decision to the Director of UPLD in a timely fashion. Specifically, the Team will determine whether the docu-

mentation verifies eligibility for UPLD services on the basis of the University's *Guidelines for Documentation of a Specific Learning Disability*. If the documentation is determined to be insufficient, the Team will delineate additional information and/or testing required to verify eligibility.

7. The Director of UPLD communicates the results of the Team review to the student and is available to consult with the student regarding the Team's recommendations about additional information/testing.

REFERENCES

Association on Higher Education and Disability (AHEAD). (1995). *Membership survey report*. Columbus, OH: Author.

Association on Higher Education and Disability (AHEAD). (1996, July). Guidelines for documentation of a specific learning disability. *Alert,* 10-12.

Brackett, J., & McPherson, A. (1996). Learning disabilities diagnosis in postsecondary students: A comparison of discrepancy-based diagnostic models. In N. Gregg, C. Hoy, & A. F. Gay (Eds.), *Adults with learning disabilities: Theoretical and practical perspectives* (pp. 68–84). New York: Guilford Press.

Feagano, L. V., & McKinney, J. D. (1991). Subtypes of learning disabilities: A review. In L. V. Feagano, E. J. Short, & L. J. Meltzer (Eds.), *Subtypes of learning disabilities* (pp. 3–31). Hillsdale, NJ: Erlbaum.

Gephart, D. (Ed.). (1997, June). Courts keep narrow interpretation of "disability," case study shows. *Disability Compliance for Higher Education, 2,* 11.

Gregg, N., Hoy, C., & Gay, A. F. (Eds.). (1996). *Adults with learning disabilities: Theoretical and practical perspectives* (pp. 68–84). New York: Guilford Press.

Harris, R. W., Horn, C. A., & McCarthy, M. A. (1994). Physical and technological access. In D. Ryan & M. McCarthy (Eds.), *The student affairs guide to the ADA and disability issues* (pp. 33–50). Washington, DC: National Association of Student Personnel Administrators.

Henderson, C. (1995). *College freshmen with disabilities: A triennial statistical profile*. Washington, DC: American Council on Education.

Hintze, J., & Passarello, D. (1997, June). *Understanding assessment information: What every good consumer ought to know*. Professional training workshop strand presented at the 9th annual Postsecondary Learning Disability Training Institute, Saratoga Springs, NY.

Korbel, D. M., & Lucia, J. H. (1996, Fall). A day in the life of a disability service provider. *Postsecondary Disability Network News, 28,* 1–2, 5.

Madaus, J. W. (1996). *Administration of postsecondary offices for students with disabilities: Perceptions of essential job functions.* Unpublished doctoral dissertation, University of Connecticut, Storrs.

Madaus, J. W. (1998). The effect of demographic characteristics on OSD administrators' perceptions of essential job functions. *Journal of Postsecondary Education and Disability, 13,* 3–22.

McGuire, J. M. (1996). *University Program for College Students with Learning Disabilities: Documentation review process.* Storrs: University of Connecticut.

McGuire, J. M., Anderson, P. L., & Shaw, S. F. (1997). *Guidelines for documentation of a specific learning disability.* Storrs: University of Connecticut Program for College Students with Learning Disabilities.

McGuire, J. M., & Brinckerhoff, L. C. (1997, June). *Crafting campus policies: Facing ongoing challenges to access and equity.* Professional training workshop strand presented at the 9th annual Postsecondary Learning Disability Training Institute, Saratoga Springs, NY.

Nezu, A. M., & Nezu, C. M. (1993). Identifying and selecting target problems for clinical interventions: A problem-solving model. *Psychological Assessment, 5,* 254–263.

Scott, S. S. (1990). Coming to terms with the "otherwise qualified" student with a learning disability. *Journal of Learning Disabilities, 23,* 398–405.

Scott, S. S. (1994). Determining reasonable academic adjustments for college students with learning disabilities. *Journal of Learning Disabilities, 27,* 403–412.

Siegel, L. (1990). IQ and learning disabilities: RIP. In H.L. Swanson & B. Keogh (Eds.), *Learning disabilities: Theoretical and research issues* (pp. 111–128). Hillsdale, NJ: Erlbaum.

Southeastern Community College v. Davis, 422 U.S. 397, 60 L. Ed. 2d 980 (1979).

Tucker, B. P., & Goldstein, B. A. (1992). *Legal rights of persons with disabilities: An analysis of federal law.* Horsham, PA: LRP Publications.

U.S. Department of Justice. (1992). *The Americans with Disabilities Act Title II Technical Assistance Manual.* Washington, DC: U.S. Government Printing Office.

3 Test Accommodations: An Administrator's View

Shelby Keiser, MS

INTRODUCTION

Testing organizations play an important national role in evaluating and credentialling students at all levels of higher education and professional training. From the Scholastic Aptitude Test (SAT) to the Graduate Record Exam (GRE) to specialty examinations for the professions, testing has become an integral step in the process by which an individual climbs the educational ladder. Especially at the top rungs, testing serves as one form of guarantee that a student has achieved sufficient knowledge to function with competence in a position that entails the public safety and trust.

While academic institutions and testing organizations are closely linked, they have inherently different goals. An understanding of those distinctions is fundamental to a discussion of issues surrounding test accommodations in postgraduate professional licensing and certification. Indeed, misunderstanding of the relationship of the testing or licensing organization to the educational process is often at the heart of confusion about accommodations in general.

Postsecondary and graduate educational institutions, indeed all educational establishments, share the singular goal of helping their students to learn. Schools seek to feed students with knowledge and skills from the first day of kindergarten to the final stages of career preparation.

If students encounter problems taking in the educational nourishment, the system is designed to come to their aid. Academic assistance is accomplished on various levels, depending on the nature of the content and of the student's deficiencies. Elementary schools, for example, have traditionally used different levels of reading and math instruction so that children could learn efficiently and at their own pace. Secondary schools frequently divide their programs into instructional tracks, offering more demanding coursework to higher achievers and less demanding courses to those who are not as accelerated.

Beyond these options, schools have provided assistance in the form of remedial training, reinforcement through tutoring and individualized instruction. Many of these services have traditionally been authorized and funded by federal and state governments under the aegis of special education laws such as the Individuals with Disabilities Education Act.

Organizations that administer tests designed to certify or license are not educational institutions. Therefore, they are not structured along the educational model that promotes a desirable outcome of successful learning. Instead, testing organizations exist to measure, fairly and impartially, the degree to which the education or training has been successful. They establish a standardized, objective benchmark against which the test-taker's skills can be compared. A college does its job well when a student successfully completes a course of study. A testing organization has performed its duty when it develops valid tests that are administered fairly and reliably.

The differences between educational institutions and testing organizations become most striking in their different approaches to disability. For elementary and secondary school students, the special education laws mandate remedial and support services to all who meet the stated eligibility criteria for disability. These criteria are typically based on a discrepancy between intellectual potential and actual achievement. Children who meet these criteria are entitled to a publicly funded education that helps them master the curriculum.

The entitlement model of special education becomes inapplicable as students move across the threshold from high school to college. Professional training and licensure require a rigorous mastery of knowledge and skills that necessarily excludes all but the most talented. Almost by definition, students in these programs are already functioning better than most in the population.

By the time students enter postgraduate programs, concerns about maintaining professional standards of competence also begin to compete with individual prerogatives. The essential requirements of the jobs for which students are preparing become easier to define as students move closer to actual employment. Thus, conditions that might not have disqualified a person for meeting the responsibilities of being a college student could become arguments for why one might not be qualified to become a doctor, lawyer, airline pilot, engineer, or architect. For all of these reasons, failure to achieve in higher education (or failure to achieve licensure after completion of training) does not trigger the entitlement to assistance that is guaranteed during earlier stages of education.

Examinees accustomed to the support of their educational institution are frequently surprised to find that the testing or licensing organization will not assist them in achieving success. Students often fail to understand that these organizations are obligated to measure outcomes of the educational process against a neutral, objective standard. These organizations would be abrogating their responsibilities if they in any way exhibited a vested interest in the success of a candidate.

Students accustomed to entitlements under special education laws often interpret the test organization's dedication to neutrality as intransigence or even as legal noncompliance. They also make the inaccurate assumption that the Americans with Disabilities Act of 1990 (ADA; PL 101-336) requires testing organizations to ensure success when, in fact, impartiality and objectivity are *required* by the law. Their confusion is mirrored in their protests to decisions by testing organizations. Administrators often hear comments like, "You have to help me do my best" or "Because I am disabled you have to make sure I finish and ultimately pass the exam." Conversations between examinees and test organizations often proceed along divergent paths because each has a different agenda. Because of this general confusion, many testing agencies are encountering an unprecedented level of frustration and animosity as they struggle to make fair decisions about requests for accommodations.

THE ROLE OF THE TEST ACCOMMODATIONS ADMINISTRATOR

The test accommodations administrator (TAA) in a testing or licensing organization acts as the agent of that organization in considering ADA requests. In many ways, the TAA and the disability service administrator (DSA) in a postsecondary educational institution have similar responsibilities because both steward the process by which each request is reviewed. But there is a critically important difference between the two roles: The DSA in the postsecondary setting may properly play an advocacy role in fostering a student's progress. Indeed, part of the DSA's job description entails direct involvement in helping students adjust and achieve. Depending on the institution's policies, the DSA might have considerable license in advocating for the student with faculty and other administrators.

In contrast, the TAA cannot take a proprietary interest in the applicant's success or failure on the test. The TAA is instead charged with determining whether the documentation adequately supports a formal diagnosis of disability and whether that disability effectively prevents the individual from equal access to the examination.

Beyond these determinations, the TAA is duty-bound not to advocate for a particular outcome. The integrity of a testing procedure depends on upholding a standard administration that is fair to all participants.

The role of the TAA is twofold: (1) to determine if the applicant requesting accommodations is a covered individual under the ADA; and (2) to determine if the requested accommodations are necessary and appropriate means of easing the impact of the identified functional limitation on the testing activity. The first question, whether or not the applicant is protected under ADA, is often the most difficult to determine.

DETERMINING COVERAGE UNDER ADA

To ensure that each request is considered under consistent criteria, the agency must develop comprehensive guidelines for what constitutes acceptable documentation. By no means, however, should agencies issue a list of tests or clinical criteria that, if provided, would guarantee the provision of the requested accommodations. Rather, the purpose of guidelines is to help the applicant (and his or her evaluator) understand the types of information required to allow for a review. Specifically, they direct the individual to provide information that addresses the following questions:

- What is the diagnosed disability?
- What are the functional limitations (those activities that the individual cannot do, or is significantly limited in his or her

ability to do) that interfere with his or her access to the testing activity?

- What is the impact of the functional limitations on the individual's ability to participate in the testing activity? (How severe is the impairment and what does the impairment prevent the individual from doing vis-à-vis the examination?)
- What accommodations or assistive devices, if any, would ease or cancel the impact of the disability on the individual's ability to participate in the testing program?

It is important to note that none of these questions address whether the individual might finish, pass, or fail the professional or licensing examination. Whether or not an individual qualifies for protection against discrimination under ADA is decided without consideration of the desired outcome.

IDENTIFYING A DISABILITY

Determining eligibility under the ADA is a two-step process. The first is to establish that a formal diagnosis of disability has been provided by a qualified professional. However, a diagnosis alone does not automatically entitle the individual to accommodations. A person can have a legitimate diagnosis of a disability but not require accommodations under the ADA. For example, a diagnosed diabetic, whose blood sugar levels are under control either by means of medication or diet, may function normally and require no accommodation or adjustment in a testing situation.

If that same diabetic required frequent monitoring and adjustment of glucose levels, accommodations may well be justified. Perhaps the examinee would require stop-the-clock breaks periodically during testing to allow for blood sugar monitoring, administration of insulin, or food intake. But the individual's documentation would need to state clearly not only the clinical basis for the diagnosis, but also how that disability would affect test taking and what accommodations would address those limitations.

The second step in the process is to determine the existence of a "significant limitation" in a major life activity as the qualifying criterion for accommodations. Regulations from both the Department of Justice and the Equal Employment Opportunity Commission that accompany the ADA and provide enforcement guidance offer many illustrations of what is meant by "significant limitation." For example, the EEOC regulations explain that an individual unable to cope with everyday tensions and stress because of bipolar disorder has an impairment. In that situation, the analysis proceeds to whether the individual's impairment substantially limits a major life activity. As stated in the EEOC regulations, "an individual is not substantially limited in a major life activity unless (s)he is unable to perform the activity or is significantly restricted in performing the activity *as compared to the average person in the general population*" (emphasis added).

A federal judge in the Southern District of West Virginia recently affirmed that principle. He ruled that, in making a determination of whether one is covered under ADA, the "significant limitation" is measured against "the average person in the general population," rather than a select group of individuals in a highly selective academic program (*Price et al. v. National Board of Medical Examiners*, 1997). It should be pointed out, however, that in another case (*Bartlett v. New York State Board of Law Examiners*, 1997), the judge, by applying regulations relative to the workplace, used a standard that allowed comparison not to the general population, but to others in law school. At the time of this writing, this case is under appeal.

DETERMINING EFFECTIVE ACCOMMODATIONS

Once the determination is made that the individual requesting accommodations is covered under the ADA, the test accommodations administrator is responsible for ensuring the delivery of effective accommodations. The most common request is for extended testing time. Most individuals believe that the extra time will allow them to finish the exam, check their answers and reduce the anxiety of working on a high-stakes task under time pressure. While extra time can certainly provide these benefits (and not only to slow readers) this accommodation is only justified if the individual has adequately documented functional limitations that directly relate to a disability. It is grossly unfair to all test takers, disabled and nondisabled alike, if some are provided with a benefit that is not clearly justified as a remedy for disability.

Sometimes examinees request extended time when the test is

perceived as speeded because they feel their reading rate is insufficient to allow them to finish. In fact, most standardized licensing exams are not speeded, but require a high level of content mastery in order for test takers to complete the exam with an acceptable level of accuracy. Step 1 of the United States Medical Licensing Examination (USMLE), for example, allows a surprisingly low reading rate of approximately 70 words per minute, far less than what is considered the "average" reading rate for a college-educated adult. Step 2 of the USMLE, which many medical students consider to be even more speeded, with longer, more complex reading passages, has an equally low reading rate of approximately 85 words per minute.

While learning disabilities and attention deficits are often identified as reasons why some fail to complete a professional exam, it should be remembered that examinees can run out of time for many other reasons. Often the difficulty in finishing or passing such an exam lies with insufficient content mastery of a large volume of complex information. Some examinees have weak test-taking strategies improperly geared to the demands of a multiple-choice recognition test. Others fail because of test anxiety or combination of all of these factors. For these examinees, whether or not extra time would be useful is a moot point because, again, the ADA does not cover them. For examinees with ADA-level disabilities, extended testing time and other accommodations of the sort discussed in the section "Accommodations and their Function" may well be justified.

ROLE OF THE DIAGNOSTICIAN

Many psychologists and psychiatrists are accustomed to approaching clinical evaluations of learning disabilities, attention-deficit/hyperactivity disorder (ADHD), and other mental health problems in an advocacy mode. They know that schools are more likely to provide services to students whose parents can present compelling evidence for remediation. Clinicians will often gear their reports to bolster the case for special services. In an educational setting this approach may be acceptable, since eligibility formulas are often liberal and the stakes are usually not high. Especially when dealing with younger children, disability criteria seem less salient than the potential benefits of extra instruction.

For ADA determinations, however, the clinician is required to operate under a different set of rules. Because the ADA definition of disability is far more conservative and the consequence more serious, the practitioner must shed the robes of advocacy and act as an impartial evaluator. While it is certainly hard for any clinician to step out of the role of patient advocate, compiling ADA-related evidence requires an evenhanded, straightforward consideration of the data. Clinicians should scrupulously adhere to professionally sanctioned diagnostic guidelines.

The serious and quasi-legal nature of ADA proceedings also requires clinicians to avoid any potential conflicts of interest. It would, for example, be unethical for an evaluator to submit a report for a patient he taught or mentored.

Clinicians who prepare reports for ADA determinations must be familiar with how the law defines disability. They must also understand the nature of the program or task for which the accommodations are being sought. Reports cannot be written in a clinical vacuum where the goal is simply to establish a diagnosis. For ADA purposes, reports must describe impairment relative to current circumstances. They must also show how accommodations would relieve the impact of impairment within the current setting.

The evaluator should also delineate between test scores on clinical measures and the patient's actual functioning. It is not sufficient to note that test scores indicate a deficit in one or more areas. Instead, the clinician must indicate how the individual is actually impaired as a result of those measured deficits. Likewise, the clinician must discuss the impact of the impairment on the particular task or in the particular setting for which accommodations are being requested.

In addition to making recommendations for effective accommodations, the evaluator should note where accommodations would *not* be effective. They should also be careful to ensure that recommended accommodations "match" the identified functional limitations rather than relate to some desired outcome. Thus, an accommodation is not justified simply because it would "benefit" the patient. Instead, it should be justified because it mitigates the impact of the impairment.

The policies of all testing and licensure organizations stipulate that professionals who submit evaluations for ADA determinations be qualified in the specific disability area and with the specific population. For example, unless a psychologist has had training in diagnostic reading assessment, he or she should not make a diagnosis of a reading-related learning disability (LD). Likewise, a professional with training in school psychology or other educational fields would not be qualified to diagnose ADHD without the requisite training and experience in making differential diagnoses across all psychiatric disorders.

In all areas of disability assessment, but particularly for "hidden disabilities" such as LD, it is especially important that the evaluator provide complete data for all the tests and subtest administered. All measures used in the evaluation should be identified and standard scores should be given wherever available. All norms used in deriving scores should be identified and explained as necessary. For physical disabilities, the physician should be sure to provide comprehensive data to identify and verify specific functional limitations and to explain the logical connection between the impairment and the recommended accommodations.

THE DOCUMENTATION REVIEW PROCESS

Testing and licensure agencies should develop and publish the procedures they use to review documentation requests. Included should be deadline dates for notification and a general description of how the agency handles the process. It is essential that the organization adhere scrupulously to its stated policies and procedures. By doing so, it ensures that all examinees are treated fairly.

Because the data are often technical and can be complex, we recommend that documentation be reviewed by professionals with training in the specific disability areas. In this way, the agency can be assured that the materials have been considered by individuals with special expertise. Their input can be particularly useful in LD and ADHD determinations since such requests are often replete with psychological testing and complicated historical information.

Some organizations have hired in-house experts to review claims based on LD, ADHD, and psychiatric illness. They might only use external consultants upon occasion. Others use a panel of outside consultants to review the documentation and to make recommendations as to its adequacy.

If outside consultants are hired, it is important to stipulate that the agency itself remains the ultimate decision maker. Administrators should be careful to communicate that, while professionals should render their opinion about the merits of a particular case, they are not the final authority, because the ultimate decision rests with the agency.

It is also important to make sure outside consultants understand that the testing organization has no vested interest in either approving or disapproving a request for accommodations. The goal of the agency is simply to ensure that people with legitimate disabilities are provided accommodations. The consultant's role is to offer an impartial opinion based on the documentation that the examinee has submitted. The agency incorporates that opinion into the overall decision-making process.

When an examinee receives a denial of an accommodations request, the role of the TAA often becomes the most demanding of time, patience, and sensitivity. Unhappy applicants will often contact the agency to learn the reasons for the denial. It is important for the examinee and the administrator to communicate directly so that the reasons for the denial can be clarified. Often the TAA must educate the applicant about the law's requirements. He or she must also explain the specific reasons why the agency and its consults felt the case did not merit accommodations (or at least the level of accommodations that were requested).

The examinee is often not the only interested party who contacts the testing or licensure agency. The evaluators themselves now emerge as active and vociferous advocates. They often express dismay that their rationale for accommodation was denied. All too often, the diagnostician fails to understand the criteria that apply in such determinations. Here again, the TAA must serve in the role of educator about the ADA and the agency's documentation criteria.

ACCOMMODATIONS AND THEIR FUNCTION

As emphasized earlier, the ADA logically assumes that the purpose of accommodations is to ease or eliminate the effect of an impairment on a specific activity, whether it be reading, walking, seeing, or something else. In order to achieve a good "match" between the functional limitation and the remedy, it is important to know what accommodations and aids might be useful. Most testing organizations offer a wide array of technological and other aids to assist those who require them. The clinician can play a key role in working with the disabled individual and the testing organization in developing creative and effective solutions where accommodations are needed. The following examples illustrate the broad range of assistance that can be provided, depending on the need and circumstances.

Assistance in Completing Answer Sheets

Individuals with visual or motor limitations may have difficulty filling in the "bubble" answer sheets typically used with computer scored examinations. The examinee may be allowed to mark answers in the test booklet itself with a proctor making the transfer to the "bubble" sheet once testing time is ended. Often this is a necessary accommodation for people who have limited vision, since the answer form cannot be produced for computer scanning in a large print format. Sometimes the examinee's motor functions are limited to the degree that dictating answers to a scribe or amanuensis is a more effective accommodation.

Audiotape or Reader

People who are blind or have limited vision may benefit from an oral rendition of an examination. An audiotaped version offers a level of quality control and consistency not available with individual readers, yet still allows the examinee the independence to reverse or skip ahead to selected questions. Also, individuals with learning disabilities who are significantly limited in their ability to read may find an audiotape or reader to be an effective accommodation. Since oral language is almost always more slowly read aloud than print can be read silently, some additional time should be allotted when an examination is delivered in this format. Voice synthesis is yet another aid that can be provided in a computer-based testing situation for individuals with reading impairments.

Extended Testing Time

Additional testing time may ease the impact of a functional limitation that impedes someone's ability to process the test questions or to respond. However, other accommodations are often more directly effective in easing the impact of an impairment. For example, off-the-clock breaks for those who must interrupt the testing period for stretching, administration of medication, distractibility, and the like more directly respond to the need at hand.

Various Technological Aids

Technological aids range from the simple to the very complex. An adjustable table or chair can provide access to wheelchair users and others who have physical or motor impairments. Trackballs, custom keyboards, and zoomtext software are just a few of the many devices available to provide greater access to learning and test taking through use of computers.

A Printed Version of Verbal Instructions

Test takers who are hearing impaired may require assistance so that verbal instructions are eliminated.

Special Seating in a Test Center

Individuals with various muscular or orthopedic conditions may require adjustments to tables, chairs, and other equipment.

Large-Print Examinations

Large print can be useful to those with visual impairments and to some learning disabled individuals. Sometimes unique accommodations can be devised to meet the needs of an examinee in unusual circumstances. Such options are developed with the cooperation of the testing agency, the examinee, and whatever outside professionals are involved (such as physicians, rehabilitation therapists, or other clinicians).

GENERAL DOCUMENTATION GUIDELINES

Presented in Appendix 3.1 is information that the National Board of Medical Examiners (NBME), a testing organization, sends examinees who request test accommodations. It provides a framework for applicants and their evaluators.

IN CLOSING . . .

Testing organizations are keenly aware that they have a legal and moral responsibility to provide reasonable accommodations to individuals with disabilities. However, they also have a strong incentive to maintain the integrity of their examinations. The desire to uphold test standards motivates administrators to establish procedures that assure compliance with the ADA's outcome-neutral stance.

Individuals who request accommodations and the evaluators who conduct assessments must always bear in mind that the ADA guarantees equal access, not success. Especially when the request involves accommodations for high-stakes professional licensing examinations, the evaluator must strive for impartiality and strict adherence to professional diagnostic standards.

Accommodations are not won on the basis of advocacy, nor does ADA embody an entitlement for personal or professional advancement. The cause of equal rights for the disabled, and the interests of all of us, are best served when objectivity, professionalism, and fairness rule.

Appendix 3.1

NATIONAL BOARD OF MEDICAL EXAMINERS DOCUMENTATION GUIDELINES

GENERAL GUIDELINES

The following guidelines are provided to assist the applicant in documenting a need for accommodation based on an impairment that substantially limits one or more major life activities. Documentation submitted in support of a request is referred to experts in the appropriate area of disability for a fair and impartial professional review.

The individual requesting accommodations must personally initiate a written request for test accommodations; requests by a third party (such as an evaluator or medical school) cannot be honored.

Source: National Board of Medical Examiners (public domain).

To support a request for test accommodations, please submit the following:

1. Completed questionnaire.
2. A detailed, comprehensive written report describing your disability and its severity and justifying the need for the requested accommodations.

Documentation must:

- *State a specific diagnosis of the disability.* The diagnostic taxonomies used by the current edition of the American Psychiatric Association's *Diagnostic and Statistical Manual of Mental Disorders* (DSM-IV) are recommended.
- *Be current.* Because the provision of all reasonable accommodations is based on assessment of the **current** impact of the examinee's disability on the testing activity, it is in the individual's best interest to provide recent documentation. As the manifestations of a disability may vary over time and in different settings, in most cases the evaluation should have been conducted within the past 3 years.
- *Describe the specific diagnostic criteria and/or diagnostic tests used, including date(s) of evaluation, test results, and a detailed interpretation of the test results.* This description should include the specific results of diagnostic procedures and tests utilized as well as relevant educational, developmental, and medical history. Where appropriate, specific test scores should be reported to support the diagnosis.

    Diagnostic methods used should be appropriate to the disability and current professional practices within the field. Informal or nonstandardized evaluations should be described in enough detail that other professionals could understand their role and significance in the diagnostic process.
- *Describe in detail the individual's limitations due to the diagnosed disability, that is, a demonstrated impact on functioning vis-à-vis the USMLE, and explain the relationship of the test results to the identified functional limitations resulting from the disability.* The current functional impact on physical, perceptual, and cognitive abilities should be fully described.
- *Recommend specific accommodations and/or assistive devices, including a detailed explanation of why these accommodations or devices are needed and how they will reduce the impact of the identified functional limitations.*
- *Establish the professional credentials of the evaluator that qualify him/*

her to make the particular diagnosis, including information about license or certification and specialization in the area of the diagnosis. The evaluator should present evidence of comprehensive training and direct experience in the diagnosis and treatment of adults in the specific area of disability.

3. If no prior accommodations have been provided, the qualified professional expert should include a detailed explanation as to why no accommodations were given in the past and why accommodations are needed now.

LEARNING DISABILITIES

The following additional information is provided to clarify the documentation process for applicants submitting a request for accommodations based on a learning disability or other cognitive impairment.

1. *The evaluation must be conducted by a qualified professional.* The diagnostician must have comprehensive training in the field of learning disabilities and must have comprehensive training and direct experience in working with an adult population.

2. *Testing/assessment must be current.* The determination of whether an individual is "significantly limited" in functioning is based upon assessment of the **current** impact of the impairment. (See "General Guidelines.")

3. *Documentation must be comprehensive.* Objective evidence of a substantial limitation in cognition or learning must be provided. At a minimum, the comprehensive evaluation should include the following:

A Diagnostic Interview and History

Because learning disabilities are commonly manifested during childhood, though not always formally diagnosed, relevant historical information regarding the individual's academic history and learning processes in elementary, secondary, and postsecondary education should be investigated and documented. The report of assessment should include a summary of a comprehensive diagnostic interview that includes relevant background information to support the diagnosis. In addition to the candidate's self-report, the report of assessment should include the following:

- A description of the presenting problem(s).
- A developmental history.

- Relevant academic history including results of prior standardized testing, reports of classroom performance and behaviors including transcripts, study habits and attitudes, and notable trends in academic performance.
- Relevant family history, including primary language of the home and current level of fluency in English.
- Relevant psychosocial history.
- Relevant medical history including the absence of a medical basis for the present symptoms.
- Relevant employment history.
- A discussion of dual diagnosis, alternative or coexisting mood, behavioral, neurological, and/or personality disorders along with any history of relevant medication and current use that may impact the individual's learning.
- Exploration of possible alternatives that may mimic a learning disability when, in fact, one is not present.

A Psychoeducational or Neuropsychological Evaluation

The psychoeducational or neuropsychological evaluation should be submitted on the letterhead of a qualified professional, and it should provide clear and specific evidence that a learning or cognitive disability does or does not exist.

- Assessment should consist of a comprehensive battery of tests.
- A diagnosis must be based on the aggregate of test results, history, and level of current functioning. It is not acceptable to base a diagnosis on only one or two subtests.
- Objective evidence of a substantial limitation to learning must be presented.
- Tests must be appropriately normed for the age of the patient and should be administered in the designated standardized manner.

Minimally, the domains to be addressed should include the following.

Cognitive Functioning

A complete cognitive assessment is essential *with all subtests and standard scores reported*. Acceptable measures include, but are not limited to, Wechsler Adult Intelligence Scale—III (WAIS-III); Woodcock–Johnson Psychoeducationalcational Battery—Revised: Tests of Cognitive Ability; Kaufman Adolescent and Adult Intelligence Test.

Achievement

A comprehensive achievement battery with all subtests and standard scores is essential. The battery must include current levels of academic functioning in relevant areas such as reading (decoding and comprehension) and mathematics. Acceptable instruments include, but are not limited to, the Woodcock–Johnson Psychoeducational Battery—Revised: Tests of Achievement; The Scholastic Abilities Test for Adults (SATA); Woodcock Reading Mastery Tests—Revised.

Specific achievement tests are useful instruments when administered under standardized conditions and when interpreted within the context of other diagnostic information. The Wide Range Achievement Test—3 (WRAT-3) and the Nelson–Denny Reading Test are not comprehensive diagnostic measures of achievement and therefore neither is acceptable if used as the sole measure of achievement.

Information Processing

Specific areas of information processing (e.g., short- and long-term memory, sequential memory, auditory and visual perception/processing, auditory and phonological awareness, processing speed, executive functioning, motor ability) must be assessed. Acceptable measures including, but not limited to, the Detroit Tests of Learning Aptitude—Adult (DTLA-A), Wechsler Memory Scale—Revised (WMS-R), information from the Woodcock–Johnson Psychoeducational Battery—Revised: Tests of Cognitive Ability, as well as other relevant instruments, may be used to address these areas.

Other Assessment Measures

Other formal assessment measures or nonstandard measures and informal assessment procedures or observations may be integrated with the above instruments to help support a differential diagnosis or to disentangle the learning disability from coexisting neurological and/or psychiatric issues. In addition to standardized test batteries, nonstandardized measures and informal assessment procedures may be helpful in determining performance across a variety of domains.

Actual test scores must be provided (standard scores where available) (see "General Guidelines").

Records of Academic History Should Be Provided

Because learning disabilities are most commonly manifested during childhood, relevant records detailing learning processes and difficulties in elementary, secondary, and postsecondary education should be included. Such records as grade reports, transcripts, teachers' comments, and the like will serve to substantiate self-reported academic difficulties in the past and currently.

Differential Diagnosis

A differential diagnosis must be reviewed and various possible alternative causes for the identified problems in academic achievement should be ruled out.

The evaluation should address key constructs underlying the concept of learning disabilities and provide clear and specific evidence of the information processing deficit(s) and how these deficits currently impair the individual's ability to learn. *No single test or subtest is a sufficient basis for a diagnosis.*

The differential diagnosis must demonstrate that:

- Significant difficulties persist in the acquisition and use of listening, speaking, reading, writing, or reasoning skills.
- The problems being experienced are not primarily due to lack of exposure to the behaviors needed for academic learning or an inadequate match between the individual's ability and the instructional demands.

A Clinical Summary Must Be Provided

A well-written diagnostic summary based on a comprehensive evaluative process is a necessary component of the report. Assessment instruments and the data they provide do not diagnose; rather, they provide important data that must be integrated with background information, historical information and current functioning. It is essential then that the evaluator integrate all information gathered in a well-developed clinical summary. The following elements must be included in the clinical summary:

- Demonstration of the evaluator's having ruled out alternative explanations for the identified academic problems as a result of poor education, poor motivation and/or study skills, emotional problems, attentional problems, and cultural or language differences.
- Indication of how patterns in cognitive ability, achievement, and information processing are used to determine the presence of a learning disability.
- Indication of the substantial limitation to learning presented by the learning disability and the degree to which it impacts the individual context of the USMLE.
- Indication as to why specific accommodations are needed and how the effects of the specific disability are mediated by the recommended accommodation(s).

Problems such as test anxiety, English as a second language (in and of itself), slow reading without an identified underlying cognitive deficit or failure to achieve a desired academic outcome are not learning disabilities and therefore are not covered under the Americans with Disabilities Act.

Each Accommodation Recommended by the Evaluator Must Include a Rationale

The evaluator must describe the impact the diagnosed learning disability has on a specific major life activity as well as the degree of significance of this impact on the individual. The diagnostic report must include specific recommendations for accommodations and a detailed explanation as to why each accommodation is recommended. Recommendations must be tied to specific test results or clinical observations. The documentation should include any record of prior accommodation or auxiliary aids, including any information about specific conditions under which the accommodations were used and whether or not they were effective. However, a prior history of accommodation, without demonstration of a current need, does not in and of itself warrant the provision of a like accommodation. If no prior accommodation(s) have been provided, the qualified professional expert should include a detailed explanation as to why no accommodation(s) was used in the past and why accommodation(s) is needed at this time.

ATTENTION-DEFICIT/HYPERACTIVITY DISORDER (ADHD)

For those applicants submitting a request for accommodations based on attention-deficit/hyperactivity disorder (ADHD), the following additional information is provided to clarify the documentation process.

1. *The evaluation must be conducted by a qualified diagnostician.* Pro fessionals conducting assessment and rendering diagnoses of ADHD must be qualified to do so. Comprehensive training in the differential diagnosis of ADHD and other psychiatric disorders and direct experience in diagnosis and treatment of adults is necessary. The evaluator's name, title, and professional credentials, including information about license or certification as well as the area of specialization, employment, and state in which the individual practices should be clearly stated in the documentation.

2. *Testing/assessment must be current.* The determination of whether an individual is "significantly limited" in functioning is based on assessment of the current impact of the impairment on the USMLE testing program. (See General Guidelines)

3. *Documentation necessary to substantiate the attention-deficit/hyper-activity disorder must be comprehensive.* Because ADHD is, by definition, first exhibited in childhood (although it may not have been formally diagnosed) and in more than one setting, objective, relevant historical information is essential. Information verifying a chronic course of ADHD symptoms from childhood through adolescence to adulthood, such as educational transcripts, report cards, teacher comments, tutoring evaluations, job assessments, and the like, are necessary.

a. The evaluator is expected to review and discuss DSM-IV diagnostic criteria for ADHD and describe the extent to which the patient meets these criteria. The report must include information about the specific symptoms exhibited and document that the patient meets criteria for longstanding history, impairment, and pervasiveness.

b. A history of the individual's presenting symptoms must be provided, including evidence of ongoing impulsive/hyperactive or inattentive behaviors (as specified in DSM-IV) that significantly impair functioning in two or more settings.

c. The information collected by the evaluator should consist of more than self-report. Information from third-party sources are critical in the diagnosis of adult ADHD. Information gathered in the diagnostic interview and reported in the evaluation should include, but not necessarily be limited to, the following:

- History of presenting attentional symptoms, including evidence of ongoing impulsive/hyperactive or inattentive behavior that has significantly impaired functioning over time.
- Developmental history.
- Family history for presence of ADHD and other educational, learning, physical, or psychological difficulties deemed relevant by the examiner.
- Relevant medical and medication history, including the absence of a medical basis for the symptoms being evaluated.
- Relevant psychosocial history and any relevant interventions.
- A thorough academic history of elementary, secondary, and postsecondary education.
- Review of psychoeducational test reports to determine if a pattern of strengths or weaknesses is supportive of attention or learning problems.
- Evidence of impairment in several life settings (home, school, work, etc.) and evidence that the disorder significantly restricts one or more major life activities.
- Relevant employment history.
- Description of current functional limitations relative to an educational setting and to USMLE in particular that are presumably a direct result of the described problems with attention.
- A discussion of the differential diagnosis, including alternative or coexisting mood, behavioral, neurological, and/or personality disorders which may confound the diagnosis of ADHD.
- Exploration of possible alternative diagnoses that may mimic ADHD.

Relevant Assessment Batteries

A neuropsychological or psychoeducational assessment may be necessary in order to determine the individual's pattern of strengths or weaknesses and to determine whether there are patterns supportive of attention problems. Test scores or subtest scores alone should not be used as the sole basis for the diagnostic decision. Scores from subtests on the Wechsler Adult Intelligence Scale—III (WAIS-III), memory function tests, attention or tracking tests, or continuous performance tests do not in and of themselves establish the presence or absence of ADHD. They may, however, be useful as one part of the process in developing clinical hypotheses. Checklists and/or surveys can serve to supplement the diagnostic profile but by themselves are not adequate for the diagnosis of ADHD. When testing is used, standard scores must be provided for all normed measures.

Identification of DSM-IV Criteria

A diagnostic report must include a review of the DSM-IV criteria for ADHD both currently and retrospectively and specify which symptoms are present (see DSM-IV for specific criteria). According to DSM-IV, "the essential feature of ADHD is a persistent pattern of inattention and/or hyperactivity-impulsivity that is more frequent and severe than is typically observed in individuals at a comparable level of development." Other criteria include:

1. Symptoms of hyperactivity-impulsivity or inattention that cause impairment that were present in childhood.
2. Current symptoms that have been present for at least the past six months.
3. Impairment from the symptoms present in two or more settings (school, work, home).

Documentations Must Include a Specific Diagnosis

The report must include a specific diagnosis of ADHD based on the DSM-IV diagnostic criteria. Individuals who report problems with organization, test anxiety, memory, and concentration only on a situational basis do not fit the prescribed diagnostic criteria for ADHD. Given that many individuals benefit from prescribed medications and therapies, a positive response to medication by itself is not supportive of a diagnosis, nor does the use of medication in and of itself either support or negate the need for accommodation.

A Clinical Summary Must Be Provided

A well-written diagnostic summary based on a comprehensive evaluative process is a necessary component of the assessment. The clinical summary must include:

1. Demonstration of the evaluator's having ruled out alternative explanations for inattentiveness, impulsivity, and/or hyperactivity as a result of psychological or medical disorders or non-cognitive factors.
2. Indication of how patterns of inattentiveness, impulsivity, and/or hy-

peractivity across the life span and across settings are used to determine the presence of ADHD.

3. Indication of the substantial limitation to learning presented by ADHD and the degree to which it impacts the individual in the context for which accommodations are being requested (e.g., impact on the USMLE program).

4. Indication as to why specific accommodations are needed and how the effects of ADHD symptoms, as designated by the DSM-IV, are mediated by the accommodation(s).

Each Accommodation Recommended by the Evaluator Must Include a Rationale

The evaluator must describe the impact of ADHD (if it exists) on a specific major life activity as well as the degree of significance of this impact on the individual. The diagnostic report must include specific recommendations for accommodations. A detailed explanation must be provided as to why each accommodation is recommended and should be correlated with specific identified functional limitations. Prior documentation may have been useful in determining appropriate services in the past. However, documentation should validate the need for accommodation based on the individual's current level of functioning. The documentation should include any record of prior accommodation or auxiliary aid, including information about specific conditions under which the accommodation was used (e.g., standardized testing, final exams, NBME subject exams, etc.). However, a prior history of accommodation without demonstration of a current need does not in itself warrant the provision of a similar accommodation. If no prior accommodation has been provided, the qualified professional and/or individual being evaluated should include a detailed explanation as to why no accommodation was used in the past and why accommodation is needed at this time.

Because of the challenge of distinguishing ADHD from normal developmental patterns and behavior of adults, including procrastination, disorganization, distractibility, restlessness, boredom, academic underachievement or failure, low self-esteem, and chronic tardiness or inattendance, a multifaceted evaluation must address the intensity and frequency of the symptoms and whether these behaviors constitute an impairment in a major life activity.

RESOURCES

College Freshmen with Disabilities, A Triennial Statistical Profile. American Council on Education Heath Resource Center, Washington, DC. 1995.

Equal Employment Opportunity Commission, 29 CFR Part 1630, Equal Employment Opportunity for Individuals with Disabilities; Final Rule

Equal Employment Opportunity Commission, EEOC Compliance Manual, Vol 2, EEOC Order 915.002, Sec. 902, 3/14/95

U.S. Department of Justice, Office of the Attorney General, 28 CFR Part 35, Nondiscrimination on the Basis of Disability in State and Local Govermnet Services; Final Rule

U.S. Department of Justice, Office of the Attorney General, 28 CFR Part 36, Nondiscrimination on the Basis of Disability by Public Accommodations and in Commercial Facilities; Final Rule

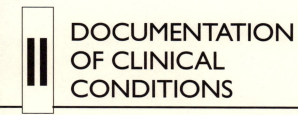

DOCUMENTATION
OF CLINICAL
CONDITIONS

Legal Requirements for Clinical Evaluations

James G. Frierson, MBA, JD

INTRODUCTION

The Americans with Disabilities Act of 1990 (ADA; PL 101-336) sets forth rules that exert a broad influence on society. The law involves five sections (or "Titles") that apply to different sectors of the economy, including general employment, local and state governmental units, public accommodations, transportation, and telecommunications. In all its aspects, however, the law embodies the same intent: to prohibit discrimination against qualified individuals with disabilities in programs, activities, and services. It prohibits eligibility criteria for such programs, activities, and services that screen out, or tend to screen out, individuals with disabilities. The law also requires accommodation of an individual's disability and the provision of necessary auxiliary aids.

While the law requires accommodations for individuals with disabilities, it does allow for certain exceptions: First, accommodations and auxiliary aids that create an undue burden on the organization or service provider are not required. For example, a student disabled by a respiratory condition may not demand that expensive air filtration devices be placed in all university buildings. Such an accommodation would place an undue burden on the university and may be denied on that basis.

Second, changes to essential job or program requirements are not required. For example, a court did not require a medical school to accommodate a blind physician who applied for a surgical residency. The court ruled that an essential requirement of surgery is to see the patient's body, thus there was no way the medical school could accommodate a surgeon who is blind. In a 1997 decision (*Guckenberger v. Boston University,* 7 AD Cases 484) the court held that "a university can refuse to modify academic degree requirements—even course requirements that students with learning disabilities cannot satisfy. . . . Neither the ADA nor the Rehabilitation Act require a university to provide course substitutions that the university rationally concludes would alter an essential part of its academic program" (pp. 516–517).

This chapter lays out the legal framework for physicians and other clinicians who are asked to provide documentation for ADA determinations. These guidelines are based on the law, court rulings, and governmental regulation and not on diagnostic criteria for the full spectrum of medical conditions. While the focus is on evaluations for physical disabilities, the reader should understand that these strategies and legal tests apply to all disabilities, physical and otherwise. You will therefore find some overlap with chapters in this book that detail assessments for mental and learning disorders because the rules set out by the law are general in scope, not specific to a type of disability.

While this book examines issues surrounding accommodations in higher education, the ADA and most of the regulatory and judicial decisions center on employment rather than on education. Fortunately, the principles involved pertain regardless of setting. The reader should understand, though, that many of these suggestions represent extrapolations from the employment arena.

Finally, many of the legal tests for qualifying an individual as disabled and for determining the appropriateness of accommodations are still uncertain. Court rulings on this matter are issued almost weekly with many of the decisions conflicting with one another. It will likely take years before a consensus of opinion emerges.

LEGAL LIABILITY OF CLINICIANS

ADA issues arise when clinicians examine, diagnose, make conclusions, and report their findings to a public service entity (such as a public university or a state or local governmental agency), to a place of public accommodation (such as a private university or testing organization), to an employer who is covered by Title I of the ADA. The ADA, Department of Justice (DOJ) regulations, and Equal Employment Opportunity Commission (EEOC) rules fail to state whether the individual clinician may be legally liable for violations of the ADA. However, a limited number of ADA court decisions, plus a much larger number of court decisions under similar laws, state that the clinician is not legally responsible, even if his or her diagnosis or conclusions are biased, unfair, or wrong.

Although clinicians, in a strictly legal sense, are not liable for their decisions, they certainly have a moral and ethical obligation to be fair and accurate in their decisions. Much of the process by which disabilities are determined hinges on valid and reliable information from practitioners. It is imperative that they become knowledgeable about how the rules affect employers, public services, and public accommodations. Without such an understanding, the clinician harms people with disabilities, as well as the employers or other entities that rely on the medical opinion of the clinician.

An illustration as to how clinicians may cause harm to all parties involved in a lawsuit is a New Jersey case brought against a grocery store. The plaintiff, an individual with epilepsy, worked as a meatcutter. One day he had a seizure at work that resulted in dropping his knife and wandering away from his job site. He was found a few moments later in the restroom with no memory of what he did. Other meatcutters complained to management, saying they felt unsafe when working with the individual. The company had the individual examined by two physicians. Both reported to the company that they would not hire or retain a person with epilepsy in a meatcutting position. One physician said that the individual "impresses me as risky and dangerous," while the other physician said that meatcutters with epilepsy are "potentially dangerous." Based on these medical findings, the supermarket discharged the meatcutter.

Evidence presented to the supermarket, and later in the court trial, showed that the individual's seizures were infrequent and mild, and that a change in medication would likely assure that he would not be subject to seizures at work. The court ruled that the supermarket violated the law by following the two physicians' recommendations. The recommendations were found to be deficient because the physicians' opinions were based on a general opinion or stereotype about people with epilepsy, and not the individual's current situation. Although the two physicians were not legally liable, their actions caused this successful lawsuit against the supermarket and harmed the meatcutter due to the time and expense of going to trial.

This case highlights perhaps the most important lesson physicians and other clinicians must take to heart when they become involved in ADA-related issues. It is a point that is reiterated in many ways throughout this chapter: *The determination of a disability and the subsequent decisions about accommodations must be considered in the educational (or occupational) context in which the individual intends to function*. It is always unwise to make assumptions about the impact of a disability without having a clear understanding of the essential demands of the educational program or job.

A clinician's diagnosis is only the first step in a determination of disability as defined by the law. In making an accommodations decision, the employer, educational institution, or testing organization needs accurate and impartial information about the individual's limitations in functioning that will affect the task in question. Neither the clinician nor the accommodating institution should assume, for example, that a person who is blind would be unable to manage training for a career in law or in sports broadcasting without understanding both the fundamental requirements of the job and the extent to which any limitations imposed by the disability could be circumvented without causing undue hardship.

This point also holds for scenarios on the other end of the disability spectrum. Under ADA, someone is disabled only if they suffer from a limitation that substantially hinders their ability to function in an educational program or job that he is otherwise qualified to manage. Consider the following example: A clinician declares a college student as learning disabled because of weakness in learning foreign languages. The evaluator advocates for the student to receive double time on all examinations throughout the student's academic career. It turns out, however, that the student is matriculated in a degree program that does not have a foreign language requirement. Furthermore, the college is understandably unwilling to provide such a broad accommodation for a limitation that is both circumscribed and largely irrelevant to academic success in the program.

WHO IS DISABLED?

The ADA protects individuals with disabilities. A disability is defined as a physical or mental impairment that substantially limits a major life activity. Major life activities as defined in the accompanying regulations include seeing, hearing, working, breathing, caring for oneself, organizing, thinking, and performing manual tasks, among others. Four types of individuals have rights under the ADA:

- Individuals who currently have a mental or physical impairment that substantially limits a major life activity. For example, a person who is paralyzed or blind.
- Individuals who have a past history of a mental or physical impairment that substantially limited a major life activity. For example, a person who had tuberculosis 20 years ago.
- Individuals who are discriminated against because they are regarded as having a disability that causes a substantial limitation on a major life activity. For example, a perfectly healthy person is covered by the ADA if an employer or educational institution discriminates against the individual because he or she incorrectly believes the individual has AIDS.
- Individuals who are discriminated against because of their association with a disabled person or group. For example, an employer who refuses to hire an applicant whose spouse is disabled because the employer is afraid the applicant will be absent from work in order to care for the spouse, or who refuses to hire an otherwise qualified person because the individual is active in an AIDS education program.

The ADA and the regulations under the ADA provide that the following conditions cannot be legal disabilities:

- Common personality traits such as poor judgment or quick temper that are not the result of a medically diagnosed mental or physiological disorder.
- Environmental, cultural, or economic disadvantages.
- Advanced age or other personal attributes such as having red hair or being left-handed.
- Compulsive gambling.
- Kleptomania.
- Pyromania.
- Psychoactive substance abuse disorders caused by the current, illegal use of drugs.
- Most sexual behavior disorders not resulting from a physical impairment, including transvestitism, homosexuality, bisexuality, pedophilia, exhibitionism, and voyeurism.
- Current drug abuse.

Alcoholism and past drug abuse may be disabilities. However, alcoholic individuals must meet the same rules applied to other people. For example, a company may discharge an alcoholic worker who brings alcohol to work, as long as the company also discharges non-alcoholic individuals who bring alcohol onto the employer's premises.

Prior to 1993, the parties to Rehabilitation Act and ADA lawsuits usually assumed that individuals diagnosed with illnesses such as epilepsy, cancer, diabetes, and other serious, chronic diseases were legally disabled. Lawsuits involved issues such as whether the defendant unlawfully discriminated on the basis of the individual's disability or failed to offer a reasonable accommodation. Typically the courts found a lack of a disability only when the plaintiff had a minor or frivolous claim, such as being left-handed, or where the impairment was not connected to the facts of the case, such as an accountant claiming that acrophobia caused a disability as an accountant.

Since 1993, federal courts have become involved in determining standards for qualifying an individual as disabled. One of the most disputed areas concerns whether an individual is legally disabled if the use of medicines and medical treatments removes the substantial limitation to the individual. Is someone with diabetes, for example, still disabled under the ADA if that condition has successfully been treated with insulin? Should an individual be considered legally disabled from depression if, with medication, those symptoms are largely absent?

The answers to these questions are still very uncertain because different courts have made different rulings. About half of the decisions apply the "medicated rule," whereby an individual with a mental or physical problem that is kept under control by modern medicine is not legally disabled. Because the individual is not legally disabled, he or she has no legal protection according to this position, even if the defendant openly discriminated based on the person's medical diagnosis, failed to accommodate the individual's impairment, or otherwise violated the ADA. The rationale is that the purpose of ADA is to protect individuals from discrimination on the basis of their disability. If their ability to function, however, is not impaired, that is, they are not disabled, then there would be no discrimination based on disability.

Under this approach, successfully treated diabetics are not disabled, nor are people with epilepsy whose medication eliminates their seizures. While such individuals suffer from legitimate medical conditions, they would not require accommodations and, according to this position, are not legally disabled.

However, the EEOC and the other half of court decisions in the past few years apply an "unmedicated test" to determine whether there is a substantial limitation on a major life activity. Under this approach, people with diabetes are legally disabled because without medical treatment, they could lose a foot or die. Obviously, life itself is a major life activity. The same point applies to many other impairments such as epilepsy, cancer, TB, learning disorders, or mental illness.

Clinicians, as well as employers, educators, and administrators, should proceed cautiously, because it is likely that an EEOC policy statement supporting the unmedicated test will increase the number of courts who use it. Additionally, if one is to err in determining whether a person has a legal disability, it may be more prudent to use the test that covers the largest number of people, that is, a disability is present when an impairment would substantially limit a major life activity when the condition is untreated (the unmedicated test).

CLINICAL EVIDENCE OF DISABILITY

Entities cannot be expected to know about a disability or provide accommodations unless individuals notify them. The burden for declaring a disability therefore falls upon the individual, not the entity. Although a disability may be obvious upon meeting someone who is in a wheelchair or blind, many disabilities are not obvious, such as diabetes, epilepsy, and so forth. Furthermore, whether or not the condition is apparent to others, it is not possible to know if the individual requires or even wishes to be accommodated in a given task or situation. When a claim of disability is made, or ADA accommodations or auxiliary aids are requested, the entity may require medical proof of disability. Unfortunately, the ADA, federal regulations on disability discrimination, and appellate court decisions offer only minor guidance as to the documentation needed to prove a disability. An EEOC interpretive guideline on employment states the following:

> If the need for accommodation is not obvious, an employer may ask an applicant for *reasonable* documentation about his/her disability. . . .

So, the applicant may be required to provide documentation from an appropriate professional, such as a doctor or a rehabilitation counselor.[1]

The only other governmental source concerning documentation of a disability begins as the one given above, then it adds a little more information:

> When the need for accommodation is not obvious, an employer may ask an employee for *reasonable* documentation about his/her disability and functional limitations. . . . A variety of health professionals may provide such documentation. . . .
>
> Example A: An employee asks for time off because he is "depressed and stressed." Although this statement is sufficient to put the employer on notice that he is requesting accommodation, the employee's need for accommodation is not obvious based on this statement alone. Accordingly, the employer may require *reasonable* documentation that the employee has a disability within the meaning of the ADA, and if he has a disability, that the functional limitations of the disability necessitate time off.
>
> The ADA does not prevent an employer from requiring an employee to go to an appropriate professional of the employer's choice if the employee provides insufficient information to substantiate that she/he has an ADA disability. . . . If an employer requires an employee to go to a health professional of the employer's choice, the employer must pay all the costs associated with the visit(s).[2]

Similar rules may be applied in cases involving public services and places of public accommodation.

The terms "reasonable documentation" and "appropriate professional" are not defined; and few, if any, court decisions have been rendered that would help define the terms. However, compliance with the following recommendations may avoid many ADA problems when dealing with applicants, employees, students, or other individuals claiming a disability:

- If the disability and extent of functional limitations are obvious, the entity should not require medical documentation that the individual is disabled. This applies when the individual is in a wheelchair, blind, deaf, or unable to speak, among others.
- If the disability is obvious, but the extent of functional limitations are not, the entity can require the individual to submit a state-

ment from a health care professional that outlines that person's functional limitations. For example, a student who claims to have a learning disorder asks for an accommodation under the ADA. The school can refuse to grant the accommodation until the student produces a statement from an appropriate health care professional that clarifies the extent of the learning disability and its impact on the student's ability to learn. Knowledge of the extent of the impairment is necessary to determine if the person is legally disabled and what accommodations might be needed. The expense of original documentation is on the individual. The entity does not have to pay.

- Where an entity suspects a lack of a legal disability, or the health care professional furnishes documentation that is not clearly stated or understood, the entity can contact the health care professional for additional information. However, the entity must obtain the individual's signature granting the clinician the right to discuss the individual's status. Clinicians should never disclose medical information without a written authorization. Appendix 4.1 at the end of this chapter may be used as a release or written authorization allowing clinicians to provide more information.

- When an individual documents his or her disability and the extent of his or her functional limitations by showing that the disability will substantially limit one or more major life activities, and the entity has no reason to question it, the entity must comply with the ADA rules banning discrimination and provide auxiliary aids and accommodations as appropriate.

- If the entity believes the health care professional's opinion is incorrect, the entity may require the individual to be examined by a health care provider chosen by the entity. In such cases, the entity must pay the expense of obtaining the health care professional's opinion.

The central point here is that the academic institution (or the employer) has the right to obtain additional information that documents the disability and the need for accommodation. Even though clinicians are not legally bound to provide that information, the "entity" has the right to request additional information if it obtains written authorization signed by the individual. Furthermore, it is important to remember that the law places the burden of documentation upon the individual claiming the disability. Therefore, a clinician who agrees to evaluate an individual seeking accommodations has an ethical responsibility to provide the entity with sufficient information to allow for a reasonable review.

An entity has a right to require the individual to go to another physician, but at the entity's expense. As stated above, a sample written authorization form appears at the end of this chapter as Appendix 4.1.

The key elements that a clinician should cover when ADA documentation is requested are the diagnosis, permanency of the problem (temporary or permanent), the specific nature and current extent of the impairment, any functional limitations, and any recommendations concerning accommodations that bear a relationship to the identified functional limitation. The doctor's role should be limited to advising the employer (or other entity) about an individual's functional abilities and limitations in relation to job (or program) functions, and about whether the individual meets the employer's (or other entity's) health and safety requirements. Although the clinician's recommendations are certainly important, the entity has no obligation to accept them at full face value. In other words, the entity has no legal duty to automatically comply with the diagnosis or recommendation.

Individuals and clinicians may request specific accommodations such as notetakers, a guide for individuals who are blind, or a wheel chair ramp. However, the entity is not automatically bound to provide the requested accommodations. The request may be denied if it will cause an undue burden on the entity, or the entity can provide other methods or devices that are effective. The legal burden remains with the service provider, university, or other entity. An EEOC manual explains:

> A doctor (or other clinician) who conducts medical exams should not be responsible for making employment (or admissions) decisions or deciding whether or not it is possible to make a reasonable accommodation for a person with a disability. That responsibility lies with the employer (or other entity).
>
> The doctor's role should be limited to advising the employer (or other entity) about an individual's functional abilities and limitations in relation to job (or program) functions, and about whether the individual meets the employer's (or other entity's) health and safety requirements.[3]

A sample standardized form for clinicians to use when providing medical documentation to public services is presented at the end of this chapter, in Appendix 4.2. The form may be used by public services (such as universities and cities), and public accommodations (such as a professional office or private school). A similar form given in Appendix 4.3 may be used in rendering opinions involving the employment of the individual with a disability. These forms may be combined with the more extensive information on clinical reports elsewhere in this book, or used as written.

Clinicians should be careful about what information it releases to employers, schools, and other third parties, even when a release or written authorization has been signed by the patient. Medical information irrelevant to the issue of disability and functional limitations should not be provided. For example, a physician is asked to render her opinion as to the impairment created by the amputation of four fingers resulting from an accident. The patient's file indicates that he had been treated for sexually transmitted diseases. The physician should not release this information.

CLINICIAN'S ADA DUTIES

The only two sections of the ADA that directly govern clinicians, such as physicians, psychologists and other experts, are the ADA regulations on public services and places of public accommodation. The public service rules apply to all state and local governmental units, while the public accommodations section applies to all clinicians in private practice and all nongovernmental hospitals and clinics. Either section of the law may apply to a clinician depending on whether the clinician works for a governmental unit or is in private practice. Although the law under the two sections presents substantially similar rules, there are some differences, which are discussed below.

According to the law, clinicians are considered an "entity" under one section of the law or another. A clinician's obligations under the law will be discussed for two reasons: First, if you are not aware of them you will need to be. Second, understanding your own obligations will illustrate the spirit and dictates of the law as it applies to others.

ACCESSIBILITY RULES

There are two types of accessibility problems addressed by sections of the ADA: (1) physical barriers to individuals with disabilities, and

(2) denial of full and equal services based on disability. A physical barrier may occur when access to a clinician's office requires climbing stairs, because people who use wheelchairs will be unable to get to the office. A denial of full and equal services may occur when the clinician or other entity treats a disabled individual differently from nondisabled people. For example, an endocrinologist specializing in diabetes refuses to see or treat an HIV-positive diabetic. In most cases this would violate ADA because HIV-positive individuals have a legal disability. However, if the refusal is based on the fact that the physician is not accepting any new patients, it is not a violation, since the disabled person is being treated in the same way as nondisabled people. Additionally, if the patient desires treatment for HIV, rather than diabetes, the physician is not required to render the treatment if it is outside his or her specialty. However, referral to a proper specialist is required, if the physician normally does this for patients.

The public services and the public accommodations sections of the ADA apply to all clinicians and other private or public entities serving the public. Unlike the rules under Title I (Employment), which require an employer to have 15 or more employees to be governed by the ADA, there are no minimum size requirements for public services or public accommodations. Even a psychologist who sees patients in his home must meet the accessibility requirements. The majority of accessibility rules imposed on clinicians concern physical and communication barriers. These rules will vary depending on whether the clinician works in a public service or a private setting. And it is in this area that Titles II and III of the ADA have different rules. The rules for public services emphasize "program accessibility." It states that a public entity may not discriminate in its programs and services because its facilities are not accessible to individuals with disabilities.

A U.S. Department of Justice (DOJ) manual states that program accessibility requires that a public entity's services, programs, and activities, when viewed in their entirety, must be readily accessible and usable by individuals with disabilities. This can be achieved by making the premises barrier-free, or moving the site where services are offered to a barrier-free site. For example, a medical school clinician sees patients in her office, which is on the second floor. The preferred change in access is to install an elevator. However, the ADA requirements on public services allow the clinician to arrange for examination in another room that is accessible to the disabled person, such as using an empty room on the first floor.

Title III (Public Accommodations) emphasizes the removal of physical barriers and the provision of communication devices that allow access and service. Clinicians in private practice and other entities subject to the public accommodations section are required to make "readily achievable" changes in removing barriers to disabled people. However, the readily achievable standard applies only to small changes in physical accessibility that do not place an undue hardship on the clinician or other entity. For example, the entrance to a psychologist's office has one step. Under the readily achievable standard, the psychologist should provide a ramp for those in wheelchairs. On the other hand, if the psychologist's office is on the second floor, ramping an entire flight of stairs is too costly to be readily achievable (and may be unworkable), therefore it is not required by the ADA. The readily achievable standard covers only smaller, less expensive alterations; however, the DOJ regulations on places of public accommodation require an annual survey of facilities and practices to determine if there are any readily achievable changes that could be made.

The ADA rules on public services and public accommodations do not require older buildings and offices to be fully accessible to disabled individuals. Physical accessibility of older structures is governed by the rules discussed previously. However, any offices and buildings that were first occupied after January 26, 1993, as well as older structures that undergo extensive remodeling, must meet the strict standards of the ADA Accessibility Guidelines (ADAAG) issued by the DOJ. State or local governments can choose to follow the ADAAG rules or very similar rules under the Uniform Federal Accessibility Standards (UFAS). Both standards appear in most looseleaf services on the ADA, and both may be ordered from the DOJ (Disability Rights Section, Department of Justice, P.O. Box 66738, Washington, DC; or phone [800] 514-0301 or [202] 616-2765).

AUXILIARY AIDS

Both the public services and public accommodations sections of the ADA require clinicians to provide auxiliary aids if necessary to serve the disabled person, unless the aid would violate the nature of the services or cause an undue burden. The issue of auxiliary aids is important in situations in which the individual's disability causes communication problems. Whether private or public, clinicians must provide reasonable auxiliary aids when it is necessary to communicate with a patient, client, or other person.

Auxiliary aids for deaf people include providing a qualified interpreter for the deaf, computer-aided transmission, assistive learning systems, notetaking, written materials, closed captioned videos, and phone devices. Auxiliary aids for blind individuals include the use of qualified readers, taped texts, audio recordings, Brailled documents, and assistance in locating items. Auxiliary aids for speech-impaired individuals may include computer terminals and speech synthesizers, among others.

As a general rule, a clinician must provide the proper auxiliary aid once the clinician knows of the individual's need for aid and it is necessary and effective. Although the ADA states that the auxiliary aid does not have to be furnished if it places an undue burden on the clinician, one should not take this too literally. Physicians have been required to provide deaf patients with qualified interpreters for the deaf even though the interpreter's fee exceeded the physician's fee. The ADA does not allow the physician or other clinician to add the cost of auxiliary aids to the patient's or client's bill.

Conformance with the auxiliary aids rules requires the clinician to determine if the aid or several aids would be effective and not cause an undue burden on the clinician. Regulations concerning public services of state and local governments require that the disabled individual's request for a specific auxiliary aid be given primary consideration, while the regulations on public accommodation state that the clinician should consult with the individual in determining necessary auxiliary aids. The following fact situations illustrate some of the requirements for auxiliary aids:

• A psychologist in private practice requires new patients to complete a written questionnaire. The psychologist is not required to have the questionnaire printed in Braille for blind patients. An effective alternative is to have a receptionist or other employee read the questions to the blind patient and record the answers. However, oral questions and answers must be given in private, so that the information is kept private, as patients who complete the written questions do so without bystanders or patients listening to the answers.

• A psychologist has patient information printed in Braille for blind patients. However, a blind patient requests an oral transmission, such as a reader or tape-recorded text. The psychologist should comply with the disabled person's request, if he or she is part of a state or local governmental unit, because the disabled individual's preference should be given primary consideration. If the psychologist is in private practice and the blind person cannot read Braille (a majority of blind people cannot read Braille), furnishing Brailled materials is not effective. Therefore, the psychologist should provide an effective alternative, such as a reader or taped text.

• A physician gives a routine physical exam of a patient who is deaf and mute. An interpreter for the deaf is not required if the physician and patient can communicate with gestures and written notes.

• A physician needs to discuss various options for cancer treatment with a deaf patient. Considering the importance of the subject, gestures and written notes would not be an effective auxiliary aid. The physician should ensure that a qualified interpreter for the deaf is used when discussing the patient's health problems.

• A patient who is deaf brings her own sign language interpreter for an office visit with a clinician. She requests that the clinician pay the interpreter's fees. The clinician is not required to pay the fee. Before auxiliary aids are chosen, the clinician must be given the opportunity to consider various alternatives that would result in effective communication.

• A blind patient insists that all written materials given to patients be printed in Braille. Because it would take considerable time and money to translate all patient documents to Braille, the ADA allows the physician to use other reasonable alternatives such as reading the written materials aloud to the blind person.

The auxiliary aid provisions apply only if the client or patient has given the clinician advance notice of a disability and the need for aid in communicating.

Although clinicians are likely to be sued only if they violate the rules for accessibility and auxiliary aids, they must understand the general ADA requirements concerning physical and mental impairments applicable to job applicants, employees, applicants for admission to programs or schools, and other areas in which the ADA applies. The case presented earlier in the chapter concerning the discharge of a meatcutter with epilepsy illustrates this. The physicians hired by the supermarket failed to properly serve the supermarket by giving incorrect opinions based on group stereotypes. To give proper advice, the physicians must have some knowledge of other sections of the ADA, so that the clinician can render useful information to an employer, state and local government, or places of public accommodation.

SUMMARY

The determination of disability based on physical or mental conditions requires clinicians to follow certain rules. These rules pertain regardless of the nature of the physical or mental condition involved. Some impairments will be easy to qualify as a disability and others, especially mental illnesses and learning disorders, will prove far more difficult. Even when the determination of disability and appropriate accommodations are less clear, professional diagnostic criteria and guidelines for accommodations are available (as discussed in the following chapters).

The biggest challenge to the clinician is to be sensitive and informed about the essential requirements of the educational program or job, and the extent to which any disabilities can be managed. Doctors should not be part of a process by which someone is excluded from an educational program or position simply because of faulty assumptions about the impact of the disabling condition. By the same token, clinicians must take care not to advocate for accommodations in the case of an individual who realistically cannot perform the essential functions of a program. Someone who is truly unqualified for a academic program is poorly served if accommodations allow for promotion despite inadequate skills. That individual will eventually (and sadly) fail in the workplace. Finally, clinicians should avoid declaring someone as disabled if there is not clear evidence of substantial impairment in relevant domains of functioning.

Appendix 4.1

WRITTEN AUTHORIZATION TO RELEASE MEDICAL INFORMATION[4]

CONSENT FOR RELEASE OF MEDICAL INFORMATION

I, [individual's name], hereby authorize [clinician's name] to release information to [name of entity] and its agents any and all information that is relevant to my disability of [name of medical condition] and the functional limitations imposed by my disability.

I desire [clinician's name] to disclose all materials that may be relevant to a determination of whether I have a disability, the extent of impairment, and possible accommodation(s).

In consideration for [clinician's name]'s act of providing medical information, I agree to release [clinician's name] and his/her agents from all legal responsibility and legal liability for any damage whatsoever resulting from the furnishing of the medical information. I promise not to make any complaint, legal or otherwise, because of any information, oral or written, released by the clinician or the clinician's agents.

_____

[Signature of individual]

_____

[Date]

Print or type the name, address, and phone number of the clinician listed in this form.

Adapted from Frierson (1995). Copyright 1995 by BNA Books. Adapted by permission in *Accommodations in Higher Education under the Americans with Disabilities Act (ADA),* edited by Michael Gordon and Shelby Keiser. Permission to photocopy this appendix is granted to purchasers of *Accommodations in Higher Education* for personal use only (see copyright page for details).

Appendix 4.2

SAMPLE GENERAL FORM FOR PROVIDING MEDICAL DOCUMENTATION CONCERNING ADMISSION, RETENTION, OR PROVISION OF ACCOMMODATION BY A PUBLIC OR PRIVATE ENTITY[5]

MEDICAL EVALUATION OF INDIVIDUAL

For Utopia University
123 Elm Street
Anytown, Homestate 00000

I have reviewed the medical status of [individual's name]. I understand that my examination or review is for the purpose of providing an opinion regarding the individual's disability, functional limitations, and their potential impact on his or her ability to participate in a program. The answers given below—the best responses circled and any additional statements made—reflect my medical judgment as to the medical status of the individual.

1. Are there any physical or mental functional limitations of the individual that will affect his or her ability to function in the program?

   Yes   No

   If yes, please explain:

Note: This form may be used by any clinician. However, other chapters in this book contain more detailed reports that may be used instead of or in conjunction with this one. Adapted from Frierson (1995). Copyright 1995 by BNA Books. Adapted by permission in *Accommodations in Higher Education under the Americans with Disabilities Act (ADA),* edited by Michael Gordon and Shelby Keiser. Permission to photocopy this appendix is granted to purchasers of *Accommodations in Higher Education* for personal use only (see copyright page for details).

2. Have you diagnosed the individual with a disability? (Please do not furnish a diagnosis or medical information that is not relevant to the public or private service listed above).

   Yes   No

   If yes, give the diagnosis:

3. If your answer to Question 1 is Yes, do you know of any accommodations that might help the individual to participate effectively in the program or services listed above?

   Yes   No

   If yes, please explain:

4. Does the individual have any physical or mental impairment that would create a current, significant risk of serious injury or death if he or she participates in the referenced program under the purpose of the evaluation contained in the first paragraph?

   Yes   No

   If yes, please explain:

5. In considering whether the individual poses a significant risk of serious injury or death, I have considered:

   a. The severity of the harm (e.g., serious injury or death).

      Yes   No

   b. The likelihood of an accident or other cause of harm occurring (e.g., a "significant" risk).

      Yes   No

   c. The imminence of the potential harm occurring (e.g., not just a future or speculative risk).

      Yes   No

6. If your answer to any part of Question 5 is yes, are you aware of any accommodations that might decrease the risk of serious injury or death?

Yes   No

If yes, please explain:

Please print or type:

_____

Name of clinician

_____

Professional designation (physician, psychologist, etc.)

_____

Highest academic degree (such as MD)

_____

Type of board certification or specialty

_____

Phone number

_____

Address

_____

Signature

_____

Date

Appendix 4.3

SAMPLE STANDARD FORM
FOR PROVIDING MEDICAL DOCUMENTATION
CONCERNING JOB APPLICANTS
AND EMPLOYEES[6]

MEDICAL EVALUATION

for Acme Company
123 Elm Street
Anytown, Homestate 00000

I have reviewed the medical status of [individual's name], and I understand that my examination or review is for the purpose of offering an opinion regarding the individual's ability to perform the essential functions of the position. The organization has furnished me information concerning the major job duties by listing the title, giving an oral explanation of job duties, giving a written job description, or providing a videotape showing necessary functions of the job. The answers given below—best responses circled and any additional statements made—reflect my medical judgment as to the medical qualification of the individual.

1. Are there any job functions the individual cannot perform because of a nontemporary mental or physical impairment?

    Yes   No

    If yes, please explain:

Note: This form may be used by any clinician. However, other chapters in this book contain more detailed reports that may be used instead of or in conjunction with this basic form. Adapted from Frierson (1995). Copyright 1995 by BNA Books. Adapted by permission in *Accommodations in Higher Education under the Americans with Disabilities Act (ADA),* edited by Michael Gordon and Shelby Keiser. Permission to photocopy this appendix is granted to purchasers of *Accommodations in Higher Education* for personal use only (see copyright page for details).

2. What are the person's functional limitations? How do they specifically relate to job performance? (Please do not furnish a diagnosis or medical information that is not relevant to job performance).

Yes   No

If yes, give the diagnosis:

3. If your answer to Question 1 is yes, what accommodations might help the individual effectively perform the job?

Yes   No

If yes, please explain:

4. Does the individual have any physical or mental impairment that would create a current, significant risk of serious injury or death if he or she performs the duties under the job listed above?

Yes   No

If yes, please explain:

5. In considering whether the individual poses a significant risk or serious injury or death, I have considered:

a. The severity of the harm (e.g., serious injury or death).

Yes   No

b. The likelihood of an accident or other cause of harm occurring (e.g., a "significant" risk).

Yes   No

c. The imminence of the potential harm occurring (e.g., not just a future or speculative risk).

Yes   No

6. If your answer to any part of Question 5 is yes, are you aware of any accommodations that might decrease the risk of serious injury or death?

Yes   No

If yes, please explain:

Name of clinician

Professional designation (physician, psychologist, etc.)

Highest academic degree (such as MD)

Type of board certification or specialty

Phone number

Address

Signature

Date

RESOURCES

Publication

Accommodating Disabilities (looseleaf service). Available from Commerce Clearing House (CCH), phone (800) TELL-CCH.

Akarbas, S., Gates, L., & Galvin, D. (1992). *Disability management.* New York: Amacon, a division of the American Management Association.

Frierson, J. (1995). *Employer's guide to the Americans with Disabilities Act* (2d ed.). Washington, DC: BNA Books.

Rothstein, L. F. (1997). Health care professionals with mental and physical impairments: Developments in disability discrimination law. *St. Louis University Law Journal, 41*(3), 973–1004.

BNA's Americans with Disabilities Act Manual (looseleaf service). Available from BNA Books, Washington, DC.

Burgdorf, R. (1995). *Disability discrimination in employment law* (1st ed.). Washington, DC: BNA Books.

Frierson, J. (1994). *Preventing employment lawsuits: A guide to hiring, discipline and discharge* (1st ed.). Washington, DC: BNA Books.

Government Sources of Information

Department of Justice
Disability Rights Section
P.O. Box 66738
Washington, DC 20035
(800) 514-0383
    Final Rule Implementing Title II of ADA
    Final Rule Implementing Title II of ADA
    Accessibility Guidelines
    DOJ Technical Assistance Manual, Title II
    DOJ Technical Assistance Manual, Title III

Equal Employment Opportunities Commission (EEOC)
1801 L Street, NW
Washington, DC
(800) 669-EEOC
    Final Rule Implementing Title I of ADA
    EEOC Technical Assistance Manual, Title I
    EEOC Interpretive Guidance on Title I of ADA
    EEOC Enforcement Guidance: Pre-employment Inquiries and
        Medical Exams
    EEOC Guidance Memorandum on Definition of "Disability"
    EEOC Enforcement Guidance on Workers' Compensation and
        ADA
    EEOC Enforcement Guidance on Benefits Application and ADA
    EEOC Enforcement Guidance on the ADA and Psychiatric Disabilities
    Fact Sheet on the FMLA, the ADA, and Title VII of the 1964 Civil
        Rights Act

NOTES

1. Guidance on Pre-Employment Disability-Related Inquiries and Medical Examinations, issued by the Equal Employment Opportunity Commission on October 10, 1995.
2. Guidance on the ADA and Psychiatric Disabilities, issued by the Equal Employment Opportunity Commission on March 25, 1997.

3. Equal Employment Opportunity Commission Technical Assistance Manual on Title I of the Americans with Disabilities Act, Section 6.4, issued on January 26, 1992.
4. Modified from a form contained in J. Frierson, *Employer's Guide to the Americans with Disabilities Act* (2nd ed.). BNA Books, Washington, DC (1995), pp. 359–360.
5. Modified from a form originally appearing in J. Frierson, *Employer's Guide to the Americans with Disabilities Act* (2nd ed.). BNA Books, Washington, DC (1995), pp. 374–376.
6. Form originally appeared in J. Frierson, *Employer's Guide to the Americans with Disabilities Act* (2nd ed.). BNA Books, Washington, DC (1995), pp. 374–376.

5 Attention-Deficit/Hyperactivity Disorder

Michael Gordon, PhD
Kevin R. Murphy, PhD

INTRODUCTION

Attention-deficit/hyperactivity disorder (ADHD) has become an increasingly popular basis for seeking accommodations under the Americans with Disabilities Act of 1990 (ADA; PL 101-336). While precise statistics are unavailable, most institutions and testing organizations are reporting at least a doubling in the number of ADHD-based claims over the past 5 years. ADHD has also become a more common comorbid condition to other psychiatric disorders and to learning disabilities.

The swelling ranks of those claiming ADHD for legal accommodations mirror the rise in ADHD identifications within the general population. Although estimates vary widely depending on methodology, the most conservative indicate that the number of children identified over the past decade has also almost doubled. Because research now documents that ADHD symptoms tend to persist beyond adolescence, assignment of the diagnosis to adults has been transformed from a rare event just 10 years ago to a popular and seemingly sought-after psychiatric label. Also, a blizzard of media stories, editorials, books, and magazine articles has propelled ADHD to star status within the orbit of mental health disorders. The increased awareness about the disorder could alone account for the burgeoning of ADHD diagnoses.

The rapid rise in identification rates, prescriptions for stimulant medications, and ADHD-based claims for accommodations have bred no small amount of skepticism and controversy about the disorder. It has been called a "diagnosis du jour," a "boutique disorder," and "psychofad." Questions have also been raised about the legitimacy of diagnostic and treatment practices.

Unfortunately, little of the public debate about ADHD has been encumbered by the weight of scientific study. Despite a voluminous research literature, much of the discourse about the disorder floats more on fancy than on fact. Nowhere is the disregard of empirical information more evident than in discussions of pharmacological interventions. Descriptions of stimulant effects in the lay press usually bear faint resemblance to documented phenomena derived from scientific investigations.

Why has ADHD become such a lightning rod for controversy? In our opinion, much of the answer lies in the nature of the disorder itself. First, the core symptoms of the disorder are also core symptoms of human nature. Everyone is prone toward some degree of inattention and impulsiveness. There is even concern for people who are not, at least occasionally, carefree and perhaps overly exuberant. The mere fact that an individual can be impulsive or inattentive is often insignificant because these are such common human traits. In essence, ADHD represents a set of common behaviors displayed to uncommon extents. As such, it is not unique, because almost all mental illnesses, from depression to mania, are normal tendencies taken to extremes.

The second characteristic of ADHD symptoms that causes some confusion is that they are typical not only of normal behavior, but also of the full range of psychiatric abnormalities. Nearly all the mental health disorders listed in the fourth edition of the *Diagnostic and Statistical Manual of Mental Disorders* (DSM-IV; American Psychiatric Association, 1994) contain at least one symptom related to inattention, disorganization, and poor concentration. Inattention is so ubiquitous a symptom of mental illness that, alone, it is wholly nondiagnostic. If anything, it is a universal manifestation of mental or physical distress.

The third characteristic of ADHD that assures a degree of complexity is its dimensionality. ADHD is not an all-or-nothing condition like pregnancy. Instead, it represents the far end of normal curves for impulse control and attention. Because it is defined by a point along a continuum, its identification inherently involves some degree of subjectivity in establishing cut points. How inattentive or impulsive one has to be to qualify for a diagnosis is therefore a matter of some judgment, especially when the intensity of problems falls within those gray zones between normal and abnormal. Whenever opinion forms the basis for important aspects of diagnostic decision making, the door is left open for a measure of uncertainty and inconsistency.

Delineating normal impulsiveness and inattention from abnormal levels is no small task except in flagrant cases of poor adjustment. It becomes an especially difficult judgment when evaluating individuals seeking academic or testing accommodations past high school. After all, many of the students who request accommodations in postsecondary settings are high functioning individuals. They have graduated from high school after having performed well enough to gain college admission, a feat accomplished by only about one quarter of the population. Only a tiny segment of Americans have the wherewithal to proceed to postgraduate training. While individuals in postsecondary programs can certainly experience serious problems, they generally have fared well, if not spectacularly so, compared to most of the population.

Despite ample room for uncertainty and disagreement, certain agreed-upon features of the disorder make the diagnosis of ADHD far from an arbitrary affair. As you will see below, research has established a reasonable footing upon which a diagnosis of ADHD for any particular patient can be constructed. In general, the key building blocks have been formed by evidence that this is a generally chronic disorder which has an early onset, affects multiple domains of functioning, and is best understood in terms of profound impulsiveness. In our view, many inappropriate ADHD-based accommodations claims could be avoided if these essential requirements were observed.

ESSENTIAL CRITERIA

The official U.S. criteria for ADHD, like criteria for all psychiatric disorders, are based on DSM-IV. Although a host of legitimate reservations have been expressed about this approach (Barkley, 1998), it nonetheless represents the current and most empirically valid standard. Any accommodations report for ADHD must describe the extent to which the patient meets DSM-IV criteria. Reports should include a statement about the number of symptoms exhibited by the patient and documentation that he or she meets criteria for early onset, impairment, and pervasiveness.

For your review and with the permission of the American Psychiatric Association, here are the criteria for ADHD:

Attention-Deficit/Hyperactivity Disorder

A. Either (1) or (2):

(1) six or more of the following symptoms of **inattention** have persisted for at least 6 months to a degree that is maladaptive and inconsistent with developmental level:

Inattention
(a) often fails to give close attention to details or makes careless mistakes in schoolwork, work, or other activities
(b) often has difficulty sustaining attention in tasks or play activities
(c) often does not seem to listen when spoken to directly
(d) often does not follow through on instructions and fails to finish schoolwork, chores, or duties in the workplace (not due to oppositional behavior or failure to understand instructions)
(e) often has difficulties organizing tasks and activities
(f) often avoids, dislikes, or is reluctant to engage in tasks that require sustained mental effort (such as schoolwork or homework)
(g) often loses things necessary for tasks or activities (e.g., toys, school assignments, pencils, books, or tools)
(h) is often easily distracted by extraneous stimuli
(i) is often forgetful in daily activities

(2) six (or more) of the following symptoms of **hyperactivity–impulsivity** have persisted for at least 6 months to a degree that is maladaptive and inconsistent with developmental level:

Hyperactivity
(a) often fidgets with hands or feet or squirms in seat
(b) often leaves seat in classroom or in other situations in which remaining seated is expected
(c) often runs about or climbs excessively in situations in which it is inappropriate (in adolescents or adults, may be limited to subjective feelings of restlessness)
(d) often has difficulty playing or engaging in leisure activities quietly
(e) is often "on the go" or often acts as if "driven by a motor"
(f) often talks excessively

Impulsivity

(g) often blurts out answers to questions before the questions have been completed

(h) often has difficulty awaiting turn

(i) often interrupts or intrudes on others (e.g., butts into conversations or games)

B. Some hyperactive–impulsive or inattentive symptoms that caused impairment were present before age 7 years.

C. Some impairment from the symptoms must be present in two or more situations (e.g., at school [or at work] and at home).

D. There must be clear evidence of clinically significant impairment in social, academic, or occupational functioning.

E. The symptoms do not occur exclusively during the course of a Pervasive Developmental Disorder, Schizophrenia, or other Psychotic Disorder, and are not better accounted for by another mental disorder (e.g., Mood Disorder, Anxiety Disorder, Dissociative Disorder, or a Personality Disorder).

Code based on type:

314.01   Attention-Deficit/Hyperactivity Disorder, Combined Type: if both Criteria A1 and A2 are met for the past 6 months

314.00   Attention-Deficit/Hyperactivity Disorder, Predominantly Inattentive Type: if Criterion A1 is met but Criterion A2 is not met for the past 6 months

314.01   Attention-Deficit/Hyperactivity Disorder, Predominantly Hyperactive–Impulsive Type: if Criterion A2 is met but Criterion A1 is not met for the past 6 months

While these criteria contain a list of relevant symptoms and embody the disorder's cardinal features, they are fraught with ambiguity. How much impairment is "clinically significant" impairment? Does a patient have to fail miserably in all academic or vocational settings to qualify? To what extent do the symptoms have to appear across settings? To qualify for the diagnosis, does there have to be evidence that ADHD-type symptoms caused impairment prior to age 7, or is it sufficient that they simply were in evidence?

Any reviewer involved in the accommodations process is fully aware that this diagnosis (and any psychiatric diagnosis for that matter) is ultimately based on clinical judgment. Because there are no unassailable markers or tests, we are all left to interpret these criteria as best we can.

While there is abundant room for subjectivity in the process, certain elements are central and form the basis for a reasonable diagnosis. They also provide the underpinnings for all of our ensuing comments regarding documentation. (Full discussions about these diagnostic guideposts are available in two books by the first author, *How to Operate an ADHD Clinic or Subspecialty Practice* and *The Diagnosis and Treatment of ADD/ADHD: A No-Nonsense Guide for the Primary Care Physician* [with M. Irwin]. Information about both of these texts is available in the Resources section at the end of this chapter.) For now, we will simply highlight each concept:

Onset

According to current theory and ample research, ADHD is a developmental disorder with a relatively early onset. While many dispute (and perhaps justifiably so) the DSM-IV's insistence that symptoms be present and impairing prior to 7 years of age, there is near-universal agreement that this is not an adult onset disorder. The only generally accepted exception to this rule comes in cases of acquired ADHD, perhaps as a result of head injury. For the vast majority of cases, however, the consensus is that ADHD-type characteristics should be present in the early years, although actual evidence of observable impairment need not surface until around middle school.

The early onset of this disorder has far-reaching implications for the diagnostic process. It dictates that the identification of ADHD in adulthood is based predominantly on evidence of the disorder in childhood. Because an early onset is a necessary although not entirely sufficient condition for assigning an ADHD diagnosis, the evaluation focuses heavily on ages 4 through 12. Without confirmation of early impairment, it is highly unlikely that an individual warrants the ADHD label. While there are credible explanations for a somewhat later onset (perhaps even into high school), these represent more the proverbial exception than the rule. As we discuss in the next section, most justifications offered for late onset are unconvincing and poorly substantiated.

Consistency

While ADHD is appropriately designated as a disorder, it more accurately represents certain traits gone awry. In other words, ADHD symptoms are normal human characteristics that become manifest in the extreme. We therefore expect that individuals who suffer from this problem will exhibit an enduring ADHD-type style over time. Although symptoms can certainly vary in their impact on a person's functioning depending on circumstance, they never abruptly arrive and depart. A credible diagnosis documents the relative temporal stability of the problem, and offers reasonable explanations for those periods during which the symptoms seem to abate.

Pervasiveness

Because ADHD is understood as a "hard-wired" feature of an individual's makeup, someone who suffers from the disorder will show significant impairment across much of his or her experience. The criteria therefore require evidence that symptoms arise in more than one setting or situation. For example, it is hard to defend a diagnosis of ADHD for an individual who had (or has) problems in only isolated classes or just when taking multiple choice examinations. While few individuals with ADHD have problems everywhere and always, virtually all show a pattern of behavior that reflects, for the most part, global impairment. For someone who truly suffers from this disorder, life is all too often characterized by disrupted interpersonal relationships, underperformance in school and at jobs, and generally inadequate adjustment. Individuals with ADHD have little problem regaling clinicians with accounts of serious impulsiveness, inattention, and poor functioning.

Severity

Establishing that the symptoms cause what the criteria describe as "clinically significant impairment" represents the single most critical and challenging component of the evaluation. But without documentation that the problems have had a serious effect on a patient's functioning, the clinician runs the risk of assigning a psychiatric label to what ultimately might embody personality traits or an individual's particular array of strengths and weaknesses. *Simply identifying that an individual can be impulsive or inattentive is not enough to justify a diagnosis*. As we indicated above, most of us can identify such tendencies in ourselves and even point to examples of how they interfered with our efficient attainment of important goals. To warrant a diagnosis of ADHD, the diagnostician must present compelling data that these symptoms significantly and seriously interfere with normal functioning.

As Gordon and Keiser discussed in Chapter 1, the ADA and its attendant regulations make it clear that these judgments of severity should be based on comparisons to the general population and not to a person's educational peer group or to a particular set of expectations. For example, let's say that on a test of attention an individual achieves a standard score of 101. While this score clearly falls in the normal range, some clinicians will claim that it actually represents a deficit relative to the patient's measured IQ and perhaps the typical score of others in that educational program. At least for ADA determinations, however, a normal score is a normal score, even if it compares poorly to other scores.

One more point about determinations of severity: The DSM-IV defines the degree of severity in part based on the number of reported symptoms. It is important that you acknowledge this particular method by stating in your report how many of the symptoms in the list your patient exhibits. But also be aware that current research supports a somewhat lower threshold for the number of symptoms required. While that threshold varies by age and gender, it falls more in the four to five range than the total of six stipulated by the official criteria (Murphy, 1996).

Impulsive/Hyperactive Behavior

Theory and research alike point to behavioral disinhibition as ADHD's core feature (Barkley, 1997). The overwhelming evidence is that individuals with ADHD first and foremost demonstrate profound and pervasive problems stopping themselves from responding to signals, events, or stimuli that are irrelevant to completing a task. Their problems with inattention are just one consequence of being unable to keep themselves from responding to whatever may come down the pike, whether it be noises, ideas, or loose threads on a sweater. According to this notion, distractibility, inability to plan ahead, disorganization, peer problems, need for novelty, certain language problems, and a seeming inability to anticipate consequences all result from poor self-control. At the heart of ADHD is the relative incapacity to keep from responding to whatever seems most interesting or rewarding at the moment.

Research has not only established that much of ADHD behavior is associated with disinhibition, it has also pointed to abnormal impulsiveness as relatively unique to children with this disorder. While inattention can surface in the presentation of many sorts of problems, impulsive/hyperactive behavior generally arises only with ADHD children. The obvious exception to this general rule comes with children suffering from a severe psychiatric disturbance (such as pervasive developmental disorder, autism, bipolar disorder, and childhood schizophrenia), developmental disabilities, or neurological impairments. Youngsters suffering from any of these conditions can be counted on to act impulsively.

Because so much evidence supports the centrality of impulsive/hyperactive behavior as the hallmark of ADHD, it is essential to establish that the patient has a consistent history of poor self-control. Reviewers understand that the nature, scope and intensity of that disinhibition will vary and that the degree of physical impulsiveness often diminishes past puberty. Some ADHD patients can point to untold numbers of times where they leaped before looking; others will provide evidence of fidgetiness or profound disorganization—some evidence of impulsive/hyperactive behavior must be present.

How about those individuals without a history of impulsiveness or hyperactivity? Can they be labeled as ADHD? The criteria do indeed allow for a diagnosis of ADHD–predominantly inattentive type. We would, however, suggest that this diagnosis be assigned only with utmost care and consideration. Why? Because individuals can be inattentive for almost every reason under the sun. It is a common symptom of nearly every psychiatric and learning disorder. It also arises within normal populations during times of physical or emotional stress. *Inattention alone does not an ADHD individual make.*

In our experience and according to available research, someone who only exhibits inattention (as opposed to inattention within the context of impulsivity/hyperactivity) is more likely to experience some other psychiatric or learning disorder or simply the frustrations that stem from failure. In our practices, we assign the diagnosis of ADHD–predominantly inattentive type only when we have first ruled out other psychiatric or learning disabilities. It is a legitimate diagnostic entity, but it should be assigned only following a careful process of elimination.

CREDIBLE CLINICAL EVIDENCE

In this section we cover the kinds of clinical information that are required to justify an ADHD diagnosis. You will notice that we do not concern ourselves much with how this information is collected. Relevant diagnostic techniques are amply covered in a wide variety of texts (see Resources section below) and we will not duplicate those efforts here. Moreover, how clinicians collect data is not as critical to reviewers as the credibility, quality, and relevance of the information they report. For example, reviewers will tend not to quibble over whether information from the parents of your patient was collected through rating scales or phone calls. They are far more focused on the validity of that information and the degree to which it is corroborated by other data.

For each domain of clinical evidence, we will present a brief rationale for its inclusion. We also highlight some of the errors we have noticed clinicians can make when they cover these topics in reports.

History

The diagnosis of ADHD in adulthood travels heavily on the wheels of symptom history. While experts differ on many ADHD-related issues, they are universal in supporting the position that this is a developmental disorder with a relatively early onset. To be credible, a report must present convincing verification that ADHD symptoms and characteristics appeared in early childhood. In other words, there has to be meaningful evidence that the symptoms surfaced early, and that, at least by middle school, they caused demonstrable interference in functioning. Without persuasive proof that impairment has been long-standing, consistent, and truly disruptive to normal functioning, reviewers will likely cast a skeptical eye on your diagnosis. There are no data like hard data.

We want to reemphasize that the requirement for an early onset does not necessary mean that the individual had to have been woefully impaired in childhood. Not all ADHD individuals were out-of-control preschoolers and unmanageable students in the early grades. Often, what parents and teachers report about this period is that the youngster showed evidence of ADHD characteristics, although not necessarily to the degree that they caused markedly poor adjustment.

For many individuals with bona fide ADHD, true signs of impairment do not surface until around middle school, when demands mount for planning, organization, and homework completion.

While credible cases can be made for onset of ADHD-type impairment beginning in the middle school years (and maybe even into high school), it is nearly impossible to justify the diagnosis when symptoms *suddenly* arise after high school graduation. It is particularly hard when the first instance of any real problems arose after graduation from college (often in a professional school and following failure on an examination). How impaired can a person be relative to the general population if the worst of his or her problems occurs in academic settings far beyond the reach of most people?

Except in cases when the ADHD symptoms are acquired because of a head injury or some other physical trauma, there must be some documentable trail of impairment that leads back to the early school years. Again, ADHD is a developmental disorder that, by definition, has roots in childhood and, in almost every case, leaves its mark on a wide swath of the individual's life.

Clinicians will typically justify adult onset of the disorder by citing arguments that are wholly unconvincing. For example, the argument is often made that the applicant's high native intelligence masked symptoms, allowing him or her to compensate successfully until current academic demands arose. Reviewers generally do not view this, by itself, as an adequate explanation, because there is little scientific evidence to support it. While IQ is related to academic achievement, it in no meaningful way is associated with the manifestation of ADHD symptoms or, for that matter, ultimate outcome. High intelligence may reduce the absolute level of academic impairment, but it does not serve as a protective factor that "shuts down" the expression of ADHD symptoms. Some of our most impaired ADHD patients have IQs in the superior range of intellectual functioning.

If individuals with high IQs are able to compensate for their symptoms, they likely are not as impaired as those who have not been able to compensate. The capacity to compensate through whatever means is itself evidence that the symptoms are not so severe that they rise to the level required for an ADA determination of disability. Except when it occurs as a result of unusual external factors (such as special accommodations or pharmacotherapy), the ability to compensate indicates that problems are either mild in their own right or easily handled by other skills and attributes. While they may justify a variety of interventions, very mild symptoms may not justify ADA-level accommodations. Put another way, someone with subthreshold problems may benefit from treatment, but they are not entitled to legal protections.

Another common but often unpersuasive argument is that the student was able to overcome symptoms successfully because he or she was highly motivated and hard working. What some clinicians suggest, then, is that symptoms can be masked by a desire to achieve. For instance, we reviewed a case in which an examinee applying for test accommodations based on an ADHD diagnosis had been the valedictorian of her high school class. The psychiatrist supporting the accommodation claimed that this level of stellar academic success was not inconsistent with an ADHD diagnosis. His rationale was the she was able to achieve a 4.0 average only with massive amounts of effort. Needless to say, we found that line of reasoning hard to accept. Outstanding academic achievement and personal success commonly require strong motivation and earnest effort. Indeed, it would be surprising if someone were able to achieve straight A's *without* burning the midnight oil.

That someone has to work hard to achieve goals is not evidence of an impairment. Conversely, the ability to overcome tendencies toward inattention and impulsiveness successfully usually proves that ADHD-type characteristics fall more in the realm of personal style than of psychiatric disability. Disability is defined by poor compensation, not by adequate compensation that requires some effort.

Are there explanations for late onset that reviewers will find convincing? Yes, but not often. They typically fall into two categories, as described below:

• *Unique environmental factors.* Some individuals achieved successfully during their primary and secondary schooling only because of medication, unusual educational programming, or psychiatric intervention. For example, an individual might have made it through high school without evidence of serious underperformance because he was on medication or because he regularly received special educational services such as tutoring. In one case, an individual's early educational history was unremarkable because he attended a special school that boasted a 6 to 1 student/teacher ratio. In another instance, an ADHD student with a miserable academic record was accepted into college because her family donated the funds for a new wing to the science center. Reviewers will accept explanations for later onset when clinicians identify special factors that are credible and well documented.

• *Heavy psychiatric costs*. Some individuals with ADHD can achieve successfully but only at a severe personal price. They may have gotten A's and B's in high school, but they showed clear evidence of clinically significant (that is, diagnosable) anxiety or depression as a consequence. In these cases, the effort to adjust took such a personal toll that other psychiatric symptoms emerged.

The evidence for a childhood onset must be more than vague self-report by the student. Most of us can look back on our education and identify times when we underachieved or were unmotivated. Self-reported memories of having been inattentive or disorganized are, in themselves, unconvincing. What they often reflect are comparisons to internal and idiosyncratic norms for appropriate behavior.

All of us are especially likely to latch onto such events when we are faced with some current academic or vocational failure. However, for the purpose of ADA documentation, the clinician must provide clear evidence of a symptom history beyond simply recounting a patient's self-report. If an individual had symptoms serious enough to warrant a claim of early impairment, there should be some paper trail. The combination of self-report with objective evidence will be compelling. The more objective the data provided about past functioning, the better the chances of approval.

What serves as credible evidence? We've listed below the sorts of information that reviewers find most convincing:

- Copies of past elementary, junior high, and high school report cards (not just selected ones but many years' worth of documentation).
- College, medical, or law school transcripts.
- Prior psychiatric evaluations.
- Prior psychological test reports.
- Prior educational testing reports.
- Prior standardized testing scores (such as SATs, LSATs, or MCATs).
- Evidence of prior academic accommodations in earlier grades.
- Any performance evaluations from past jobs or clerkships.
- Military records.

- Descriptions (in narrative or via rating scales) from parents, spouses, teachers, friends, roommates, coworkers, and/or supervisors.

We cannot emphasize enough how important it is to provide as much hard evidence as possible supporting an ADHD-type history. But as we emphasize in the next section, historical evidence of impairment must be linked to evidence of current impairment. For example, that a student received accommodations in high school does not *necessarily* justify the provision of accommodations in a new or different setting. The earlier accommodations might have been easier to achieve or were granted in a setting less concerned about formal definitions of disability.

Current Symptoms

Even though we have made mountains out of the need for documenting a childhood onset, we do not intend to overlook requirements for providing evidence of current impairment. Although ADHD is considered a chronic disorder, its symptoms do not always persist into adulthood. (While estimates vary, somewhere between 50% and 70% of children identified with ADHD in childhood will still show symptoms serious enough to warrant an ongoing diagnosis.) It therefore behooves the clinician to make a case that the ADHD symptoms have indeed continued to cause impairment.

For those individuals who have a clear early history of ADHD, it is often not difficult to establish that problems persist. It is more difficult however, when the evidence of early ADHD-type impairment is weak or nonexistent. And it becomes even more questionable when claims of current dysfunction are circumscribed to a specific academic activity or test format.

We have read many reports in which the only evidence of impairment offered is that the patient is unable to finish certain exams or assignments. As we indicated above, individuals cannot fairly claim to suffer from ADHD simply because they perform poorly on a test or in a particular course of study. It is just as likely in those instances that the cause of the underperformance relates more to transient situational/environmental events, inadequate preparation, or a poor match between abilities and academic demands. Patients who truly suffer from this disorder can provide ample evidence of pervasive limitations in their ability to adjust across the broad spectrum of their experience.

Testing

Many ADA-oriented documentation reports are chock full of scores from psychological and psychoeducational testing. Sometimes the write-ups contain little information other than test results. In other cases, no such data are included at all. What's the appropriate role of psychological testing for the assessment of ADHD?

Opinions vary widely on the validity, utility, and overall relevance of psychological testing for this particular diagnosis (Gordon & Barkley, 1998). In addition, while published research on the topic offers some overall direction, the jury is still out on the exact contributions of standardized testing to the diagnostic process. We offer below some general guidelines for the consideration of test data.

• *No one test or test score alone can document the disorder.* While psychological assessment might play a meaningful role in the diagnostic enterprise, there is absolutely no evidence that it can serve as a litmus test for identifying ADHD, especially in adults. Scientific studies have failed to establish that any score or combination of scores is sufficiently sensitive and specific to warrant much faith in them as diagnostic indicators. In fact, with the possible exception of computerized tests of attention, the vast array of psychological tests commonly administered are largely irrelevant to the identification of ADHD (although, as we point out below, they may be crucial when considering alternate or comorbid diagnoses). Consequently, reviewers will be unimpressed when clinicians attempt to justify the identification of ADHD based almost entirely on test data. Research simply does not support this practice.

Perhaps the most common test-based rationale for the ADHD diagnosis comes from references to the so-called Freedom from Distractibility factor of the Wechsler scales. However, considerable research has shown that relative suppression of this subtest combination can occur across the full range of diagnostic categories as well as within the normal population. The same holds for subtest scores from the Woodcock–Johnson Psychoeducational Battery—Revised, tests of reading speed and comprehension such as the Nelson–Denny Reading Test, and traditional neuropsychological batteries (such as the

Luria–Nebraska and Halstead–Reitan). Again, while these measures may have relevance to other diagnostic decisions, they play little if any role in the identification of ADHD per se. One or two low scores on a psychological test do not an ADHD diagnosis make. They are especially unconvincing when they are reported without collaborative evidence from history and descriptions of actual impairment.

• *Computerized tests of attention may be relevant but they are not diagnostic.* Computerized measures such as the Test of Variables of Attention (TOVA; Greenberg & Kindschi, 1996), and the Gordon Diagnostic System (GDS; Gordon, 1983) have become popular additions to ADHD-oriented assessment batteries. While each differs in format and presentation, they all seek to develop information on the subject's ability to sustain attention and to exert self-control. It may well be that these tests, when considered in the context of other information, provide some useful information, especially about the severity of the disorder (see Gordon & Barkley, 1998) and perhaps also medication response. Attentional measures also have the advantage of providing the clinician with the opportunity to observe the patient performing tasks specifically designed to require attention and disinhibition.

While results of computerized testing may help to confirm the diagnosis, they should never be considered in isolation or offered as proof positive that the patient suffers from ADHD. A circumspect treatment of such data is especially warranted when testing adults because the literature on older patients is limited and not overwhelmingly encouraging. Even the developers of these measures (the first author included) openly discourage overreliance on quantitative scores.

• *Psychological testing is most useful for ruling out alternate or comorbid diagnoses.* While no test score or scores alone can identify the disorder, some are critical to the diagnostic and administrative process. In particular, testing can be essential in ruling out the possibility that failure on examinations (and perhaps other academic endeavors) is due to limitations in intelligence and/or the acquisition of academic skills. Some students are accepted into institutions of higher education or professional training without the necessary abilities, cognitive or otherwise. It is not unusual for us to review documentation of examinees who have IQ scores in the borderline to low-average range of intellectual functioning. These students could therefore fall almost two or three standard deviations below the norm for their educational cohort. Recasting inappropriate educational or vocational placement as ADHD ultimately benefits no one.

Testing can also play a role in documenting the presence or absence of other psychiatric disorders. For example, one approach to ruling out anxiety, depression, or perhaps more serious psychopathology as the primary cause of poor performance is to provide psychological test data regarding affective functioning. It may well bolster the case for ADHD if personality testing substantiates that an individual is free of major psychopathology.

- *A trial of stimulant medication is not a test for ADHD.* In all too many instances, a response to medication (and sometimes its mere prescription) is offered as proof that the diagnosis is appropriate. Such practice flies in the face of available research. Except for patients who are psychotic or intensely anxious, the beneficial effects of stimulant medication will likely surface across the diagnostic board. Pharmacotherapy can also enhance the performance of nonimpaired individuals. Although reviewers are interested in learning about the treatment history, they are unlikely to consider medication effects alone as diagnostic.

Exploration of Alternative or Comorbid Conditions

Reviewers require some assurance that the clinician has diligently considered explanations for the symptoms other than ADHD. How do we know that the applicant's inattention and fidgetiness are not better explained by anxiety, depression, substance abuse, or bipolar disorder? Has the clinician fairly explored the possibility that the examinee is not simply overwhelmed by academic demands that outstrip his or her cognitive abilities? When reviewers fail to detect a reasonable consideration of alternative diagnoses, they often conclude that the clinician either overrelied on test results or single-mindedly advocated for the ADHD diagnosis. To address this issue, clinicians should provide evidence that they conducted a full psychiatric evaluation and considered a range of diagnostic options before settling on ADHD.

In addition to pursuing alternative diagnoses, the clinician should also explore psychiatric disorders that might coexist with ADHD. The research literature suggests a high likelihood that ADHD will indeed be joined by other psychiatric disorders. Presenting the full panorama of the patient's problems helps administrators make decisions about appropriate accommodations. For example, knowing that a student not only has ADHD but also a specific learning disability gives administrators a sense of the range of services required.

DIAGNOSTIC REVIEW SHEET

To summarize the essential elements of a convincing report, we present a form we often use when we review documentation (see Figure 5.1). In addition, guidelines for documenting ADHD are provided in Appendix II to this book.

REASONABLE ACCOMMODATIONS

The treatment of choice for ADHD in most instances is pharmacotherapy, especially with stimulant medications such as methylphenidate and dexedrine. In head-to-head comparisons with nonmedical interventions for children, pharmacotherapy almost always wins because it produces more positive benefits in less time. We have not seen such comparative studies for adult populations, but would imagine that the same general findings would emerge.

Because pharmacological treatment is not considered an ADA accommodation, we will instead concentrate on nonmedical interventions. What makes such a focus tricky is that we are not aware of any empirical research that provides steady guidance on that accommodations are likely to be effective for any particular individual. As a matter of fact, we are not aware of any studies that are especially relevant to this topic.

Since research provides little direction, we instead must rely on extrapolations from the literature on child-oriented interventions. A review of that research and our own clinical experience leads to the following conclusions:

• *No single intervention is of surefire benefit for every individual with ADHD.* Managing patients with this disorder gives one a fine sense of individual differences in treatment response. What can be extraordinarily helpful for one patient can easily be counterproduc-

Early childhood history	
Was there early onset of impulsive, hyperactive, and inattenttive behavior?	
Is there convincing evidence that symptoms caused significant impairment?	
Were symptoms consistent over time?	
Were symptoms relatively pervasive across situations?	

Current functioning	
Are ADHD-type symptoms currently in evidence?	
Is there convincing evidence that symptoms cause significant impairment?	
Have symptoms been consistent/ pervasive over time?	
Is there evidence that symptoms are not due to other disorder(s)?	
Is current remediation insufficient?	

Adequacy of clinical assessment	
Is the psychological testing/psychiatric assessment current?	
Are the clinicians qualified?	
Were appropriate tests administered?	
Were appropriate conclusions drawn?	
Was there reasonable consideration of alternative diagnoses?	
Was there reasonable consideration of comorbidity?	

Accommodations	
Do requested accommodations address functional impairments?	
Is there evidence that similar accommodations have alleviated symptoms in the past?	

FIGURE 5.1. Diagnostic review sheet.

tive for another. As an example, some individuals with ADHD perform at their best in extremely quiet environments where distractions are few. But at least as many (if not more) individuals with ADHD actually perform better in settings that are not particularly quiet. In no case is there one universal accommodation that helps all.

Perhaps the most common request for accommodations, especially for testing, is extra time. In the case of ADHD, it is hard to prove either in individual cases or by citing research that extra time on an exam is necessarily helpful. Our bona fide ADHD patients have often commented that they fail because they work too quickly just to be finished. Even when they have the time, they often fail to read questions or check their work because they simply want to leave. For these patients, additional time would be unproductive.

Of course, the next logical question is, "Then how do you know which accommodation or set of accommodations to recommend?" Perhaps the best answer is, "Those that have worked in the past." Most individuals with ADHD have received accommodations prior to college. Perhaps they were in special education or participated in some other form of remedial program. At a minimum, they have enough of a track record dealing with their symptoms that they, or those who have worked with them, have a sense of what helps. As always, past experience is the best guide for future programming. If extra time on exams, a distraction-free environment, or access to word processors have helped before, chances are good that they will help again.

Part of the problem in judging requests is that many of the applicants have not had prior accommodations, because they did not need them. At most, their statements report having had to work extra hard or having to reread passages often. In these cases as in most others, it is hard to predict whether a program of accommodations will be successful without a test drive of sorts. Most effective strategies follow a process of trial and error whereby all involved experiment with a range of options.

• *ADHD-related accommodations are generic, commonsense adjustments to an impulsive and disorganized style.* In our review of the literature, we have been unable to identify an accommodation or intervention that uniquely benefits individuals with ADHD. While many of us experts write books that convey the impression that there are special techniques for educating, parenting, or supervising people with this disorder, the truth of the matter is quite different. Who wouldn't perform better on a long, complicated essay exam, for instance, if they had extra time to edit and review? Wouldn't anyone benefit from clear rules and expectations, from compelling course materials, from structured work settings, from emotional support, from extra tutoring for challenging subjects, from permission to use a word processor in a written exam, or from the services of a note taker? Unlike accommodations such as wheel chair ramps or elevator signs written in braille, ADHD accommodations are universal in their potential benefit even for people without the disorder.

We make this point to put the accommodations enterprise for ADHD in some perspective. More than any specific or novel strategy, students with ADHD must learn to use good study, organizational, and test-taking skills. They require an environment that provides instruction and support for implementing those skills effectively. In addition, they need opportunities to secure extra help, review, and feedback during the course of their learning. In essence, individuals with ADHD benefit from an educational (or work) setting that is flexible enough to allow for a heightened degree of structure, instruction, and reasonable compensation.

• *Accommodations must address the intersection of functional impairments and task demands.* According to the laws and regulations governing this process, it is not enough simply to establish the diagnosis and then rattle off a series of accommodations. The clinician is required to demonstrate that those accommodations flow logically from the diagnostic formulation and will serve to counter the manifestations of the identified impairments. In other words, you must provide a justification for why a particular set of accommodations makes sense given the diagnostic picture and the specific tasks confronting the student. Reports often falter because the accommodations requested are not in proportion to the characterization of the disability.

Here's a common scenario: A clinician conducts a full evaluation and determines that the student has a mild problem paying attention and also a history that suggests a possible anxiety disorder. The psychologist then recommends an extensive list of accommodations that includes double time and a quiet room for all examinations, provision of a note taker for all classes, and a waiver from certain degree requirements. It is understandable that an administrator would question whether this represented a reasonable set of accommodations for that student.

As we have emphasized throughout this chapter, the best way to justify an accommodation is to point to past benefits from that accommodation. For instance, did the person receive extra time on standardized tests in the past? If so, how much time? Is there reason to believe it made a difference? If there were no prior time dispensations required, why would one expect that they be necessary for the upcoming examinations? Reviewers are looking for some explanation for why your recommendations are reasonable.

PARTING SHOTS

By way of summary, we list below many of the conclusions we have drawn from our experience both as reviewers but also as clinicians who have submitted documentation materials on behalf of patients. You will see that we state them bluntly and without the qualifications we've woven into our overall presentation:

- No early history of ADHD symptoms, no ADHD.
- IQ is not a viable explanation for late onset.
- Inattention *alone* does not an ADHD individual make.
- The consequences of having talents insufficient to attain certain goals should not be labeled as ADHD.
- Having to work harder than others is not necessarily a symptom of ADHD.
- Failing an important test is not a surefire symptom of ADHD.
- Psychological testing alone does not justify an ADHD diagnosis.
- The diagnosis of ADHD is founded upon evidence of significant impairment and not simply the identification of certain personality characteristics.
- Claims based solely on self-reported symptoms are hard to establish as credible.

SAMPLE REPORT

We present below a report that, in our opinion, embodies many of the elements we've covered throughout this chapter. It not only describes someone who meets the criteria, but also contains a level of documentation that would allow a reviewer to arrive at an informed judgment.

Patient's name: Larry Lewan
Medical record number: 10-20-30
Date of birth: 1/30/76
Date of evaluation: 2/10/96

Reason for Referral

Larry Lewan is a 20-year-old, single, white male who was referred by his counselor from the Student Disability Office at Heritage University for symptoms suggestive of attention-deficit/hyperactivity disorder (ADHD). He has had problems with concentration, distractibility, impulsivity, hyperactivity, disorganization, and following tasks through to completion dating back to early childhood. He has been struggling at Heritage University this year and, despite concerted effort, is at risk for failing out of school. He wanted to determine if ADHD was a factor that at least partially accounted for his longstanding academic struggles.

Assessment Procedures

- Semistructured interview with Mr. Lewan.
- Semistructured interview with Mrs. Lewan (the patient's mother).
- Standardized rating scales completed by Mr. Lewan, his mother, and roommate.
- The Kaufman Brief Intelligence Test.
- The Wide Range Achievement Test (which measures academic achievement in spelling, arithmetic, and single word reading).
- The SCL-90-R (a measure of general psychological adjustment).
- A computerized test of sustained attention and distractibility (continuous performance test).
- A review of Mr. Lewan's prior report cards, past evaluations, and several performance reviews from prior employment.

Developmental History

Larry was the product of a normal, full-term pregnancy with no major complications. He had some problems with stuttering and speech as a child, but otherwise reached all of his major developmental milestones at age-appropriate times. Larry described himself as having been an extremely high-energy and disruptive child who was often in trouble at school. He remembers being moody, easily frustrated, and prone to temper tantrums as a child. He also describes himself as having been highly unpopular with peers. According to him, he never was able to maintain a close relationship with any of his classmates. He ascribes his peer problems to his tendency to irritate and alienate others.

Larry described a lifelong history of impulsiveness. He says that family members still comment on how he always seemed to have bruises from ill-considered ventures. As he got older, he blurted out comments he would quickly regret. Despite his strong efforts to be less impulsive and improve his social relationships, he has never achieved much success.

Larry's mother confirms his self-descriptions. She indicated that he was always a "difficult" child who had trouble regulating his behavior and keeping on task. She described him as being extremely intense, driven, hyperactive, spirited, and feisty. She said that he forever marched to his own drummer and found himself in trouble, often because he failed to consider the consequences of his actions.

Health History

Larry describes himself as free from any significant health problems. He has no history of heart problems, seizures, high blood pressure, head injury, migraine headaches, or thyroid condition. Larry's mother indicated he was taken to the hospital emergency room on numerous occasions during his childhood for stitches, sprained ankles, and broken bones. He broke his leg at age 8 after falling out of a tree and has broken his left arm twice in bicycle accidents. He has no known allergies and is not currently taking any medications.

Family History

Larry is the second oldest of four children (two brothers and a sister). His parents are married. His father, a salesman, graduated from high school, attended several different colleges, and earned a bachelor's degree. His mother, an administrative assistant for an insurance company, has an associates degree. The family history is positive for ADHD: Larry's younger brother has been diagnosed with ADHD and takes methylphenidate with a positive response. Larry and his mother suspect that his father may also have symptoms of ADHD in that he is highly disorganized and scattered. A maternal aunt has had problems with depression and was treated with Prozac. Both his grandfathers and a maternal uncle have abused alcohol. No other significant medical or psychiatric conditions were reported for either side of the biological family. Larry has never been married and has no children.

Past Psychiatric History

Larry has never been formally diagnosed with ADHD in the past. However, this diagnosis had been suggested to him by two different psychologists. His mother stated that she knew something was different about Larry from early on but did not know what it was. He first saw a counselor at age 8 at the Center for Youth Services in Boston, because of school and behavioral difficulties. He has seen several other psychologists since then, mostly for school and behavior/temper problems. These problems were usually viewed as reflective of internal conflicts or family dysfunction. Because of academic underachievement, he was also evaluated on three occasions by his district's committee on special education, but never received formal services, although, informally, he did attend several resource room classes. He was most recently tested in twelfth grade for academic problems and has been seeing Dr. Jones at Heritage University for the past 6 months for issues related to academic performance and anxiety.

Larry has never been hospitalized for a psychiatric problem. He has had some chronic low-grade depressive symptoms and has felt a longstanding sense of frustration and demoralization. He has also had low-grade anxiety symptoms mostly associated with school performance and test anxiety.

Larry has experimented with drugs in the past including marijuana and cocaine, but denied having any significant problems presently. He has abused alcohol on occasion, but both he and his mother denied that it has caused any significant disruption to his life presently. His mother indicated that Ritalin was suggested by two different doctors in the past, but she was reluctant to put him on medication. He has never been on any psychotropic medication. He was arrested on one occasion at age 18 for possession of alcohol, but these charges were dropped.

School History

Larry is currently a junior at Heritage University. He has a history of problems with school including inconsistent performance, distractibility, impulsivity, inconsistent concentration, poor reading comprehension, hyperactivity, and some behavior problems that began in early elementary school. He also has a history of performing below his potential in school; his teachers always thought he could do better. He had chronic difficulty completing his homework and rarely did it. He stated that it was extremely difficult for him to sit still and focus long enough to complete most assignments. When he did persist with a task, it was often done at the last minute just to get it in.

Larry received mostly B's with some C's during elementary school but began getting C's, D's, and F's during high school. He has struggled in college and his grades have ranged from A's to F's depending on his level of interest in the course. His current GPA is 2.0, despite above-average intelligence. He described having trouble focusing his attention in class, listening to teachers and taking notes, having to read textbooks numerous times before comprehension occurs, and problems with memorization. He stated that no matter how hard he tries, he cannot sustain his concentration or effort, which is extremely frustrating to him. He has walked out of classes on occasion because of his frustration at not being able to pay attention. He has always had great difficulty with projects such as papers or other things that require long-term effort.

Larry stated that he has known for a long time that something was wrong with his ability to learn but was not sure what. He is fearful that his academic performance will worsen if he does not learn to cope. Copies of report cards and school records Larry provided indicated longstanding and classic ADHD symptomatology beginning in kindergarten and continuing throughout his school history. Themes that were evident from teacher comments on his report cards included insufficient effort, not working up to his potential, missing homework assignments, behaving disruptively in class, talking and socializing too much, not paying attention, and generally underachieving. His mother echoed the comments on the report cards and stated that she was often called in for teacher/parent conferences to discuss Larry's troubles. Larry believes he would have done far better in school if he could have focused and concentrated more effectively.

Vocational History

Larry worked at a local golf course for the past 3 years both in the pro shop and out on the course. He described having problems following directions, losing his temper with his coworkers, being distractible and thrown off task easily, and being easily bored. He frequently needs directions repeated, which has caused some to wonder if he has a hearing problem. He has had several other jobs ,mostly at fast food restaurants, which he has quit after a short time out of boredom. Larry also worked as a waiter but was unsuccessful because of forgetfulness, poor planning, and his short fuse. He is unsure of his future vocational plans but hopes to complete his college degree. He stated that he cannot see himself doing anything professional because he does not have the patience to sit at a desk all day. He believes he has a high need for variety, constant movement and change, and enjoys the outdoors.

Mental Status

The patient was a well-groomed, casually dressed male who was friendly and cooperative throughout the evaluation. His mood was normal to mildly agitated at times and his affect was appropriate to content. Thought process and content were normal. There was no evidence of formal thought disorder. Speech was rapid and loud, and he was quite talkative, often going into minute detail and sometimes losing track of what he was saying. He denied any current suicidal ideation. He displayed a great deal of restlessness and fidgeting during the interview and testing. He often switched positions in his seat, interrupted on several occasions, and got out of his seat to walk around the office on two occasions. He tended to work slowly on a number of the tests and attempted several verbal compensatory strategies to assist him in taking certain tests.

Due to his rather rapid and pressured speech, I carefully reviewed the symptoms of bipolar disorder with him. He clearly did not meet criteria for bipolar disorder, nor did he appear to have ever met criteria for major depression in the past. He denied ever having an eating disorder. His appetite and sleeping patterns were within normal limits. He described himself as being chronically high strung, frequently having emotional overeactivity, and always being loud, driven, and aggressive. These characteristics, combined with his history of impulsivity, have contributed to his uneven social relationships.

Other symptoms Larry described included being easily bored, having trouble memorizing and following lectures at school, having poor reading comprehension, having trouble sitting through classes to the point where he sometimes had to get up and leave, having trouble finishing his work, losing things, being messy and disorganized, having low self-esteem, having to work much longer and harder than his peers to accomplish tasks, and having trouble sustaining his effort over long periods of time. Larry has also had difficulty with daily adaptive functioning, including paying bills on time, being unable to balance a checkbook, cooking, cleaning, and organizing his apartment. He denied ever having any delusions or hallucinations, manic episodes, or clinically significant obsessions or compulsions.

Test Results and Interpretation

During the diagnostic interview, the patient indicated that he has exhibited eight of the nine criteria associated with attention-deficit/hyperactivity disorder, inattentive type, and all nine of the nine criteria of ADHD, hyperactive/impulsive type. Overall, he endorsed the following symptoms:

- Fails to pay close attention to details or makes careless mistakes.
- Has difficulty sustaining attention.
- Often does not listen when spoken to directly.
- Has trouble following through on instructions and often fails to finish school work, chores or work place duties.

- Has difficulty organizing tasks and activities.
- Avoids tasks that require sustained mental effort.
- Is easily distracted.
- Often fidgets or squirms in seat.
- Has difficulty remaining seated.
- Experiences feelings of physical restlessness.
- Has difficulty engaging in leisure activities quietly.
- Is always on the go, as if driven by a motor.
- Often talks excessively.
- Blurts out answers before questions have been completed.
- Has difficulty waiting in lines or awaiting turn.
- Interrupts or intrudes on others.

His mother endorsed eight of the inattentive symptoms and eight of the hyperactive/impulsive symptoms and corroborated many of the difficulties Larry described. The rating scale provided by a dorm mate also confirms that these symptoms are frequently in evidence.

Results of the Kaufman Brief Intelligence Test indicated that Larry's composite score fell in the 85th percentile, which corresponds to the above-average range of intelligence. WAIS-R results from a prior test report during high school indicated a Verbal IQ of 115, a Performance IQ of 120, and a Full Scale IQ of 117. Results of the Wide Range Achievement Test indicated that Larry fell in the 81st percentile in spelling (above-average range) the 60th percentile in arithmetic (average range), and in the 81st percentile in single word reading (above-average range). These results are indicative of strong native intelligence and solid proficiency in the basic skill areas of math, spelling, and reading and are not suggestive of any gross learning disabilities.

Larry's responses to a test of general psychological adjustment indicated that he is experiencing some significant psychological distress presently in the areas of hostility, interpersonal sensitivity, and anxiety. His responses to this questionnaire also suggested that he was having difficulties with attention and concentration. Results of a computerized test of sustained attention and distractibility showed that the standard error of his responses was significantly higher at the end of the test than at the beginning, indicating a loss of attention. Further, his omission error rate was significantly higher at the end of the test, indicating that attention was not maintained. He also had a high error commission rate, suggesting a tendency toward impulsive responding.

Summary and Impressions

Larry Lewan is a 20-year-old, single white male of above-average intelligence with a long history of inattention, distractibility, impulsivity, hyperactivity, poor peer relationships, and academic underachievement since early childhood. His school, behavioral, and work history, mood and temperament difficulties, less than satisfactory social relationships, problems with daily adaptive functioning (cooking, cleaning, paying bills, forgetfulness, general organization), and chronic problems with impulsivity, attention, and distractibility all support a diagnosis of attention-deficit/hyperactivity disorder (ADHD), combined type. Moreover, he endorsed 17 (and his mother, 16) of the 18 criteria that are associated with a diagnosis of ADHD. The early childhood onset and lifelong duration of these symptoms, and the pervasiveness of them across school, social, and work domains are strongly suggestive of the presence of an underlying ADHD. He has also experienced longstanding feelings of demoralization, frustration, and anxiety which appear to be a direct consequence of his underlying ADHD symptoms. His symptoms do not appear to be better explained by any other psychiatric or medical condition. Further, school records and report cards documented longstanding and classic symptoms of ADHD throughout his school history. Although Larry has worked hard at compensating for his deficits, his symptoms have continued to significantly interfere with his life.

Recommendations

1. Because being fully educated about the disorder is the foundation of effective coping, Larry and his family should first become knowledgeable about ADHD. This can be accomplished in part by reading literature on adult ADHD; some of which can be provided by the Heritage University Medical Center. I have also provided a bibliography of resources.

2. Stimulant medication can be helpful to children and adults to assist them with their inattention, distractibility, restlessness, and concentration. A medication consultation with a local psychiatrist who is experienced at treating ADHD in adults is recommended to determine an appropriate treatment plan. It is possible that a medication trial would result in a significant improvement of Larry's symptoms.

3. Compensatory behavioral strategies may be used to address some ADHD problems prior to their occurrence. Strategies that may be helpful to Larry include (1) making a daily list of what he wants to accomplish to help organize and structure his life more effectively; (2) posting visual reminders in strategic locations (refrigerator, bulletin board at work or home, etc.) to jog his memory and remind him of commitments; (3) keeping an appointment book or daily planner/organizer to write down appointments and schedules. In short, any behavioral strategy that serves to remind, better organize, and help structure his life might well bring about some benefit.

4. Given that Larry is presently experiencing some psychological distress, it is recommended that he seek individual counseling specifically aimed at improving his self-esteem, exploring anger-control strategies, and helping him develop more effective self-management and organization skills.

5. Compensatory behavioral strategies and accommodations should be implemented at school to help Larry perform more effectively. Larry should discuss this report with his academic counselor at Heritage University and begin to develop strategies for intervention. Consideration should be given to the following:

a. His teachers should be educated about ADHD and understand its impact on Larry. His teachers might consider allowing him alternative ways of demonstrating his knowledge that are consistent with his learning style. Given that he has always had difficulty writing and finishing tests in a timely manner, it may be helpful for him to take tests orally or to be allowed extended time on certain tests. There is evidence from past efforts that these accommodations can be especially helpful to him.

b. He is clearly a visual learner and has much better verbal strengths than written. In general, allowing him to demonstrate his knowledge in ways that are consistent with his strengths would be important for him. Without doubt, Larry should learn to use a word processor with a spelling and grammar checker.

c. Larry may benefit by being taught specific study skills in a one-to-one tutoring format. Target skills might be learning conceptualization of main ideas and making an outline, note taking, cognitive and verbal rehearsal of material he has learned, test taking, communication, listening, and the like.

d. Because people with ADHD become bored easily and lack the proper motivation to complete uninteresting tasks, it is often necessary to provide them with a lot of ongoing feedback about their performance. Larry's teachers should consider providing him with more feedback (both positive and negative) than might be necessary for other students. Positive reinforcement, when warranted, and other incentives should be used as much as possible.

e. It is recommended Larry read the literature on ADHD in college students that was provided to him and highlight areas of need to discuss with his academic advisor. I am available to consult with his counselor for more specifics on accommodations and can be reached at 555-2345.

Disposition

I discussed portions of the above findings and recommendations with Mr. Lewan. He seemed most relieved and indicated that he will work with his counselor to develop a treatment plan. He is also considering a trial of medication.

Diane Jones, PhD
Department of Psychiatry
Attention Deficit Disorder Clinic
Barkley University Medical Center

REFERENCES

American Psychiatric Association. (1994). *Diagnostic and statistical manual of mental disorders* (4th ed.). Washington, DC: Author.

Barkley, R. A. (1997). *ADHD and the nature of self-control.* New York: Guilford.

Conners, C. (1995). *The Conners Continuous Performance Test.* North Tonawanda, NY: MultiHealth Systems.

Gordon, M. (1983). *The Gordon Diagnostic System.* DeWitt, NY: Gordon Systems.

Gordon, M., & Barkley, R. A. (1998). Tests and observational measures. In R. A. Barkley, *Attention-deficit/hyperactivity disorder: A handbook for diagnosis and treatment* (2nd ed.). New York: Guilford Press.

Greenberg, L. M., & Kindschi, C. L. (1996). *T.O.V.A. Test of Variables of Attention: Clinical guide.* St. Paul, MN: TOVA Research Foundation.

Murphy, K. R., & Barkley, R. A., (1996), Prevalence of DSM-IV symptoms of ADHD in adult licensed drivers: Implications for clinical diagnosis. *Journal of Attention Disorders, 1*(3), 147–161.

RESOURCES

Books and Chapters about ADHD in Adults

Barkley, R. A. (1998). *Attention-deficit hyperactivity disorder: A handbook for diagnosis and treatment* (2nd ed.). New York: Guilford Press.

Gordon, M. (1995). *How to operate an ADHD clinic or subspecialty practice.* Syracuse: GSI Publications.

Gordon, M., & Irwin, M. (1997). *The diagnosis and treatment of ADD/ADHD: A no-nonsense guide for the primary care physician.* Syracuse: GSI Publications.

Murphy, K. R., & Gordon, M. (1998). Assessment of adults with ADHD. In R. A. Barkley, *Attention-deficit/hyperactivity disorder: A handbook for diagnosi and treatment* (2nd ed.). New York: Guilford Press.

Nadeau, K. (Ed.). (1995). *A comprehensive guide to attention deficit disorder in adults: Research, diagnosis, and treatment.* New York: Brunner/Mazel.

Weiss, G., & Hechtman, L. T. (1986). *Hyperactive children grown up: Empirical findings and theoretical considerations.* New York: Guilford Press.

Wender, P. (1995). *Attention-deficit hyperactivity disorder in adults.* New York: Oxford University Press.

Books for Adults with ADD — Legal Issues

Latham, P. S., & Latham, J. D. (1992). *Attention deficit disorder and the law: A guide for advocates.* Washington, DC: JKL Communications. (Phone, 202-223-5097)

Latham, P. S., & Latham, J. D. (Eds.). (1994). *Succeeding in the workplace: Attention deficit disorder and learning disabilities in the workplace: A guide for success.* Washington, DC: JKL Communications. (Phone, 202-223-5097)

Latham, P. S., & Latham, J. D. (1994). *Higher education services for students with learning disabilities and attention deficit disorder: A legal guide.* Washington, DC: JKL Communications. (Phone, 202-223-5097)

Language-Based Learning Disabilities

Barbara J. Lorry, PhD

INTRODUCTION

The Americans with Disabilities Act of 1990 (ADA; PL 101-336) provides protection from discrimination for individuals with learning disabilities (LD). It allows them to request accommodations that will modify the learning environment and the conditions under which they are tested. The law guarantees the learning disabled population an equal opportunity to learn and to demonstrate learning.

For individuals with disabilities to qualify under the ADA, they must show evidence of "a physical or mental impairment which substantially limits one or more major life activities." Learning disabled individuals are therefore covered under the ADA if evidence exists that their LD seriously impedes skill acquisition. Much of the debate surrounding determinations under the ADA focuses on the definition of what actually constitutes "substantial limitation." Grossman (1994) highlights this issue as follows:

> Many impairments, even those affecting a major life activity, do not adversely affect an individual's life to the degree necessary to constitute a disabling impairment. Nonetheless, the inability to do what most people can do is highly relevant to determining who is disabled within the meaning of the ADA. . . . The inability of an uneducated person to read anything will not be evidence of a disability. But if an educated person cannot comprehend the first written page of a book, there is strong inference of an impairment that substantially limits a major life activity. . . . It makes sense that these laws do not cover persons with insubstantial impairments or persons whose impairments affect them only in the narrowest of situations. (p. 22)

The first goal of this chapter is to provide a definition of learning disabilities that reflects current research and practice. Most of the emphasis will fall on language-based learning disabilities, specifically reading disorders, because they represent by far the largest segment of this population. Reading disabilities are also the most likely of all the learning disabilities to serve as a basis for an accommodations claim in higher education.

The second goal is to provide a practical strategy for determining whether an identified learning disability rises to the level of impairment required by the Americans with Disabilities Act. The ADA imposes a set of rules for qualifying an individual as disabled that requires an especially close adherence to certain fundamental principles. Thus, a diagnosis of LD may or may not be sufficient to establish protection under the law. In fact, Equal Employment Opportunity Commission (EEOC) regulations state the following:

> A diagnosis is relevant to determining whether a[n individual] has an impairment. It is important to remember, however, that a diagnosis may be insufficient to determine if the [individual] has a disability. (EEOC Regulations, Sec. 902.2)

DEFINING LEARNING DISABILITIES

Learning disabilities as a diagnostic category describing individuals with learning problems was first defined in 1962 by Samuel Kirk (Kirk, 1986). Prior to his efforts, low academic attainment was ascribed primarily to generalized cognitive limitations or to insufficient motivation. The only formal designation of a cognitive condition that could produce academic problems was "dyslexia." In its earliest form, this inability to read was considered to result from a "word blindness" that precluded an individual from decoding words (see Goldstein, 1997).

Since Kirk's introduction of the LD concept, professionals in both psychology and education have struggled to refine and operationalize a meaningful definition. The definition that perhaps comes closest to representing a consensus was developed by the National Joint Committee on Learning Disabilities (NJCLD), a group of professional and advocacy organizations. The most recent version of their definition is as follows:

Learning Disabilities is a general term that refers to a heterogeneous group of disorders manifested by significant difficulties in the acquisition and use of listening, speaking, reading, writing, reasoning, or mathematical skills.

These disorders are intrinsic to the individual and presumed to be due to a central nervous system dysfunction, and may occur across the life span. Problems in self-regulatory behaviors, social perception, and social interaction may exist with the learning disabilities but do not, by themselves, constitute a learning disability.

Although learning disabilities may occur concomitantly with other disabilities (e.g., sensory impairment, mental retardation, serious emotional disturbance), or with extrinsic influences (such as cultural differences, insufficient or inappropriate instruction), they are not the result of those conditions or influences. (NJCLD, 1990, p. 29)

This definition underscores certain cardinal features of learning disabilities. First, it defines a learning disability as a problem in the acquisition and use of language. While it acknowledges that problems can occur in various aspects of language acquisition and skill, it construes the disorder as language based. Mathematics was included because of evidence that it, too, requires solid language abilities.

Secondly, the definition assumes that learning disabilities are related to some underlying central nervous system dysfunction. In so doing, the definition limits the disorder to problems that are intrinsic to the individual's cognitive makeup, as opposed to other psychiatric or environmental factors. Indeed, the definition acknowledges that individuals can achieve poorly for many reasons, including sensory impairment, mental retardation, serious emotional disturbance, cultural differences, and insufficient or inappropriate instruction. It reserves the LD term to cover those causes of insufficient learning that relate to specific cognitive dysfunctions.

The NJCLD definition specifically excludes retardation as a basis for a LD diagnosis. Therefore, to be labelled as LD, an individual must have general intellectual abilities that are at least within the average range. If a person has generally low-average cognitive abilities, his academic attainment may also be below par. What characterizes the learning-disabled individual is that problems with language, usually reading, stand out against a backdrop of significantly better abilities in other areas (Stanovich, 1988). The reading problem is not just another instance of poor academic skills, but is unexpected in light of average to above-average cognitive ability.

Although the NJCLD definition does not make an explicit statement to this effect, it assumes that learning disabilities are a developmental phenomenon (NJCLD, 1997). The reason a childhood onset was not indicated in the actual wording is largely because the definition was developed for children and adolescents. Nonetheless, learning disabilities are widely considered to be associated with cognitive dysfunctions that, by their nature, would have impact during childhood. Research substantiates the notion that children with learning disabilities demonstrate a range of early-appearing vulnerabilities in functioning (Blumsack, Lewandowski, & Waterman, 1997).

While this consensus definition presents a solid foundation for conceptualizing LD, it is not so specific that it can serve as a basis for developing diagnostic criteria. What constitutes "significant difficulties"? How does one establish that a language problem stems from a "central nervous system dysfunction"? What measures are appropriate for documenting problems in "listening, speaking, reading, writing, reasoning, or mathematical skills"?

The definition alone also does not address other critical issues. How should practitioners determine the impact of other conditions that can impact learning? Researchers and practitioners alike have struggled with establishing guidelines that provide a meaningful foundation for clinical assessment.

Competing with the NJCLD definition are discrepancy models of learning disabilities that have emanated from special education mandates. These laws, specifically PL 94-142 (now rewritten and designated the Individuals with Disabilities Education Act, or IDEA; 1975, PL 101-476), have used relative differences between aptitude and achievement as a basis for identifying those children in need of remedial services. While discrepancy formulas vary from state to state depending on local preferences and resources, they all use a gap between ability and performance to qualify a student for educational interventions.

The problem with a discrepancy approach for diagnostic purposes is that it focuses only on test scores and not on the underlying cognitive deficits that may be creating the learning problems. It does not acknowledge the many reasons why a student can have problems mastering a curriculum, including, but not limited to, those tied to a specific learning disability. It would not make sense, for example, to diagnose an individual as learning disabled if he or she had trouble learning as a result of inadequate education or serious emotional problems. A documented discrepancy may indicate that a problem exists, but it does not suggest that it is necessarily related to cognitive deficits. Also, a discrepancy is not, in itself, proof of substantial limitation as defined by the ADA.

Another limitation of a discrepancy model is the undue faith it places on intelligence test scores as predictors of academic potential. While measures of intelligence are associated with general academic performance perhaps through high school, they contribute little to the variance in predicting ultimate educational and occupational success. Outcome is associated more with social abilities, motivation, socioeconomic status, psychiatric functioning, and circumstance than with scores on measures of cognitive functioning (Neisser et al., 1996). IQ scores are therefore a tenuous method for measuring a person's aptitude. The IQ/achievement duality is also confounded because performance on IQ measures is partially dependent on acquired knowledge.

Discrepancy models have also been criticized for being generally unsuited to adults. Over time, a learning disability can suppress performance on tests of intelligence and thus reduce aptitude–achievement discrepancies. Consider the following example: As a second grader, Robin was administered a standard psychological diagnostic test battery which generated a Full Scale IQ of 130 but also evidence of difficulties in acquiring beginning reading skills. Because reading was difficult for her, she read as little as possible. She would read only when it was necessary to complete assignments, never for recreation.

As a senior in high school, she requested testing in order to obtain extended time on the SATs. This evaluation found her Full Scale IQ to be 110, a decline of 20 points from the earlier assessment. As a result of her years of very limited reading, Robin's general fund of knowledge, math abilities, and vocabulary had not kept pace with development. Applying a discrepancy formula in this case would not demonstrate a significant gap between measured aptitude and reading achievement, even though she was clearly reading disabled.

Brackett and McPherson (1996) also point out that another weakness of the ability–achievement discrepancy model is its tendency to overidentify students with above-average aptitude. Many bright individuals show variability in academic skills, and their relatively lower achievement in some areas will be discrepant from overall high cognitive ability.

Although discrepancy models provide an unsatisfactory basis for conceptualizing learning disabilities, they focus attention on the thorny issues involved in defining impairment. Because much of the population experiences intra-individual variations in abilities, consideration must be given to the point at which those skill differences can be fairly characterized as a disability. Within educational and clinical settings, the guidelines for judging severity of impairment vary widely. They depend on interpretation of special education laws, local funding, and individual approaches to clinical management.

For purposes of defining a learning disability under the ADA, however, the matter is somewhat less complicated because the law firmly establishes the "average person" standard as the basis for judging impairment. Therefore, to be protected under the ADA with a diagnosis of LD, a person must demonstrate that certain essential skills fall well below what is expected for the average person (as opposed to peers in a particular college or training program). Conversely, the ADA would not consider an individual as disabled based on intraindividual differences if the lowest skills still fell within an average range. Thus, the diagnosis of LD is not commensurate with disability as defined by the ADA. While many might bristle at this stringent standard, it nonetheless stands as the legal test of disability.

Because definitions vary across the educational, clinical, and legal landscapes, it is entirely possible that a student who meets criteria for a learning disability in one environment may not qualify in another. Which cutoff for determining a disability is most justified stands as a question that extends well beyond the scope of this chapter. For ADA determinations, clinicians must understand that the law sets a relatively specific standard for defining disability that may differ from the diagnostic criteria for LD.

Another factor can complicate the diagnosis of LD in postsecondary settings. Many programs present students with educational demands that are so challenging that even those with above-average abilities might falter. Failure to achieve in a demanding academic environment in and of itself is not indicative of a learning disability. These scenarios are often better understood in terms of a mismatch between the individual's abilities and the demands of the program. Regardless, a person of at least average abilities would not qualify for ADA accommodations simply because he or she experienced failure in a competitive academic setting.

Based on all of these concepts as well as legal requirements, the assessment of a learning disability for ADA determinations must follow four steps: The first establishes that the individual has underlying cognitive deficits that limit learning despite at least average intellectual abilities. Although other noncognitive factors may come into play, a substantial component must derive from certain cognitive impairments. Because LD is a developmental disorder, the assessment must next demonstrate that the individual experienced "significant difficulty in the acquisition and use" of language skills as a child, as well as currently. The third step involves documenting that the disability limits the individual's performance relative to the general population. The last step indicates how the requested accommodation helps the individual to overcome the impact of the impairment.

The task of defining LD continues to challenge the professionals involved in both research and assessment. Definition and diagnosis are particularly daunting for those who work with adults in postsecondary programs. Nevertheless, there is a basis for providing credible evidence of a learning disability. That documentation requires evidence of an underlying cognitive dysfunction that interferes with language processing, visual and/or auditory processing, or working memory.

THE READING PROCESS

As indicated in the introduction, most LD are language based and are largely related to reading. Language-based learning disabilities are the most difficult to define because they can manifest themselves in different ways. Historically, difficulty with learning to read, experiencing letter and word reversals, and poor use of spoken and written language are the hallmarks of dyslexia or specific language disability (Doris, 1996). Samuel Orton, a neurologist who practiced in the 1920s, attributed these reading problems to a lack of development of cerebral dominance. Although his hypothesis has been questioned based on current neurobiological research, he was one of the first in the field to associate reading difficulties or dyslexia with language (Clark & Uhry, 1995).

More recent research in the many aspects of language, language processing and other psychological processes, involved in reading have brought to light an expanded view of the etiology of reading and language disorders. Current research holds that reading is a complex process that involves extracting and constructing meaning from text (see Figure 6.1). Initially, reading is a perceptual process requiring automatic, effortless word recognition. Visual, auditory, and phonological processing are important components of fluent word recognition. Phonemic awareness—the awareness of and the ability to manipulate the phonemes within words—is an essential skill and is thought to be crucial to learning to read. Indeed, a prominent characteristic of the disabled reader, whether child or adult, is lack of phonemic awareness.

In addition to decoding words, the skilled reader must have a well-developed vocabulary and a wide information base. Two other components of the process that distinguish the good reader are reliable working memory and what Perfetti and Lesgold (1979) refer to as "verbal efficiency" and "lexical access." Working memory is that aspect of short-term memory that holds information until it is stored. When reading long, complex material, one must be able to retain information from the beginning of sentences or paragraphs until the end of those sentences or paragraphs. Phonological processing is a necessary aspect of working memory because meaning is carried, in part, by the phonology of the words that are read and thus allows the reader to hold information in short-term memory until meaning is processed and data is stored. Verbal efficiency refers to speed of decoding, while lexical access refers to the speed at which an individual can retrieve information from his or her personal lexicon.

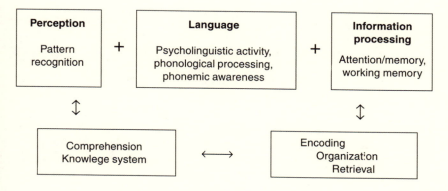

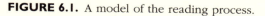

FIGURE 6.1. A model of the reading process.

In sum, linguistic processes are at the heart of the reading process. Deficits in one of many language abilities can interfere with one's ability to decode and comprehend reading material. Slow decoding or slow retrieval of information from one's knowledge base, for example, can create what Perfetti and Lesgold (1979) call "a bottleneck" which can slow reading rate and inhibit comprehension. Another view of the reading process, put forth by Gough and Tumner (1986) describes reading (R) as the product of decoding (D) and comprehension (C): $D \times C = R$. While this model is an oversimplification of a very complex process, it does capture the essence of what one must be able to do to read effectively and efficiently. It also conveys the importance of characterizing the nature of information processing deficits during the course of an LD evaluation.

ESSENTIAL CRITERIA

The official criteria for learning disorders, particularly reading disorders, are found in the fourth edition of the *Diagnostic and Statistical Manual of Mental Disorders* (DSM-IV; American Psychiatric Association, 1994). They represent the accepted clinical basis for assigning an LD diagnosis. With the permission of the American Psychiatric Association, they are presented below:

Reading Disorder

A. Reading achievement, as measured by individually administered standardized tests of reading accuracy or comprehension, is substantially below that expected given the person's chronological age, measured intelligence, and age-appropriate education.
B. The disturbance in Criterion A significantly interferes with academic achievement or activities of daily living that require reading skills.
C. If a sensory deficit is present, the reading difficulties are in excess of those usually associated with it.

Despite differences in wording, the DSM-IV and the NJCLD definition presented earlier share certain features. They both focus on intraindividual differences between aptitude and performance as one basis for establishing a learning disability. The two approaches also require "significant" interference with academic performance and assume that the problems are intrinsic to the individual. Finally, the

DSM-IV and the NJCLD acknowledge, at least implicitly, that language disorders do not exist in isolation, but rather interfere with a wide range of functions. Their impact can indeed be identified in academic areas that are not obviously tied to language skills, including mathematics and the sciences.

Alongside these similarities reside some important differences. The DSM-IV criteria simply gauge reading achievement as measured by a standardized test. As such, it is based on a simple discrepancy model and therefore suffers from inherent limitations of the sort described earlier. The psychiatric definition unfortunately poses no requirements that the underachievement be tied to underlying neuropsychological dysfunction. It also fails to stipulate in the formal criteria that other factors, such as those related to psychiatric disorders or insufficient education, be ruled out. However, it does imply that the cause of the disorder is inherent in the individual because, after all, the diagnosis appears in a list of mental conditions.

A limitation of both sets of criteria is that they do not specifically address the obvious developmental nature of the disorder. Although both suggest that it is developmental in nature (the DSM-IV by putting it in the "Disorders Usually First Diagnosed in Infancy, Childhood, or Adolescence" section), no age delineations are offered. It is just accepted that the disorder appears before the end of adolescence.

In this regard, criteria for learning disabilities are different from those for attention-deficit/hyperactivity disorder (ADHD). For ADHD, there is a discrete cutoff for age of onset, presumably because deficits in response inhibition typically manifest themselves very early in life. Because demands for reading and other language skills arise with schooling, the appearance of a reading-based learning disability will necessarily be somewhat later and perhaps more inconsistent across individuals and academic settings. Nonetheless, common sense and standard diagnostic practice requires a true disability in language acquisition to become manifest during the development period in which such skills are typically mastered.

Another limitation of the DSM-IV criteria for academic disorders is especially relevant to ADA determinations. While the criteria for ADHD acknowledge that impairment can persist across the life span (by including work-related symptoms), the same cannot be said for learning disorders. They do not address how the diagnosis is applied to adults.

The absence of a life-span model is particularly problematic because the DSM-IV criteria hinge in part on evidence derived from standardized measures of academic underachievement. However, most tests of academic skills are normed on individuals up to age 18. While a few standardized tests are normed for adults, they are more suited to assessing baseline functioning than for examining the nature of a given disability and how it affects activities of daily living. Indeed, the entire field of LD is restricted by the relative absence of solid assessment tools and of robust research on the nature of language processing in postsecondary populations.

ESSENTIAL STEPS IN THE IDENTIFICATION OF A LANGUAGE-BASED LEARNING DISABILITY

This section elaborates on the actual components of an LD evaluation. The process involves a combination of clinical assessment (including a complete review of symptoms and history) and psychological testing. While most evaluations focus almost entirely on test results, the examiner should not forget that formulating an LD diagnosis requires ruling out noncognitive explanations for poor achievement. The process of identifying a learning disability is therefore, in part, a process of eliminating psychiatric, family, or educational factors.

For psychological diagnostic instruments, examiners have a range of reading and language measures available to them. Individual tests as such will not be discussed here, because it is more important to identify the overall assessment targets in the areas of reading and language processing. Some common misinterpretations of testing will also be presented.

History

It is essential to obtain a detailed educational, medical, and family history. This information enables the clinician to understand how symptoms have affected an individual's functioning over time. Historical accounts of learning difficulties also drive the selection of assessment tools.

Of particular importance are data regarding early speech development, including the age of articulation of first words and sentences as well as the quality of articulation. In addition, evidence of early deficits in phonemic awareness, such as rhyming, syllable segmentation, and manipulation of phonemes, including both deletion and substitution, may point to problems in reading and language. The clinician should also inquire carefully about early hearing problems that may have interfered with either language acquisition or finely tuned perception of speech sounds.

Another key area of inquiry concerns a possible family history of speech and language deficits or of overall academic difficulties. A learning disability in a child often represents the next edition of a family's oft-repeated pattern of academic underperformance. Genetic predispositions can create vulnerabilities in the learning of language and, later, reading skills.

Reading difficulties in school-age children can appear as early as kindergarten or first grade but may not emerge until grade three or four. These children fail to acquire the beginning components of the reading process, including learning letter names, corresponding letters with sounds, or grasping the alphabetic principle. Students with such fundamental reading problems are usually identified quickly and receive special reading instruction. While many children with early reading weaknesses progress to a level of fluency, some are plagued with reading difficulties throughout their education. Such early problems should be carefully documented for adolescent or adult LD–ADA evaluations

Some children acquire the essentials of the decoding process but begin to experience difficulty, usually in fourth grade, with the shift to reading for concepts and understanding of abstract content. This group is characterized as having reading comprehension problems, slow reading rates, and lack of interest in reading, all of which lead to limited reading experience. While some children show reading problems later than others, rarely would a student with significant reading problems graduate from high school without having shown some prior academic difficulty related to reading.

Current Symptoms

The most common LD-type symptoms that undergraduate and graduate students report are avoidance of reading, inability to complete reading assignments, slow reading rate, and difficulty with concentration on or recall of material read. To qualify as a learning disability, the reading problems must be associated with factors tied to the reading process, including gaps in vocabulary, fund of knowledge, or conceptual understanding.

At the postsecondary level, the source of a reading problem must be carefully investigated because it may be related to poor study skills or lack of background in a given subject, rather than to an actual learning disability. The NJCLD definition of LD makes clear that learning problems caused by poor instruction or other extrinsic factors do not qualify as specific disabilities. In its discussion on operationalizing the LD definition (NJCLD, 1997), the NJCLD notes that some learning problems (as opposed to learning disabilities) stem from "mismatches between the student's abilities and important learning demands at a particular point in time" (p. 32). The more demanding the program requirements of graduate and professional training become, the more likely academic problems can be attributed to these "mismatches."

To document an actual disability, the evaluator must rule out noncognitive factors and provide evidence of identifiable reading-related deficits. A longstanding history (as outlined in the prior section) is instrumental in substantiating the persistent role of reading problems.

Often the argument is made that the absence of early learning difficulties reflects successful compensation, perhaps due to superior intelligence or high motivation. As Gordon and Murphy point out in Chapter 5 (this volume), individuals with developmental disorders will, by definition, manifest symptoms of that disorder during childhood, regardless of cognitive ability or hard work. Although there are some exceptions to this rule (primarily cases in which the student had been placed in highly unusual educational settings), individuals with LD can produce ample evidence of symptoms across their educational experience. Even if they were able to work around those limitations during their early schooling, those limitations would still have been demonstrable.

A careful analysis of current functioning should pinpoint the specific circumstances under which the student manifests language-based (i.e., reading) problems. How consistently during the years of postsecondary education have reading problems interfered? Do they occur in all courses requiring reading or only during examinations? For those courses in which the student performs well, how much extra effort was required? What is the evidence that problems with comprehension are associated with trouble reading as opposed to problems understanding the material regardless of how it is communicated? Answers to these kinds of questions are critical to documenting the nature of academic limitations.

Testing

Psychological testing should provide information to address four essential questions:

1. *Are the student's overall intellectual abilities at least in the average range and generally sufficient to meet specific academic demands?* To qualify for a learning disability, a student's Full Scale IQ should fall within one standard deviation from the mean on any accepted measure of intellectual functioning. These may include, but are not limited to, the Wechsler Adult Intelligence Scale (WAIS-III), Kaufman Adolescent and Adult Intelligence Test (KAIT), and Woodcock–Johnson—Revised (WJ-R) Tests of Cognitive Ability. Any test must be administered according to standard instructions and must use norms based on the general population.

It is important to present information about all aspects of cognitive processing including short- and long-term memory, verbal and nonverbal problem-solving skills, visual and auditory memory, general working memory, knowledge base, and inspection time (Deary & Stough, 1966). Written language, although not an integral part of the reading process, can be examined as well, particularly when language processing appears to be the source of the reading difficulties. Often written language assessment can confirm problems in language comprehension when production is limited or language use is immature or incorrect. On the other hand, receptive language (e.g., reading comprehension), is often superior to expressive language skills in individuals with language-processing problems.

In interpreting the results of cognitive testing, consideration must be given to the match between a student's overall aptitude and the demands of the academic program. For example, a student may have a measured Full Scale IQ of 94 but compete in a program in which the average student's IQ falls in the superior range. Someone cannot be considered learning disabled simply because he finds himself surrounded by classmates who are generally more able.

2. *Are the individual's general academic skills in the average to above-average range and sufficient to satisy academic demands?* An LD assessment must provide an overall profile of the individual's academic skills. It should include an evaluation of all basic skills, including word recognition, spelling, reading comprehension, and written expression, as well as math computation, concepts, and application. Achievement batteries such as the Woodcock–Johnson Psychoeducational Battery—Revised Tests of Achievement (WJ-R) or the Scholastic Abilities Test for Adults can provide these data.

The examiner must consider not only the individual's abilities but the academic demands facing the individual. That assessment should determine the specific skill requirements of the academic program. Once again, the evaluator must consider whether the student has elected a course of study that is an appropriate fit for his general achievement profile.

3. *Do test scores indicate specific and substantial weaknesses in the ability to read?* To qualify as disabled under the ADA, evidence must be presented that an individual's language abilities, specifically reading decoding and/or comprehension, fall below the norm. Admittedly, documenting specific weaknesses from test data is challenging because no well-normed measures of skilled reading above the secondary level are currently available in print, nor are there accurate measures of reading rate. The Nelson–Denny Reading Test, which has been standardized for a 4-year undergraduate population, is primarily a screening tool. Low scores on this test serve only to alert the examiner to investigate reading difficulties further. A thorough investigation of reading skills will include assessment of phonological awareness, vocabulary, and rapid automatized naming. The Lindamood Auditory Conceptualization Test and the Boston Naming Test are two measures with adult norms.

4. *Do tests provide evidence of weaknesses in underlying processes related to reading?* All components of the reading process require assessment, from word recognition to comprehension. Automaticity of word recognition is essential before fluent comprehension is possible. When a slow reading rate is reported, decoding problems must be ruled out first as the source of the slow rate. If decoding is labored, the evaluator should explore the person's knowledge of phonics as

well as phonemic and phonological awareness, using measures normed on adult populations.

Exploration of Alternate Explanations and Comorbid Conditions

As mentioned earlier, part of what substantiates an LD diagnosis is evidence that the clinician has carefully explored and ruled out the wide range of other factors that can cause poor achievement. In some cases, poor preparation, lack of background, or inadequate study skills are more likely the primary cause of the individual's difficulties, rather than a specific language disability per se. Individuals can also perform poorly because of ADHD (see Chapter 5), mood disorders (see Chapter 7), substance abuse, family problems, and financial pressures. A comprehensive evaluation considers all of these factors and, for an LD diagnosis, eliminates them as more convincing explanations.

In some cases, a student with a legitimate learning disability exhibits co-occurring psychiatric or social problems. When multiple factors are involved, it is important for the clinician to explain the evidence to support each individual component and to demonstrate how they interact.

DIAGNOSTIC REVIEW SHEET

The following checklist includes key areas that should be investigated as part of the overall diagnostic workup.

1. Early childhood history
   - Delayed speech development or articulation problems
   - Hearing impairment
   - Visual impairment
   - Lack of interest in reading or related activities

2. Current functioning
   - Average or above-average cognitive ability
   - Memory and retrieval ability
   - Word recognition skills

- Phonemic and phonological awareness
- Reading comprehension ability
- Language comprehension and language processing
- Written language ability
- Psychological functioning

3. Adequacy of psychological and academic assessment
   - Appropriate tests administered
   - In-depth evaluation of deficit areas
   - Explanation of inconsistencies or discrepancies in test results
   - Appropriate conclusions drawn
   - Reasonable consideration of alternative diagnoses
   - Reasonable consideration of comorbidity

REASONS FOR DENIAL OF ACCOMMODATIONS

Clinicians who have never submitted documentation for ADA accommodations are sometimes surprised by the diagnostic rigor required by colleges, universities, and testing organizations. Reports that might well have passed muster to justify classifying elementary or secondary students for services may be dismissed by institutions of higher education or by licensing groups. Requests are denied for many reasons, but most fall into certain categories, as follows:

- *Improper test selection and administration.* Requests are often denied because the clinician used inappropriate tests or procedures. Sometimes measures are administered that have inappropriate age norms. It is obviously an error to administer to adults measures that are normed only for children.

A common mistake involves improper administration or misuse of a given measure. For example, the Nelson–Denny Reading Test (ND) has an extended time administration, but only for Forms G and H. The amount of extra time for each subtest is specifically noted in the manual. In addition, the norms for extended time are different from those for scores from the strictly timed administration. An examiner who provides extended time using older forms of the ND or gives the examinee as much time as needed to complete the test is presenting invalid data, from which diagnostic conclusions may not be properly drawn. To illustrate, here is a statement from an actual LD report:

> When the ND was given to Susan, she performed at the 6th percentile on the comprehension section, but when she was allowed to finish the test without time limits, her comprehension score was at the 90th percentile.

The clinician interpreted these results even though the administration clearly violated the standardized procedures. Because there are no norms for administration under conditions of unlimited time, the comprehension score at the 90th percentile is irrelevant. It could just as easily be that Susan's test score was still abnormal compared to others who were allowed unlimited time.

Another example: Many examiners use the Reading Rate score on the ND to support the claim of slow reading rate. First, the Reading Rate score is based on only *1 minute* of reading a passage, the content of which may be unfamiliar to the examinee. As it is commonly recognized that rate is related to familiarity with or prior knowledge of a subject, 1 minute of contact with new material is not sufficient to draw a conclusion about an individual's reading speed. In fact, one needs more than 1 minute to adjust reading rate to meet the demands of the content. Furthermore, in spite of a slow start, an individual often goes on to complete the entire test within the time limit and does not require the extended time allowance. The initial low Reading Rate score is meaningless, but examiners will often use a low score as evidence of slow reading and, in turn, as justification for extended time on standardized tests.

• *Overinterpretation of test results.* Clinicians will sometimes justify accommodations based on strained logic or limited data. The most common examples come from overinterpretation of Verbal–Performance splits on the WAIS-R/WAIS-III. Evaluators often make interpretations about uneven functioning based on differences between the subscales that are essentially trivial. While it is true that 12 points represent a statistically significant Verbal–Performance discrepancy, almost 40% of the normal population demonstrate a difference of at least 10 points (see the technical manual to the WAIS-III).

Moreover, while significant Verbal–Performance discrepancies are often seen in individuals with learning disabilities, they are not diagnostic of a LD. Rather, discrepancies provide information about strengths and weaknesses in problem solving that may or may not confirm the existence of a learning disability.

To illustrate both appropriate and inappropriate interpretations of test scores, presented below are two more statements culled from actual evaluations:

> His Verbal IQ was 111, Performance IQ 93, and Full Scale IQ 102. In view of the results obtained by this psychologist indicating good spatial visualization ability (based on results of other visual–spatial measures) the significant difference between the Verbal and Performance scores is most likely related to the fact that the Performance Scale subtests are strictly timed.

The evaluator offers no convincing evidence that the lower Performance scores were due to time demands. An individual can score poorly on the Performance subscales for many reasons, not just time interference or impaired visual–spatial ability. Contrast the unsubstantiated conclusion of the prior statement with this more credible justification. Note that this examiner explains how and why the time limits generated lower Performance subtest scores:

> Low-average scores to average scores (on the WAIS-R) were obtained across subtests associated with visual–motor speed and problem solving. On such tasks, however, his responses were usually correct, but the time he took to complete or recheck his responses penalized his overall score.

The same care is required for interpreting differences between individual subtest scores. First, a difference of three points or less between subtests does not constitute a strength or a weakness. Only when the scaled score is at least three points higher or lower compared to the *mean* of the Verbal or Performance subscale is it appropriate to consider it a relative strength or weakness. Furthermore, interpretations of test scores must be supported by the data from which the interpretations are made.

The case for impairment is always stronger if the examiner can point to research that substantiates a clinical conclusion. Conversely, statements derived from pure speculation or hefty leaps in logic are more vulnerable to being dismissed.

The overinterpretation of Verbal–Performance discrepancies, individual falloffs in single subests, or isolated academic problems all rely on scores or events that, in themselves, are not sensitive or specific to the disorder. For example, while it is true that, in group studies, learning disabled students may be more vulnerable to discrepant subscale scores, no evidence exists that these differences are diagnostic of a learning disability. Unfortunately, clinicians often point to these nonspecific features as conclusive.

• *Failure to demonstrate functional impairment relative to the general population.* Perhaps the single most common reason that accommodations are denied is that evaluations fail to make a convincing case for "a substantial limitation in a major life activity." As indicated throughout this chapter, the law requires evidence that the individual suffers from significant deficits relative to most people. Students who cannot offer such evidence will find accommodations under the ADA to be elusive.

Certain justifications for designating someone as impaired are especially weak. The most frail is the "had to work harder than others" rationale. This reasoning suggests that someone is learning disabled if he or she had to expend more effort than classmates to achieve satisfactory results. As indicated earlier, having to study hard or to find ways to compensate for relative weaknesses is not a sufficient basis for declaring a disability. Most students struggle to master certain aspects of their academic program.

Another questionable approach to judging impairment relies on discrepancies between isolated subtest scores and the aggregate assessment of achievement and aptitude scores. For example, when all scores on the WJ-R are within one standard deviation of each other except for a single subtest, some examiners will identify a learning disability because of that one outlier. Discrepant scores from one or even two subtests are insufficient evidence on which to base a diagnosis. Rather, data must be gathered from more than one test or measure. If anything, the presence of outlier scores suggests the need for further testing in the discrepant area.

More important, the examiner must show how measured weaknesses are tied to evidence of actual functional impairment. Accommodations are not justified under ADA for individuals who show isolated weaknesses that do not substantially interfere with a major life activity.

Weaknesses in auditory or visual processing are also offered as evidence of processing deficits sufficient to justify a request for accommodations. The visual-processing subtests on the WJ-R (Visual Matching and Cross Out) are essentially clerical tasks and have no real impact on one's reading behavior because they do not require the processing and understanding of information. The auditory processing cluster (Sound Blending and Incomplete Words), if lower than other subtest scores, may be suggestive of phonological-processing problems, but without further exploration are of little use in making a diagnosis. Additional information about phonological processing and phonemic awareness must be presented to demonstrate the presence of reading-related auditory-processing problems.

NONVERBAL LEARNING DISABILITIES

Although most LD involve specific language deficits, nonverbal deficits do have an impact on reading comprehension and thus deserve mention. Individuals with nonverbal LD (NLD) usually acquire word identification skills early and show advanced decoding and spelling abilities because auditory perception and memory capacities are well developed. Difficulties in reading comprehension arise, however, when higher-level inferential thinking is required. Concept formation, analysis and synthesis of information, and strategy generation are generally deficient, as are other aspects of linguistic performance such as appropriate prosody and functional language (Rourke, 1989). Although these deficits are often extremely difficult to diagnose in adults, Rourke (1989) found that "adults who exhibit the NLD syndrome were much more deficient (relative to age-based norms) on tests for psychomotor coordination, problem solving, and concept formation. [They] performed at similar levels (relative to age-based norms) on tests of linguistic functioning" (p. 100).

While a Verbal IQ higher than the Performance IQ on the WAIS-R might signal the possibility of NLD, far more evidence is required to document the diagnosis. In general, NLD is a subtle and elusive syndrome which necessitates careful test selection and interpretation.

REASONABLE ACCOMMODATIONS

Because a slow reading rate is the most common presenting complaint, extended time for tests is the accommodation usually requested.

A separate room might also be sought when an individual has the need to subvocalize while reading. Other accommodations are available, however, that might actually better serve someone with a learning disability. These include audiotape versions of examinations, a reader, assistance in completing answer sheets, extended breaks, large-print examinations, or a printed copy of verbal instructions read by the proctor.

Regardless of the exact accommodations requested, the examiner must explain how they specifically address the individual's identified functional limitations. Providing a rationale for recommended accommodations is therefore a critical component of an LD evaluation. The examiner has the advantage of actual contact with the applicant and can explain, on the basis of both test behavior and test results, why a given accommodation is necessary.

SUMMARY

Although research data are sketchy at best, the number of adults with LD in the United States is estimated to range from 5% to about 15% of the total population (Craig, 1990). The percentage of students in graduate and professional programs with LD is undoubtedly smaller, but those students with significant learning problems can succeed with accommodations that allow them to demonstrate their mastery of coursework. What do reviewers look for to justify granting accommodations?

- History of learning problems.
- Consistency of test scores that record information processing deficits.
- Accurate administration of appropriate tests.
- Accurate interpretation of test results.
- Thorough explanation of results including aggregation of both consistent data and inconsistencies and/or discrepancies that appear in the data.

What prompts reviewers to deny requests for accommodations?

- Statements reporting difficulties with only one aspect of an academic program, such as low scores on timed, standardized tests.

- Apparent absence of academic problems until a failure occurs on a test, the passage of which is necessary to proceed with one's education.
- Misuse and/or misinterpretation of tests and test results to reach a diagnosis that is not in fact supported by the results.

The purpose of LD-related accommodations under the ADA is to provide equal access to learning. The challenge to examiners is to provide accurate and valid evaluations that document *both* the stated disability *and* the way in which that disability "substantially limits one or more [of the individual's] major life activities."

REFERENCES

American Psychiatric Association. (1994). *Diagnostic and statistical manual of mental disorders* (4th ed.). Washington, DC: Author.

Blumsack, J., Lewandowski, L., & Waterman, B. (1997). Neurodevelopmental precursors to learning disaiblities: A preliminary report from a parent survey. *Journal of Learning Disabilities, 30*(2), 228–237.

Brackett, J., & McPherson, A. (1996). Learning disability diagnosis in post-secondary students: A comparison of discrepancy-based models. In N. Gregg, C. Hoy, & A. F. Gay (Eds.), *Adults with learning disabilities: Theoretical and practical perspectives* (pp. 68–84). New York: Guilford Press.

Clark, D. B., & Uhry, J. K. (1995). *Dyslexia: Theory and practice of remedial instruction* (2nd ed.). Baltimore: York Press.

Craig, J. L. (1990, November). The hidden handicap: Learning disabilities. *Menninger Clinic Perspective*, pp. 5–9.

Deary, I. J., & Stough, C. (1996). Intelligence and inspection time: Achievements, prospects, and problems. *American Psychologist, 51*(6), 599–608.

Doris, J. (1996). *Dyslexia: Evolution of a concept*. Paper presented at the Spectrum of Developmental Disabilities XVIII: Dyslexia: Practitioner's dilemma; researcher's delight (or vice versa), Johns Hopkins Medical Institutions, Baltimore.

Goldstein, S. (1997). *Managing attention and learning disorders in late adolescence and adulthood: A guide for practitioners*. New York: John Wiley & Sons.

Grossman, P. G. (1994). Developing issues for the learning disabled community under employment discrimination laws. In P. J. Gerber, & H. B.

Reiff (Eds.), *Learning disabilities in adulthood: Persisting problems and evolving issues*. Stoneham, MA: Butterworth-Heinemann.

Gough, P. B, & Tumner, W. E. (1986). Decoding, reading and reading disability. *Remedial and Special Education (RASE)*, *7*(1), 6–10.

Kirk, S. A. (1986). *Educating exceptional children*. Boston: Houghton Mifflin.

National Joint Committee on Learning Disabilities (NJCLD). (1990). Operationalizing the NJCLD definition of learning disabilities for ongoing assessment in schools: A report from the National Joint Committee on Learning Disabilities. *Perspectives: The International Dyslexia Association, 23*(4), 29.

Neisser, U., Boodoo, G., Bouchaard, T. J., Boykin, A. S., Brody, N., Ceci, S. J., Halpern, D. F., Loehlin, J. C., Perloff, R., Sternberg, R. J., & Urbina S. (1996). Intelligence: Knowns and unknowns. *American Psychologist, 51*(2), 77–101.

Perfetti, C. A., & Lesgold, A. M. (1979). Coding and comprehension in skilled reading and implications for reading instruction. In L. B. Resnick & P. A. Weaver (Eds.), *Theory and practice early reading* (Vol. 1). Hillsdale, NJ: Erlbaum.

Rourke, B. P. (1989). *Nonverbal learning disabilities: The syndrome and the model*. New York: Guilford Press.

Stanovich, K. E. (1988). Explaining the difference between the dyslexic and the garden-variety poor reader: The phonological core variable-difference model. *Journal of Learning Disabilities, 21*, 590–604.

7 | Mood and Anxiety Disorders

Lauren Wylonis, MD
Edward Schweizer, MD

INTRODUCTION

Mood and anxiety disorders are more common in the general population than any other category of mental illness except for alcohol and substance dependence/abuse. The lifetime prevalence of affective illness (comprising major depressive disorder, dysthymic disorder, bipolar disorder, and cyclothymic disorder) is estimated, conservatively, to be in the range of 10–15%. Anxiety disorders (comprising panic disorder, obsessive–compulsive disorder, generalized anxiety disorder, social phobia, specific phobias, and posttraumatic stress disorder) become manifest at about the same rate (Robins & Regier, 1991; Kessler et al., 1994). The consensus estimate from a series of epidemiological surveys is that at least 25% of the population will experience an affective illness or anxiety disorder (or both) at one point during the lifespan (Kessler et al., 1994). It is therefore not surprising that these conditions are frequently the basis upon which individuals request accommodation under the Americans with Disabilities Act of 1990 (ADA; PL 101-336).

Although Congress clearly intended the ADA to cover psychiatric illnesses, the government has been slow to clarify how the law applies to these disorders. It was only in March of 1997, 7 years after the law's passage, that the Equal Employment Opportunity Commission (EEOC) issued guidelines for mental conditions. By most accounts, these guidelines represent a belated and somewhat ungainly attempt to reduce the confusion that had emerged around applying the ADA to psychiatric disorders.

Ironically, these new regulations have become a lightning rod for a public backlash against extending ADA protections to feelings and behaviors that differ dimensionally, not categorically, from the normal range of human responses. This media attention has included well over 100 articles in the print media, many discussions on the Internet (see Kramer & Satel, 1997), and a flurry of television stories. A representative and high-profile television segment on the new ADA guidelines was aired in the summer of 1997 on ABC's *PrimeTime Live.* Diane Sawyer, serving as the incredulous Everyperson, queried the director of the EEOC about how he would interpret specific psychiatric disability cases. His awkward and tongue-tied explanations of the guidelines served as powerful evidence of their impracticality in the hurly-burly world of the workplace. At the same time, the *Wall Street Journal* (Davis, 1997) reported that courts are widely rejecting cases brought before them by psychiatrically disabled plaintiffs.

The uproar around the ADA's application to psychiatric disabilities has unfortunately obscured the wisdom of providing accommodations to individuals with legitimate mental illnesses (Kramer, 1997). The problem appears, in part, to stem from the fact that much of psychiatric illness represents the extreme end of a spectrum, at whose other end are fluctuations in normal human emotions of, for example, anxiety and depression. Familiarity with milder, normal mood fluctuations appears to lead many people to underestimate just how disabling the more severe forms of anxiety and depressive illness can be (Wells et al., 1989; Katon et al., 1995). In fact, the disability associated with psychiatric illness has been found to be equal to that of most chronic medical illnesses (Wells et al., 1989).

ADA DOCUMENTATION OF MOOD AND ANXIETY DISORDERS

To properly document a need for accommodations under ADA for individuals with affective and anxiety disorders, clinicians should consider certain key issues. These are the same concepts, of course, that apply to the verification of all disorders under the ADA (see Chapter 1, this volume). They involve establishing the credibility of the diagnosis, the severity of impairment, and the suitability of the accommodations for the tasks at hand. Once the clinician understands the law's requirements for documentation, the path to a reasonable determination is cluttered only by the normal vicissitudes of psychiatric diagnosis.

As much as clinicians would prefer institutions to accept diagnostic determinations without careful documentation, rarely will a brief statement of two suffice. Credible documentation of the presence of a mood and anxiety disorder cannot be made by assertion, regardless of the practitioner's special qualifications or clinical experience. A clinical report cannot simply state that panic disorder or major depression is present and that accommodations are justified.

In this chapter, we provide a road map for documenting mood and anxiety disorders by addressing three questions:

- How should clinicians validate and document the presence of the mood or anxiety disorder?
- What are the best approaches to establishing the degree of severity and disability associated with the illness?
- How can clinician's prove that the accommodations requested are reasonable?

DOCUMENTATION OF THE DIAGNOSIS

Markers of the diagnosis are less well established for mood and anxiety disorders than for other medical illnesses or conditions. Therefore, confidence in the validity of the diagnosis increases in direct proportion to the ability to document the presence of the following:

- A characteristic pattern of clinical symptoms that meet DSM-IV criteria.
- The presence of a verifiable genetic and family history.
- Documentation of the characteristic age of onset and course of illness for each disorder.
- Evidence of characteristic biological, psychological, and neuropsychological test results, where applicable.
- Documentation of characteristic treatment response.

Current Clinical Symptoms

As for all psychiatric diagnoses, close adherence to formal criteria substantially increases the accuracy and reliability of identification.

Field trials for the various versions of the DSM (e.g., DSM-IV; American Psychiatric Association, 1994) diagnostic criteria, as well as for their international cousins ICD-9 and ICD-10 (Spitzer, Forman, & Nees, 1979; Hiller, Dichtl, Hecht, Hundt, & von Zerssen,1993; Regier, Kaelber, Roper, Rae, & Sartorius, 1994), suggests that they provide a reasonable basis for making a reliable and valid diagnosis. All evaluations for mood and anxiety disorders must report the extent to which the patient meets DSM-IV criteria.

Ideally, a structured psychiatric assessment such as the Structured Clinical Interview based on DSM-IV (SCID; First, Spitzer, Gibbon, & Williams, 1990) should be employed. Convincing evidence exists that the reliability and validity of a diagnosis made by this method is higher than for less formal psychiatric evaluations. If information from structured interviews is not provided, it is acceptable to rely on a less formal psychiatric evaluation, but only if the specialist's report provides a detailed list of the DSM-IV criteria that were reviewed and found to be either present or absent.

The reader is referred to DSM-IV for a summary of the criteria for the key mood and anxiety disorders. The mood disorders consist of unipolar depression, dysthymic disorder, cyclothymic disorder, and bipolar disorder. The anxiety disorders consist of panic disorder, agoraphobia, social phobia, specific phobias, obsessive–compulsive disorder, generalized anxiety disorder, and posttraumatic stress disorder. Adjustment or stress disorders are unlikely to form the basis for an ADA accommodation request because of their transience.

The diagnosis of agoraphobia is also unlikely to form the basis of a request. Someone who is so house bound that he or she is unable to venture forward to take the test is also unlikely to be able to perform the essential features of any profession. Besides, the only imaginable accommodation would be to administer instruction or tests in the individual's own home.

Perhaps the area of greatest diagnostic confusion concerns the issue of test anxiety. Anxiety is an almost universal response to the test-taking situation. In fact, some degree of anxiety may increase arousal and translate into enhanced performance, although excessive anxiety may clearly impair performance. What is important for clinicians to keep in mind is that test anxiety is not a psychiatric disorder per se. Therefore, simply scoring poorly on a test, even if it is due to anxiety, is not sufficient evidence of a mental illness as classified by DSM-IV. The burden of proof falls on the clinician to document a preexisting, anxiety-driven disorder that has manifested itself in other antecedent spheres of activity. In other words, the patient must meet criteria for generalized anxiety disorder or one of the other anxiety-related illnesses.

A related issue concerns depression associated with past academic and testing difficulties. Reactive depression is an understandable consequence of failure, especially when such failure seriously jeopardizes career plans. However, the fact that someone is depressed (or anxious) because he or she has not fared well academically is not alone a basis for a psychiatric diagnosis. While this circumstance is certainly a cause for sympathy, it cannot justify a claim of depression-related disability. Requests for accommodations that invoke test-related anxiety and reactive depression as their primary evidence subscribe to the faulty notion that there must be a clinical explanation (which is, in turn, actionable) for every setback. We caution clinicians against falling into this mind set because, as Gordon and Keiser point out in Chapter 1 (this volume), this entitlement philosophy is not true to the intent of the ADA.

Another stumbling block for some evaluators involves false presumptions of causality. Consider the student with a social phobia who performs poorly on a test. Unfortunately, some clinicians will automatically assume that the test failure serves as retrospective evidence that the social phobia was the proximate cause. But social phobics can perform poorly for reasons other than those associated with their disorder. Some causes are no more profound than an inadequate knowledge base. As with other conditions, the clinician must entertain the full range of etiological possibilities.

A final pitfall concerns making assumptions about the impact of a disorder on learning or evaluation that may not necessarily hold true. A good example comes from the case of social phobia. Even though social phobia is characterized by marked anxiety in social situations, the majority of social phobics experience no particular problems with test taking in public. Most social phobics, especially those with the "social-interactional" subtype, have no problem whatsoever being in a group situation as long as they are not called upon to interact verbally or socially with others (especially with ·strangers, authority figures, or the opposite sex). In a testing environment, the social phobic only has to sit and, like other examinees, be careful *not* to interact with others, since this would be against the rules.

One important method of establishing the credibility of the impairment is to cite published research that establishes a relationship between a specific mood or anxiety disorder and a specific impairment within an educational or testing environment. For example, there is good evidence that some individuals suffering from social phobia will have marked impairment in concentration and functioning in classroom or test settings. Similarly, some forms of depression have been shown to be associated with impairment not only in concentration, but also in cognitive functioning (Tarbuck & Paykel, 1995). In the absence of any previously established link, the documentary requirement for establishing a direct etiological link between the psychiatric cause and the disability is much more stringent.

Genetic or Family History

Adoption and twin studies suggest that there is a genetic or family history loading for most mood and anxiety disorders. Documentation of the presence of first-degree relatives who have been hospitalized in the past or have otherwise received specific treatment for a mood or anxiety disorder constitutes useful external validation of the presence of the disorder. Reports should therefore include a section detailing family psychiatric history. However, we must emphasize that although the presence of a family history can be informative, it is not diagnostic of a mood or anxiety disorder. Such data could help clinch an otherwise ambiguous diagnosis, but they cannot be taken in isolation as definitive.

Age of Onset and Course of Illness

Specific mood and anxiety disorders have characteristic (mean and modal) ages of onset. For example, bipolar disorder tends to have an earlier age of onset than unipolar major depression, with the majority of individuals suffering from bipolar disorder reporting their first episode under the age of 21. Similarly, social phobia has a modal age of onset in the early teenage years, while the modal age of onset of panic disorder is in the mid-20s.

Each illness also tends to exhibit a distinctive course of illness pattern, both in terms of its chronicity or episodic nature, as well as in terms of characteristic comorbidity that develops over the course of the disorder. For example, panic disorder frequently is complicated over time by agoraphobic avoidance. As with family history, documentation of age of onset and course of illness features serves as useful supportive evidence in favor of the presence of a valid diagnosis. These typical ages of onset, however, are not in and of themselves evidence for or against the presence of an illness.

Biological, Psychological, and Neuropsychological Tests

Well-established biological markers validating the presence of a mood or anxiety disorder diagnosis are generally not available. A wide range of tests have reported abnormal results in those with mood disorders, including dexamethasone suppression, blunted TSH (thyroid stimulating hormone) response to TRH (thyroid releasing hormone) stimulation, shortened REM (rapid eye movement) latency, and altered regional cerebral blood flow and metabolism. In anxiety disorders, they include exaggerated MHPG (3 methoxy 4 hydroxyphenylglycol) response to yohimbine challenge and blunted growth hormone and saccadic eye movement response to diazepam challenge. But both the expense of these tests and the lack of definitive evidence for their diagnostic specificity and sensitivity make them only useful, at present, as research tools.

Psychological testing may provide supportive evidence for the presence of a mood or anxiety disorder. Such psychological testing may include assessment scales predating the DSM-III (American Psychiatric Association, 1980) such as the Minnesota Multiphasic Personality Inventory (MMPI). But it is far more useful to have illness-specific measures such as the Yale–Brown Obsessive–Compulsive Scale (YBOCS; Woody, 1995) for obsessive–compulsive disorder, the Liebowitz (Clark et al., 1997) or the Brief Social Phobia Scale (Davidson et al., 1991) for social phobia, or the Beck Depression Inventory (BDI; Beck, Steer, & Garbin, 1988) or the Hamilton Depression Rating Scale (HAM-D; Hamilton, 1960) for depression. The inclusion of these scales as part of a psychiatric or psychological assessment is an especially desirable form of documentation if no structured interview was completed.

Treatment Response

Documentation of treatment history is another essential component of an adequate report. Evidence that an individual has previously sought and received treatment assists in establishing the antecedent nature of the disorder. It also demonstrates that the disorder has previously been perceived as having sufficient severity to warrant seeking help.

The lack of any previous history of treatment is not necessarily definitive in determining a current need for accommodations because the diagnosis as well as the determination of severity hinge on current functioning. In addition, many individuals who actually meet criteria for depression will avoid treatment for fear that they will be stigmatized. However, regardless of whether the individual has declined or even pursued available treatment for the mood or anxiety disorder, the determination of disability and need for accommodation will still turn on the individual's current functional limitations. The clinician should also explore what might represent a reasonable accommodation in the absence of medication or other therapeutic treatment.

DOCUMENTATION OF FUNCTIONAL IMPAIRMENT

The sine qua non of disabilities determinations under the ADA is evidence that a diagnosis causes substantial limitation relative to others. Because mood and anxiety disorders fall along a normal continuum, it is absolutely essential for the clinician to document that the disorder significantly interferes in areas of functioning relevant to the learning or test-taking situation. It is certainly possible that a patient might meet a clinical diagnosis of a mood or anxiety disorder without being "significantly limited" according to the ADA.

More important, a person could meet even the law's standard of disability but not show impairment in ways that would affect the opportunity to learn or to take an exam. For example, a student could have a classic case of generalized anxiety disorder (GAD), which causes him chronic and excessive worry accompanied by various psychosomatic symptoms (e.g., insomnia, tension, irritability). He worries about everything, including test performance, but never to the degree that it impairs performance. Like most individuals with GAD, he does not suffer from impairments in memory, cognitive function, or concentration. In fact, he worries so much about his performance that he studies harder than is required. He actually performs better than some of his friends who do not worry and obsess enough about the significance of examinations.

The most reliable way to demonstrate the current severity of an illness is to utilize one of the diagnosis-specific scales cited previously. These scales are generally well validated and provide normative estimates of severity. Global impression of severity provided by an experienced clinician is acceptable, but it is much more idiosyncratic since the range of patients seen varies so greatly and is so dependent on practice setting. Some formal statement of the severity of the mood and anxiety disorder is an essential component of the documentation and should be supported by clear evidence, whether by scale scores or clinical detail.

Documentation of disability requires several components. First, it is essential that the clinician document the extent of functional impairment. As mentioned previously, empirical field trials have been conducted of DSM-III, DSM-III-R, DSM-IV, ICD-9, and ICD-10. These field trials have included assessment of the reliability of the V code used to index disability. The results of this research (Goldman, Skodol, & Lave, 1992) found, at best, moderate interrater reliability among psychiatrists who were asked to record the functional impairment caused by a psychiatric illness. More disturbingly, psychiatric ratings of degree of disability appear to be frequently confounded with symptom severity (Roy-Byrne, Dagadakis, Unutzer, & Ries, 1996). In other words, clinicians often confuse the extent to which symptoms are present with the degree to which those symptoms cause impairment. While it is true that there is a correlation between the two, severity of disability (i.e., functional impairment) is an independent domain only partly determined by illness severity, given all the many factors that can affect adjustment. Documentation of illness severity should therefore be supported by evidence that the psychiatric disorder has caused impairment in actual functioning.

A second key component involves the presentation of information about the extent and nature of the disability. To document precisely how the disability manifests itself requires reporting specific details and not simply global impairment. The documentation should, except in rare instances, include examples of functional impairment that come from non-test-related activities.

Finally, the manifestations of disability should bear a clear etiological relationship to the mood or anxiety disorder that has been documented. Ideally, there should be evidence from the empirical literature to support that the mood or anxiety disorder in question has been shown to cause the specific functional impairment being claimed.

THE APPROPRIATENESS OF ACCOMMODATIONS

The final requirement in the process of requesting accommodations is to provide a justification for their provision. Any proposed accommodation should be specifically targeted to the illness-caused disability. The clinician should also demonstrate that there is a reasonable amount of evidence that the proposed accommodation will actually remedy the disability.

Depending on the nature of the disability and the educational circumstances, any number of accommodations might apply for an individual with a mood or anxiety disorder. For example, a student with an anxiety disorder who faces a licensing examination may require one or more of the following changes:

- The examination environment (e.g., the test could be administered apart from the main testing group).
- The duration of the exam (e.g., by giving additional time or by allowing breaks).
- Examination format (e.g., orally instead of in written form).

How does the clinician determine which would be most suited to the patient? What type of documentation would most institutions find convincing?

Building a solid argument for a particular remedy (or set of remedies) is not always as simple as it might seem. The clinician must provide evidence that the proposed accommodation will actually remedy the functional impairment caused by the mood or anxiety disorder.

There are two useful principles to keep in mind when assessing the appropriateness of mood and anxiety disorder-related disability accommodations. The first is the *principle of specificity*. It states that an accommodation must be targeted to alleviate the impact of specific impairments on access to education or fair testing. The crucial element here is to document that the proposed accommodation is specifically targeted at the illness-caused disability. By requiring a match between impairment and accommodation, the ADA discourages requests for accommodations that represent nonspecific aids in performance that might help anyone, disabled or not. The convincing argument for accommodation identifies the impairment and then describes how the accommodation would alleviate the impact of that impairment within the educational or testing context.

The second concept we call the *principle of minimal effective accommodation*. This principle stands as a reminder that the goal of accommodation is not to optimize performance, but to level the playing field by removing obstacles to performance that are inequitable. It is not sufficient to show that performance would be improved if certain accommodations were implemented. Improving or optimizing performance is not the goal of ADA accommodations. Instead, accommodations should remedy the illness-caused disability so that the individual has an equal opportunity to learn and to demonstrate competence.

This second principle also recognizes a need for reasonableness and practicality. For example, in the case of a college student with social phobia, one might propose that the teacher lecture the student individually. However, this would be exceptionally time consuming for the teacher and would provide the student with a one-to-one teaching experience that the other students clearly do not receive. Taping the regular lecture in this case would be an example of the minimal effective accommodation.

To illustrate the application of these principles, here are statements from two different reports about students seeking accommodations based on an anxiety disorder:

Because Kenneth is so anxious, he will do much better on exams if he is allowed extra time. He will perform even better if he is allowed not only extra time but also a separate testing room.

One manifestation (among many) of Allen's generalized anxiety disorder is that he consistently develops symptoms when he takes exams that barely allow enough time to finish. Under these conditions, he is unable to concentrate on anything other than his sense of panic. When he knows he has extra time, he is able to stay calm enough to respond to test items. Therefore, providing him extra time will allow him to have an equal opportunity to demonstrate his competence.

In the first instance, the clinician tries to justify the accommodation based on performance enhancement. The position he offers is that the accommodation should be provided because it will lead to better scores. He also has not tied the proposed accommodation to a specific disabling feature of the anxiety disorder. He simply offers a nonspecific performance aid (that is, extra time) which conceivably would help anyone.

In the second, the practitioner identifies the specific impairment and indicates how the accommodation is tied to that aspect of the disability. The wording of the statement indicates that the accommodation is designed to enable equal opportunity as opposed to improved chances for success. The power of his argument is also enhanced because he indicates that this remedy has proven effective for the patient in the past.

Because decisions about appropriate and reasonable accommodations can be complex, we offer some additional examples that illustrate the process:

Case 1. A graduate student with a social phobia finds it difficult to concentrate or even remain in a required course because the teacher repeatedly asks questions and interacts with an audience of 100 students. The student has an intense fear of being embarrassed or humiliated if asked a question in this forum. Even if he is not called on, the mere possibility causes him extreme anxiety. His psychiatrist recommends that the student be permitted to have a friend or the teacher tape the lecture. This specific accommodation would remedy the functional impairment by eliminating the need for the student to be present in the classroom where he is so anxious and unable to concentrate. This would allow him to listen to the class lectures at home where he is comfortable and able to focus on the information presented by the lecturer. In this way, his phobia will no longer hinder his opportunity to learn. However, some classes may have a laboratory or class participation requirement that is an essential element of the program. In such cases, the individual may not be able to fulfill the course requirement and thus may not be considered "otherwise qualified."

Case 2. In a common performance subtype of social phobia, individuals may develop intense and paralyzing anxiety and self-consciousness when they are asked to write in public. Elaine has such a fear of being observed and becomes preoccupied that she will make a fool of herself. Her fear becomes a self-fulfilling prophesy, because she trembles so much that she is unable to write even a simple check at a retail store. Her psychiatrist uses her social phobia as a basis for requesting extra time but does not give a rationale for how having extra time would make her any less anxious. For example, her anxiety disorder may be more suitably accommodated by placing her in the furthest back row in the examining room so that there is no one behind to observe her.

Establishing the appropriateness of the proposed accommodation is almost always challenging. The example of panic disorder, and the related diagnosis of agoraphobia, illustrates the difficulty. An individual who suffers from panic disorder is susceptible to unexpected panic attacks. The frequency of panic attacks varies greatly and may occur as often as several times per day, in unusual cases. However, the modal frequency of attacks is less than two per week, even among untreated individuals. The actual risk of having an attack during an exam is relatively modest, but clearly present. Anticipatory anxiety concerning the *possibility* of having an attack is also part of the clinical picture, especially as it relates to fears of not being able to escape or do something to control the attack.

The question then becomes, "How can one craft an accommodation that targets the specific nature of anxiety for an individual suffering from panic disorder. In this instance, providing extra time or a separate testing room may not be appropriately targeted remedies. Instead, the ability to stop the exam, leave the room for up to 1 hour, and perhaps even to take medication to treat the attack may be more appropriate. This accommodation may even serve to reduce distracting levels of anticipatory anxiety since it provides the individual a sense of flexibility and of being able to take some action to control the attack when and if it comes. The take-home point is that the accommodation should be structured in a way that grows logically out of the clinical problem that is causing the functional interference with performance.

SUMMARY

Fraudulent "up-coding" of diagnoses and services has, in the past few years, been an endemic problem in the mental health industry. It is therefore possible that such practices are equally endemic among ADA accommodation requests that are based on claims of psychiatric disability. Nowhere are temptations for overstatement greater or diagnostic boundaries more blurry than for the categories of mood and anxiety disorders. Unwavering insistence on careful, detailed documentation is the only possible means of establishing the legitimacy of accommodation requests. Perhaps in no other diagnostic category is the percentage of adequately documented and justified accommodation requests so low as among the mood and anxiety disorders. Below is a brief summary of some key points to remember in assessing the documentation of mood and anxiety disorders.

1. The presence of a full-fledged DSM-IV mood or anxiety disorder must be documented.
   a. Adjustment reactions, stress reactions, anxiety or depression limited to, or a reaction to, the test-taking situation itself are rarely, if ever, a sufficient justification for an accommodation.
   b. A structured psychiatric interview is preferred. In the absence of such a structured interview, an itemized review of DSM-IV diagnostic criteria must be present.
   c. Supportive documentation of the mood or anxiety disorder should include review of family history, age of onset and course of illness, psychological tests (especially illness-specific assessments), and the history of treatment for the disorder. This supportive documentation is essential to provide external validation of the presence of the disorder. It is unacceptable for the documentation of the mood or anxiety diagnosis to be limited to a description of current symptoms.
2. The functional impairment caused by the disorder must be documented.
   a. Diagnosis-specific rating scales should be provided whenever possible, although global clinical assessments of severity may be acceptable.
   b. Detailed documentation should be provided of precisely how the mood or anxiety diagnosis causes impairment in functioning.
   c. Detailed documentation should be provided about the extent to which the diagnosis of a mood or anxiety disorder is

linked to pervasive and disabling impairment. Note that it is rarely if ever acceptable for documentation of a disability to be limited to the test-taking situation or to have arisen (essentially de novo) around the time of the test-taking situation.

3. Documentation should be provided concerning what accommodation is being requested, and how this accommodation will specifically remedy the illness-caused disability.

   a. Accommodations are not generally acceptable unless they are targeted toward remedying the illness-caused functional impairment.

   b. Individuals may have well-documented disabilities for which no targeted accommodation is available.

REFERENCES

American Psychiatric Association. (1980). *Diagnostic and statistical manual of mental disorders* (3rd ed.). Washington, DC: Author.

American Psychiatric Association. (1994). *Diagnostic and statistical manual of mental disorders* (4th ed.). Washington, DC: Author.

Beck A. T., Steer, R. A., & Garbin, M. G. (1988). Psychometric properties of the Beck Depression Inventory: Twenty-five years later. *Clinical Psychology Review, 8,* 77–100.

Clark, D. B., Feske, U., Masia, C. L., Spaulding, S. A., Brown, D., Mammen, O., & Shear, M. K. (1997). Systematic assessment of social phobia in clinical practice. *Depression and Anxiety, 6*(2), 47–61.

Davis, A. (1997, July 22). Courts reject many mental-disability cliams. *Wall Street Journal,* p. B-1.

Davidson, J. R., Potts, N. L., Richichi, E. A., Ford, S. M., Krishnan, K. R., Smith, R. D., & Wilson, W. (1991). The Brief Social Phobia Scale. *Journal of Clinical Psychiatry, 52*(Suppl), 48–51.

First, M. B., Spitzer, R. L., Gibbon, M., & Williams, J. B. (1997). *Structured Clinical Interview for DSM-IV.* Washington, DC: American Psychiatric Press.

Goldman, H. H., Skodol, A. E., & Lave, T. R. (1992). Revising Axis V for DSM-IV: A review of measures of social functioning. *American Journal of Psychiatry, 149,* 1148–1156.

Hamilton, M. A. (1960). A rating scale for depression. *Journal of Neurology and Neurosurgical Psychiatry, 23,* 56–62.

Hiller, W., Dichtl, G., Hecht, H., Hundt, W., & von Zerssen, D. (1993). An empirical comparison of diagnoses and reliabilities in ICD-10 and DSM-

III-R. *European Archives of Psychiatry and Clinical Neuroscience, 242,* 209–217.

Katon, W., Hollifield, M., Chapman, T., Mannuzza, S., Ballenger, J., & Fyer, A. (1995). Infrequent panic attacks: Psychiatric comorbidity, personality characteristics and functional disability. *Journal of Psychiatric Research, 29,* 121–131.

Kessler, R. C., McGonagle, K. A., Zhao, S., et al. (1994). Lifetime and 12-month prevalence of DSM-III-R psychiatric disorders in the United States: Results from the National Comorbidity Survey. *Archives of General Psychiatry, 51,* 8–19.

Kramer, P. D., & Satel, S. (1997, June 5). Mental illness on the job. *Slate* [On-line serial]. Available: http://www.slate.com

Regier, D. A., Kaelber, C. T., Roper, M. T., Rae, D. S., & Sartorius, N. (1994). The ICD-10 clinical field trial for mental and behavioral disorders: results in Canada and the United States. *American Journal of Psychiatry, 151,* 1340–1350.

Robins, L. N., & Regier, D. A. (1991). *Psychiatric disorders in America: The epidemiologic catchment area study.* New York: Free Press.

Roy-Byrne, P., Dagadakis, C., Unutzer, J., & Ries, R. (1996). Evidence for limited validity of the revised global assessment of functioning scale. *Psychiatric Services, 47,* 864–866.

Spitzer, R. L., Forman, J. B., & Nee, J. (1979). DSM-III field trials: I. Initial interrater diagnostic reliability. *American Journal of Psychiatry, 136,* 815–817.

Tarbuck, A. F., & Paykel, E. S. (1995). Effects of major depression on the cognitive function of younger and older subjects. *Psychological Medicine, 25,* 285–295.

Wells, K. B., Stewart, A., Hays, R. D., et al. (1989). The functioning and well-being of depressed patients: Results from the Medical Outcomes Study. *Journal of the American Medical Association, 262,* 914–919.

Woody, S. R. (1995). Reliability and validity of the Yale–Brown Obsessive–Compulsive Scale. *Behaviour Research Therapy, 33*(5), 597–605.

Zuckerman, D., Debenham, K., & Moore, K. (1994). *The ADA and People With Mental Illness: A Resource Manual For Employers.* Washington, DC: American Bar Association and National Mental Health Association.

8 Physical Disabilities

Stanley F. Wainapel, MD, MPH

INTRODUCTION

The heterogeneity of physical disabilities make them challenging to document. They encompass a wide variety of medical/surgical conditions that affect multiple body organs and systems. Depending on the circumstances, almost any medical problem could cause impairment sufficient to justify accommodations.

As medicine itself has become more specialized, the range of subspecialists involved in disabilities determination has broadened. While most of the other disabilities discussed in this book likely fall within the province of one or two disciplines (for example, psychiatrists or psychologists for mental disorders), physical disabilities can be evaluated by any number of medical specialties. These might include rehabilitation medicine, neurology, neurosurgery, orthopedic surgery, rheumatology, ophthalmology, optometry, audiology, otolaryngology, cardiology, gastroenterology, nephrology, endocrinology, and internal or family medicine.

This variety of disorders and practitioners has limited the development of universal guidelines for assessment. Each disorder harbors its own diagnostic nuances which can defy easy classification. Moreover, medical specialization has, to some extent, narrowed the physician's focus from a more holistic view to specific body systems or disease entities. Competent disability assessment, however, requires a comprehensive and thorough understanding of the patient's overall lifestyle and adjustment.

While the evaluation of physical disabilities can be complex, it does offer some advantages over the assessment of many learning and psychiatric disorders. The symptoms of most physical problems are more amenable to objective measurement. Their impact on functioning is also more visible and, for the most part, easily verifiable. Finally, physical disorders are less apt to provoke the levels of public skepticism so commonly reserved for mental health and learning disorders.

In 1980, the World Health Organization (WHO) published the International Classification of Impairment, Disability, and Handicap (ICIDH; WHO, 1980). This framework for classification is regarded as the worldwide standard. It is founded upon the definition of three key terms: *impairment, disability,* and *handicap.* Although they are usually used interchangeably, they actually represent distinct concepts. They are defined as follows:

Impairment: The absence of or abnormal function of an organ or body part, representing disease at the organ level.

Disability: The physical disadvantage that results from an impairment; the difficulty in performing physical tasks.

Handicap: The social disadvantage that results from an impairment; the difficulty in fulfilling a social role that is considered normal.

In this context, an *impairment* requires medical attention but not necessarily rehabilitation or accommodation. For example, patients with arthritis of the hand can suffer from various degrees of impaired dexterity. In some cases, the impact of that impairment on the ability to learn, work, and otherwise adapt is negligible. Patients whose arthritis manifests itself in mild morning stiffness may have an impairment, but not a disability.

An impairment reaches the level of a *disability* when the individual requires rehabilitation and possibly accommodation in order to function as well as others. If the arthritic patient were unable to perform routine life tasks without special accommodations, the WHO system would classify him as having a disability. Therefore, someone can manifest symptoms of a wholly legitimate medical disorder without necessarily meeting criteria for a disability. Obviously, not all physical conditions are disabling.

The WHO definition of a *handicap* addresses the social consequence of having an impairment. To carry forward the example of an individual with arthritis: Let's say that our arthritic male patient lives in an agricultural community where the general expectation is that men work the farm. Although he could perhaps work at other non-physical jobs if they were available, he might be considered handicapped as a farmer if his arthritis were severe enough to keep him from farming.

While the WHO system of classification is a well-accepted approach to categorizing disabilities from a medical perspective, it is not directly tied to the definition of disability under the Americans with Disabilities Act of 1990 (ADA; PL 101-336). The law reserves the term *disability* for conditions that cause significant functional limitations relative to the average person. The ADA requires both a formal definition of the impairment (that is, a diagnosis) and proof of substantial limitation. The WHO definition simply categorizes how an impairment affects an individual's functioning. Therefore, an individual who meets the WHO definition of *disability* may not satisfy the ADA standard of "substantial limitation in a major life activity."

THE CLASSIFICATION OF PHYSICAL DISORDERS

Physical disorders are typically grouped into five general categories according to the affected organ or body system: neurological, musculoskeletal, visual, auditory, and miscellaneous medical.

Although this scheme is somewhat simplistic, it covers most of the physical problems postsecondary students will likely present. The most commonly encountered conditions within each of these categories are as follows:

Neurological

- Traumatic spinal cord injury with resultant paraplegia or quadriplegia
- Traumatic brain injury (TBI)
- Stroke syndromes
- Sequelae of cerebral palsy
- Multiple sclerosis (MS)
- Muscular dystrophy and other myopathies
- Peripheral neuropathy or nerve injury

Musculoskeletal

- Rheumatoid arthritis or other arthritic disorders
- Collagen diseases such as systemic lupus erythematosus
- Scoliosis and other spinal deformities
- Lower extremity or upper extremity amputation
- Sequelae of major bone fractures or ligamentous injuries
- Lower back pain syndrome
- Cervical spine pain syndrome
- Congenital limb deficiencies

Visual

- Diabetic retinopathy
- Glaucoma
- Cataract; macular degeneration
- Retinitis pigmentosa
- Congenital conditions such as retinopathy of prematurity
- Strabismus
- Neuro-ophthalmologic sequelae of MS and TBI

Auditory

- Sensory–neural hearing loss
- Otosclerosis
- Congenital hearing loss

Miscellaneous Medical

- Diabetes mellitus and its complications
- Chronic renal failure
- Cardiac diseases
- Pulmonary diseases (e.g., asthma)
- Gastrointestinal disorders (e.g., irritable bowel syndrome, ulcerative colitis, Crohn's disease)

THE DOCUMENTATION OF DISABILITY

A clear and credible diagnosis is the starting point for the documentation process. The physician must demonstrate that the patient meets generally accepted criteria for the medical condition. This is particularly necessary in the case of "invisible" disabilities such as those whose primary manifestations are pain and fatigue (as in fibromyalgia and multiple sclerosis, respectively). Confirmatory evidence from tests such as X-ray or neuroimaging studies should be included in any reports. Also required is evidence that the physician is indeed qualified in the identification and treatment of that particular disorder.

Although arriving at a diagnosis is certainly important, it represents just the first step. One should always remember that a diagnosis is not synonymous with a disability. A disorder becomes disabling when it causes meaningful and substantial impairment in normal life activities. Therefore, a proper ADA-based disabilities evaluation moves systematically from clinical diagnosis to functional assessment.

Determining the extent of functional impairment requires a careful analysis of the interaction between physical symptoms and environmental demands. It is not enough simply to describe the typical consequences of having one disorder or another. Instead, the evaluator must detail the specific nature of the patient's limitations and how they might become manifest within the context of that patient's daily life.

A large number of assessment scales and systems have evolved over the years that can be useful in the documentation process. Some are highly disease-specific, such as the American Spinal Injury Association (ASIA) criteria for spinal cord injury (ASIA, 1992). Other measures, such as the Functional Independence Measure (FIM), are applicable to a considerable number of disabling conditions (Deutsch, Braun, & Granger, 1997). But it is not enough for a physician to cite a FIM score as an adequate assessment. While this score may be helpful for monitoring progress during rehabilitation treatment, it is not specific enough to use as a basis for designing accommodations in higher education.

In my work as a physiatrist, I have developed a five-category classification system. While this method lacks the quantifiable elements of the ASIA or the FIM, it does promote a more problem-focused, individualized approach to assessing functional impairment. It divides deficits into the following groups:

- *Mobility*: Difficulty in ambulation (e.g., paraplegia, hemiparesis) or joint range of motion (e.g., hip flexion contractures, joint fusion)

- *Manual dexterity*: Difficulty using hands for purposeful activities (e.g., arthritis of hands, finger muscle weakness, sensory loss in hands).
- *Information retrieval*: Difficulty in receiving data due to sensory (visual or hearing) or processing deficits (such as dyslexia).
- *Communication*: Difficulty communicating due to deficits in articulation (e.g., dysarthria, unintelligible speech due to deafness) or expressive language (e.g., aphasia).
- *Endurance*: Difficulty tolerating activity for appropriate duration due to factors such as fatigue (e.g., MS), pain, or medical issues (e.g., pulmonary/cardiac limitations, frequent need to monitor blood glucose in unstable diabetes mellitus).

This system allows the clinician to characterize the impact of a disability on a patient's functioning both in the past as well as the present. The following are the sorts of questions the physician can ask to determine levels of impairment and/or disability in each category:

Mobility

- How far can you comfortably walk without fatigue?
- What walking devices (cane, crutches, walkerette) do you use?
- Do you use a wheelchair? In what situations?
- Can you climb stairs by yourself? If so, how many flights?
- What symptoms prevent you from walking farther?
- How long does it take you to walk a distance of one block?
- Does movement limitation of any of your joints interfere with your function? If so, which joint and which function?

Manual Dexterity

- Can you use your hands for writing, handling papers, or typing?
- Do you use any splints, braces, or similar devices for your hands? If so, why?
- Does your hand fatigue easily when it is used for writing or typing? If so, after how long?
- Does your hand problem interfere with the legibility of your handwriting?
- Do you frequently drop things you are holding?

Information Retrieval

- Is your vision adequate to read ordinary newspaper print?
- Do you have difficulty reading or walking in environments with low lighting levels?
- Do you have difficulty hearing spoken voices in classrooms or groups of people?
- Do you use any special equipment due to vision or hearing loss? Please specify.
- Do you have problems reading despite having normal eyesight? Have you always had them?

Communication

- Do you require an interpreter when speaking with others, as a result of hearing loss?
- Do you use writing or a computer to facilitate communicating with others?

Endurance

- Is your sitting tolerance limited? By what?
- Is your writing tolerance limited? How long before you have to rest?
- Do you become fatigued during the day so that you cannot continue your usual activities? When does this occur during the day? Is it affected by specific environmental factors such as temperature and humidity?
- Do you become breathless with only slight activity? Can you climb a flight of stairs without being short of breath?

Although this list of questions is not exhaustive, it illustrates a function-focused approach to history taking. As you will see in the sample report below, this method can also serve as the basis for reviewing possible accommodations.

Physical examination will depend on the nature of the disability. When mobility and/or manual dexterity are the primary problems, the musculoskeletal and neurological examinations should be particularly thorough. Problems related to information retrieval and/or communication will tend to require more detailed evaluation of vision and hearing function.

Difficulties related to endurance or tolerance are often the most problematic to identify and treat. They require a particularly comprehensive examination. For relatively "invisible" disorders such as repetitive strain injury or chronic fatigue syndrome, the documentation process is made all the more difficult because it is not always clear which particular specialist would best handle the referral. Each of these disorders falls on the fringes of general acceptance.

If the limited tolerance stems from cardiopulmonary factors, an internist, cardiologist, or pulmonologist can be consulted. When pain or fatigue is the primary etiology, the underlying diagnosis may determine who the physician most suited for assessing the patient is. Unfortunately, the diagnosis is often not immediately evident.

Physicians tend to focus mainly on physical symptoms, but they should not overlook the fact that physical disabilities can coexist with cognitive or psychiatric disorders. In some cases, a single etiology accounts for both, as in TBI patients or in MS patients for whom cortical demyelination has produced cognitive problems. In others, the relationship is more indirect. For example, a person with chronic intractable pain may become clinically depressed as a result of the chronicity of the problem or even as a side effect of strong narcotic analgesic drugs. Drug dependence can also arise as a complicating factor. The physician should be careful to consider these cognitive and psychiatric comorbidities during the course of the disabilities evaluation.

ACCOMMODATION STRATEGIES

Accommodation for the postsecondary school student involves attention to the physical environment, technology, and personal assistance in varying proportions. In general, the neurological and musculoskeletal groups have their greatest negative impact in the areas of mobility and manual dexterity. Visual and auditory disorders affect information retrieval and communication while endurance problems cut across all five impairment groups. Some of the more frequent accommodations for each disability category will be summarized below.

Mobility

The physical environment can often be the primary problem with mobility impairments. Buildings, classrooms, and living quarters that are not accessible to those in wheelchairs create a formidable physical barrier. The same is true when extensive stair climbing is required from someone with cardiopulmonary limitations or fatigue.

Mobility accommodation begins with the school building itself, which should be as user friendly for these students as possible. Doorways may need to be widened or replaced with automatically opening doors at building entrances. Lighting conditions also need to be considered in terms of their potential for limiting the mobility of students with visual problems.

When standing is limited or impossible, it inevitably reduces the person's vertical reach and can interfere with educational activities. For example, a medical student in a wheelchair may not be able to fully examine a patient who is sitting or lying on an ordinary-height examination table. Four possible strategies in such a case would be:

- Providing a nurse to place instruments for the student.
- Installing an electrically controlled table whose height can be adjusted to an appropriate level.
- Purchasing devices that extend the student's reach (e.g., a stethoscope with elongated rubber tubing or a reflex hammer with a long handle).
- Constructing a simple, portable plywood ramp and platform to elevate the wheelchair user to an accessible level.

Of these various options, the adjustable table represents considerable technology and expense, but it is likely to benefit the patient as much as the medical student since it makes it easier to get on or off the table. Special wheelchairs have been developed that allow the user to stand up with good trunk support for extended periods; in the hypothetical medical student's case such a chair could give him or her the opportunity to observe or even participate in surgery despite significant neuromuscular limitations.

Manual Dexterity

Dysfunction of the hand results in major limitations in activities such as writing, touching, and perceiving objects. Imagine the difficulties that would ensue if our medical student could not grasp the reflex hammer or could not perform the delicate movements required to tie a suture during surgery. The least problematic limitation would be writing, such as in taking tests or writing reports. Here technology provides us with voice-activated computers that can be used even by those with bilateral problems such as repetitive strain injury or paralysis.

Tests can be administered orally or an assistant can write answers based on the student's dictation. Turning pages in a book may also require personal or technological assistance. Skilled activities such as those described for the medical student above may not be able to be performed without the assistance of an intermediary person. When the dexterity is only mildly or moderately impaired, functions may take longer to complete and require periodic rest.

Information Retrieval

Vision and hearing deficits interfere with obtaining information but since most affected individuals are not totally blind or deaf a number of enhancement devices or techniques can reduce the problem significantly. These include magnifiers, visual field expanders, and glare reducing and contrast enhancing devices (for vision problems), and hearing aids, amplification systems, and other auditory enhancements.

The environment should also be optimized through adequate illumination and reduced noise levels. When the vision or hearing loss is severe or total, more sophisticated and complex technology or skills will be required. Computers with optical-character recognition and synthetic speech software or with Braille output allow totally blind persons to read and perform word-processing activities. Personal assistance in the form of readers or audiotapes for the blind and interpreters for the deaf are accommodations that may be considered as well.

Communication

Computers have been adapted to allow people with unclear speech to use voice-activated devices in spite of their problem. However, it may be necessary to resort to human assistance in the form of interpreters for optimal communication. Sign language is not widely known outside of the deaf community and its relatives and friends, so signing is not ideally suited to direct communication without intermediaries. Time factors must be considered in these instances, as communication may take considerably longer than normal.

Endurance

Architectural barriers and environmental considerations are highly pertinent to problems of limited endurance. Cardiopulmonary problems may render stair climbing difficult or impossible. A hot environment may exacerbate the fatigue associated with multiple sclerosis. These and similar factors should be eliminated or minimized for optimal access to the disabled student. Rest periods or time off the clock for examination situations should be considered when clearly documented endurance problems exist. Devices such as wheelchairs and scooters can be viewed as ergonomically efficient ambulation aids which can increase endurance.

ADMINISTRATIVE CONSIDERATIONS

Administrators at postsecondary institutions and testing organizations most likely do not have medical degrees; nevertheless, they can conduct informed reviews of documentation for physical disorders. Regardless of the nature of the medical condition, reviewers can determine whether the documentation addresses certain basic questions. If the complexity of the medical information makes it hard to answer those questions, the administrator can direct consultants to provide feedback. In some cases, of course, the physician who provided the original documentation can be asked for clarification or elaboration.

Those essential questions are as follows:

- Is there convincing evidence that the patient suffers from a legitimate medical condition?
- Does the report document that the medical conditions cause substantial limitation relative to most people?
- Has the physician detailed how the physical disorder would limit the patient's functioning for the learning or testing environment in question?
- Does the report address whether the disability would interfere with the person's ability to meet the essential requirements of the job or educational program (if applicable)?
- Are the accommodations proposed reasonable means of alleviating the impact of the disability?

Because students may ask administrators, "Where should I go for an evaluation?," perhaps a few words on referral are worthwhile. Generally, any physician can conduct a disabilities evaluation. A student need not seek a specialist if all that is required is documentation, for example, that the individual indeed has a broken leg and requires an extra chair so he can elevate his foot. As the disorders become more subtle or exotic, it may be wiser for the individual to seek out a specialist in that field. However, individuals should be encouraged to find a specialist whose expertise extends beyond diagnosis. The physician must also be familiar with the classification of disabilities and with the essential elements of disability law.

PITFALLS AND CONTROVERSIES

Underlying most of the disputes around accommodating to physical disorders are disagreements over whether a condition represents an impairment only or an impairment combined with a disability. These disagreements are less controversial than most, because physical disabilities are highly visible, with verifiable diagnoses affecting neurological, musculoskeletal, visual, and auditory functioning. But what about a diagnosis such as irritable bowel syndrome? Do frequent diarrhea and abdominal symptoms constitute a disability that warrants some form of accommodation? And if accommodations are warranted, what might they involve other than perhaps allowing the student some time off the clock while in an examination setting? The line between impairment and actual disability is often not easy to draw, even when the medical condition itself is obvious.

A troubling issue that can arise involves fair assessment of whether the disability is so serious that it renders the individual no longer "otherwise qualified." While these determinations are less common in educational settings, they can still confront the physician with some thorny questions: Is the brain damage this student suffered so extensive that I should counsel him to terminate his law school career? Will this quadriplegic patient be able to meet the technical standards of being a medical student and, ultimately, a physician? Fair answers to these questions require careful investigation of functioning and expectations. However, they might also put the physician in an uncomfortable position vis-à-vis a patient who is intent on pursuing options that may be ill advised.

A final factor to consider is the stability or instability of the disease process. A static disability such as traumatic paraplegia is easier to accommodate than one that waxes and wanes like multiple sclerosis or progressively deteriorates like amyotrophic lateral sclerosis. The latter two scenarios require frequent reevaluations of the patient's needs and hence entail periodic reassessments to document any changes in their requirements.

SAMPLE REPORT

M.S. is a 28-year-old right-handed female with a diagnosis of multiple sclerosis who is entering her first year of medical school and is being seen for recommendations regarding appropriate accommodation for her disabilities.

History

Ten years ago she had an episode of transient monocular visual loss which completely resolved. Two years ago she developed sudden lower extremity weakness with loss of bladder control. Neurological evaluations included visual evoked responses (abnormal), lumbar puncture with cerebrospinal fluid evaluation (positive for oligoclonal bands), and an MRI of the brain (multiple focal areas of demyelination). Her leg weakness improved slightly but did not resolve. She also noted blurred vision and was found by ophthalmologic evaluation to have bilateral evidence of optic neuritis. Mild spasticity was treated with low-dose baclofen; urinary incontinence was controlled with ditropan and a schedule of intermittent catheterizations every 6 hours, which she was able to perform herself.

Functional History

The patient reports that she is able to walk relatively short distances (e.g., across a classroom or up a few steps) using metal Canadian crutches. For outdoor ambulation she uses a motorized scooter. Because of decreased visual function she reads large-print books and uses a portable magnifier for reading ordinary-sized print. She also utilizes the Talking Books program of the Library of Congress for her recreational reading. She notes fatigue particularly in the late afternoon and when in indoor or outdoor environments with high temperatures.

Social History

The patient is unmarried and lives alone in an elevator-accessible apartment. She is able to drive a car that has been modified to utilize hand controls.

Examination

M.S. is a slender, well-groomed young woman who arrived in the office using her power scooter but was able to get on and off the exam table independently with her Canadian crutches. Her speech is mildly scanning in type but is easily understood. The extraocular movements are full, with no nystagmus or evidence of intranuclear ophthalmoplegia. Corrected visual acuity with her glasses is 20/100 in the right eye and 20/80 in the left eye. Visual fields are grossly normal using quadrant confrontation. The upper extremities show full range of motion and normal muscle strength. I note very mild intention tremor which is more evident in her nondominant left arm, but finger dexterity is quite good bilaterally.

The lower extremities show 3+ deep tendon reflexes but no ankle clonus. Muscle strength is only 2/5 at the hips and 3/5 at knees and ankles. She is wearing bilateral plastic ankle–foot orthoses which appear to fit her well. She is able to stand with her crutches for a few minutes, after which she becomes tired and needs to sit down. She can ambulate 150 feet in about 60 seconds using an alternate two-point crutch gait pattern.

Impression

Multiple sclerosis with resulting spastic paraparesis, bilateral optic neuritis and consequent low vision, mild upper extremity tremor, and neurogenic bladder dysfunction.

Comments/Recommendations

Mobility

The patient has limited standing tolerance and a slow walking speed with capacity for indoor ambulation only. Her orthotic devices, crutches, and a power scooter are appropriate for her needs. She will need to use her scooter between classrooms and therefore needs to be in a fully accessible building. If standing is required, as with anatomical dissection (1st year) or assisting at surgical procedures (3rd and 4th year) a special wheelchair that converts to standing position can be used. Clinical rotations in her 3rd and 4th years need to be done in hospital centers that are fully wheelchair accessible.

Manual Dexterity

The mild intention tremor of her nondominant hand should not interfere with her handwriting or technical procedures such as drawing blood, assisting at surgery, or anatomical dissection.

Information Retrieval

The degree of visual acuity deficit indicates the need for enlarged print handouts and course syllabus materials. Alternatively she can utilize either a 3x magnifier, possibly with a built-in halogen light, or, for more sustained reading at home, a closed-circuit television videomagnifier (CCTV). The latter may be of particular value for reading textbook-length materials.

Communication

The patient's scanning speech is very mild and poses no problem for effective communication.

Endurance

Fatigue associated with high ambient temperature is common in multiple sclerosis and may explain this patient's late-afternoon fatigue, since core body temperature is at its maximum at around 4:00 P.M. She needs to avoid excessively warm environments for this reason, and her clinical rotations should preferentially be planned at facilities that have consistent air conditioning systems and that do not require prolonged outdoor travel during warmer parts of the year. She should also have a parking space as close to buildings as possible. If possible, she should be allowed to take tests earlier rather than later in the day to avoid her late afternoon fatigue symptoms.

Miscellaneous

This patient needs to catheterize her bladder every 6 hours; time provision needs to be made for this, should she have prolonged classes or examinations; in the latter case she will need time off the clock to complete the needed catheterization.

REFERENCES

American Spinal Injury Association (ASIA). (1992). *Standards for neurological and functional classification of spinal cord injury.* Chicago: Author.

Deutsch, A., Braun, S., & Granger, C. V. (1997). The Functional Independence Measure (FIM instrument). *Journal of Rehabilitation Outcome Measurement, 1,* 67–71.

World Health Organization (WHO). (1980). *The international classification of impairments, disabilities, and handicaps —A manual of classification relating to the consequences of disease.* Geneva: Author.

9 | Visual Disorders, Dysfunctions, and Disabilities

David A. Damari, OD, FCOVD

INTRODUCTION

This chapter offers guidelines for documenting a visual problem when the patient is claiming a visual disability as defined under the Americans with Disabilities Act of 1990 (ADA; PL 101-336). It should be understood from the beginning that disabilities requiring academic accommodations need a higher level of documentation than most physicians customarily provide. A simple narrative letter that lists the diagnosis or diagnoses and perhaps describes the condition is *not* adequate for the purposes of requesting accommodations under the ADA.

In order to determine if certain accommodations are actually required, it is necessary to provide documentation of all relevant tests given and the results of that testing. The March 1995 update of the EEOC Compliance Manual (Equal Employment Opportunity Commission, 1995) states that "the determination of whether an individual has a disability is not necessarily based on the name or diagnosis of the impairment the person has, but rather on the effect of that impairment on the life of the individual." Some impairments may be disabling for particular individuals but not for others, depending on the stage of the disease or disorder, the presence of other impairments that combine to make the impairment disabling, or any number of other factors (Garzia, 1996). This is especially true with visual conditions: Because of the combination of sensory, perceptual, and motor factors, visual deficits can create very individualized circumstances for any diagnosis. These determinations are difficult or even impossible to make without having the raw data or standard scores available.

CATEGORIES OF DISABLING VISUAL CONDITIONS

There are three basic categories of disabling visual conditions that may be present either in isolation or in some combination for a particular patient. These conditions will be categorized for the purposes of this chapter as the following:

- Conditions that restrict central visual acuity.
- Conditions that restrict peripheral vision.
- Conditions that cause difficulty with functioning necessary to maintain a clear, comfortable, single image of a page of print.

To allow educators, educational administrators, and psychologists to better understand the visual conditions that students may claim as disabling, a glossary of terms is provided at the end of this chapter. A word that appears in **boldface** here can be found in the glossary. For more complete and detailed information on the complex relationship between reading and specific visual deficits, see Garzia (1996) and Scheiman and Rouse (1994).

Acuity Loss

Conditions such as **macular** degenerations or dystrophies, **strabismic** or refractive **amblyopia**, optic neuropathies, or certain retinal vascular disorders can cause a loss of central visual **acuity** in one or both eyes. These cases are easily documented. However, the extent of disability created by some of these conditions, especially if only one eye is affected, can be difficult to demonstrate. Monocular visual acuity loss has been shown to have little or no effect on reading facility. In fact, there is a good deal of evidence that readers who suffer from amblyopia or constant strabismus have a lower prevalence of reading difficulties than people with more subtle visual dysfunctions, such as **convergence** insufficiency. However, if the onset of the acuity loss was acute and developed within weeks of an important examination, it can be argued that the condition is indeed temporarily disabling.

Visual Field Loss

Visual field losses are clearly disabling for many life activities. The Social Security Administration currently only takes into account the quantity of field loss in determining the "loss of visual efficiency." However, the amount of disability experienced when reading can vary greatly with different areas of loss. For example, bilateral right-field **hemianopsia**, where a patient has lost peripheral vision to the right side, is quite disabling to a reader because this is the area of the visual field used to plan the extent of the next reading **saccade** during a **fixation**. Because such a reader cannot decide where to gather the next chunk of information, he or she typically demonstrates extremely poor reading eye movements and the attendant difficulties with comprehension and reading facility. Patients with the same extent of visual field loss, to the left side instead of the right have much less difficulty with reading because they can better plan their next fixation. These individuals typically only have difficulties with the return sweep to get to the beginning of the next line. Therefore, even though both types of conditions are graded equally under the American Medical Association (AMA) guidelines (AMA, 1995), the accommodations would be very different. Because of the profound effect their visual field loss has on their reading facility, the person with a right hemianopsia frequently needs extra time, transcription of the answers to the Scantron sheet, and possibly even a reader. The person with a left hemianopsia would simply need a line guide.

Visual field losses must extend to within 30° of the macula even to begin affecting reading function, although field losses that are less extensive may be very detrimental to mobility in new environments or to driving. Therefore, the extent of visual field loss may be disabling for some significant life functions but not for others.

Monocular visual field deficits have not been demonstrated to have any significant effect on reading speed or comprehension (Sheedy, Bailey, Muri, & Bass, 1989), just as is the case with unilateral losses of visual acuity. Therefore, documentation must demonstrate the individual's functional limitations. Patients with this type of visual defect are not likely to warrant academic accommodations unless they have additional sequelae, such as binocular vision dysfunctions

Visual Dysfunctions

Conditions affecting eye movements, **accommodation** (which, for clarity's sake, will hereafter be referred to as "focusing"), or **binocular coordination** can clearly have an adverse effect on reading facility and comprehension. However, these dysfunctions exist on a continuum that is generally described by a bell curve. Therefore, as with any developmental or psychometric measurements, it must be documented that a particular patient's condition is severe enough to cause actual impairment.

The physician or optometrist should use objective measures to gauge whether the severity of the condition matches the degree of disability. Fortunately, verification is fairly straightforward, as almost all measures of the functioning of these three systems have been standardized. It only requires that the examining specialist actually performs the tests of these functions and provide the data as part of a written evaluation. For eye movement dysfunctions, pursuit dysfunction is largely irrelevant because pursuit movements are insignificant during reading. Therefore, as a general rule, only saccadic eye movement dysfunctions will create a visual disability that has a significant impact on reading facility and comprehension.

As mentioned earlier, research shows that people with amblyopia or strabismus are *less* likely to have reading difficulties related to their visual conditions than those with less "severe" binocular dysfunctions. This is probably because reading is essentially a two-dimensional task. Therefore, binocular vision is not necessary for good reading facility. However, if one normally uses both eyes together but is struggling to do so during near-point visual tasks, then discomfort, confusion, and avoidance result. The person who habitually uses only one eye is still well adapted for the visual task of seeing high-contrast objects in a two-dimensional presentation. Individuals who struggle to use both eyes encounter nothing but frustration. They are trying to use what, for them, is an inefficient mechanism built to examine three-dimensional space in a task that offers little feedback to assist them. Therefore, the system fatigues and fails, resulting in diplopia, headaches, confusion of the print, and intermittent blur.

CLINICAL EVIDENCE AND TESTING
REQUIRED FOR PROPER DOCUMENTATION

The level of documentation required by an educational, testing, or certifying organization to determine the level of disability and the appropriateness of any requested accommodations is higher than physicians generally provide. A simple statement of the diagnosis or diagnoses is insufficient. As a general rule for *all* visual conditions, the physician should provide the following, at a minimum:

- A history of the patient's symptoms and signs.
- A list of the tests that were administered.
- The data obtained from testing.
- Any unusual circumstances of the testing that may have affected the validity of test results, as well as the patient's subjective responses to the testing.
- Diagnostic conclusions.

Patients' subjective reactions to the test are especially important to document in a disability case, not only because of the clinical insights we can gain from those observations, but because the courts appear to be recognizing the importance of those clinical insights when deciding the merits of individual requests for academic accommodations.

Acceptable tests for each of the visual-condition categories are given below. The list of tests given in this section is not intended to be exclusive, nor is it intended to be all-inclusive. It is an example of the minimal data base required to document the various visual conditions that could possibly be claimed as visual disabilities to reading, learning, and test-taking.

Acuity Loss

A decrease in central visual acuity is the most obvious visual disability. When people think of someone who is visually disabled, they typically assume that decreased visual acuity is the only manifestation possible. Reduced visual acuity can be quite disabling for a reader (Henderson, McClure, Pierce, & Schrock, 1997). The reader uses the macula to gather identifying information during a fixation with input from the peripheral retina to the right of the target so that the most efficient saccadic eye movement can be made for the next fixation. Most tests are printed in a typeface that requires the equivalent of 20/60 acuity.

During testing, the patient's visual acuity through the *best* possible **refractive** compensation should be recorded, as well as the method used to test that acuity. Because of the nature of acuity loss, acuity in both eyes tested monocularly and binocularly, at distance and near, should be given. The level of near vision acuity is especially important for determining the appropriateness of any reading accommodations requested, such as the size of enlarged print or any special lighting requirements. If special lighting is requested, a demonstration of reduced **contrast sensitivity** should also be provided.

Visual Field Loss

A visual field loss can be devastating to the average reader. As was previously mentioned, a right-field hemianopsia makes it impossible for the reader to make any clear determination about where to make the next fixation. Therefore, information is gathered in an extremely haphazard fashion. A left-field hemianopsia, although less disabling, makes it very difficult to identify which line was next on a return sweep. Other types of visual field loss can also create some disability during reading.

The neurological cause of the visual field loss is important to know, because many conditions that cause visual field loss have other sensory, functional, or mental health sequelae. If the visual field instrument used is capable of generating a printout, a copy of that printout should be provided. If field testing was done in a Goldmann perimeter, a copy of the examiner's diagram of the field loss should be provided. Tangent screen visual fields are generally not acceptable for the purpose of determining disability because of the ease of malingering on that test, especially as automated visual field testing instruments are so widely available (Committee on Vision, 1994). As with the loss of visual acuity, a summary of the patient's history should also be provided.

Visual Dysfunctions

These dysfunctions, because of their complex and controversial nature, require somewhat more extensive documentation. As with acuity and visual field losses, review of the patient's history and chief complaint should be provided. It should be clear from the history that the condition created difficulty with reading for a long period of the examinee's life. If the condition was acquired, the incident that caused the condition should be identified. If the condition was ameliorated with vision therapy, lenses, or prisms, but the patient is still requesting accommodations, the history and testing should be updated to demonstrate that the condition remains at a level that may still create problems in a reading situation despite completed therapy or lens management.

Certain medications can also interfere with efficient functioning of these visual systems. Focusing is especially sensitive to medications. For example, tricyclic antidepressants and two central nervous system stimulants used for attention-deficit/hyperactivity disorder therapy, methylphenidate (Ritalin) and dextroamphetamine (Dexedrine), have been associated with differing degrees of focusing dysfunction (Physicians' Desk Reference, 1997). Any iatrogenic focusing disabilities should be fully documented.

For eye movement dysfunctions (including **nystagmus**), the best acceptable test instrument that is generally available is the Developmental Eye Movement (DEM) test. This test is valuable because it controls for difficulties with rapid automatic naming or number-naming automaticity. The New York State Optometric Association King–Devick saccadic eye movement test is also acceptable if accompanied by some documentation that the patient has normal speech automaticity. If some other measurement of saccadic eye movements during reading has been performed, such as the VisiGraph Eye Movement Recording System. or the OBER2 eye movement recording system, those printouts and the examiner's interpretations should be given. All statistics obtained from those programs, such as number of fixations, number of regressions, average duration of fixation, and words per minute (with level of comprehension) should also be reported.

Focusing dysfunctions should be demonstrated with the following tests: accommodative facility tested with ±2 diopter lenses over the patient's best distance correction for 1 minute, with documentation of whether the monocular or binocular test was administered; accommodative amplitude should be tested monocularly and with minus lenses to avoid the confounding factor of retinal image size changes, which occur when amplitude is tested by the push-up method; and the comfortable binocular accommodative range should be tested using the negative relative accommodation/positive relative accommodation (NRA/PRA) tests. If **near-point retinoscopy** is performed, for example, the Monocular Estimation Method (MEM) to demonstrate any unusual accommodative lag, or book **retinoscopy** to directly view accommodative response when reading, this data should also be provided. Of course, students over the age of forty are typically **presbyopic,** so for them the tests of focusing become less crucial.

Binocular functioning can be demonstrated in a variety of ways. The minimum that should be determined is the near point of convergence, giving both the break point and the point where the patient recovers fusion, with documentation of the type of target used (accommodative or nonaccommodative). Fusional vergences should be given using prism bars in free space or Risley prisms in the phoropter. Distance and near VonGraefe **phorias** should be given. If a bifocal has been prescribed, the phoria through that prescription should also be given. Any tests that demonstrate **suppression**, anomalous correspondence, or noncomitance should also be listed and the data provided.

JUSTIFICATIONS FOR ACCOMMODATIONS

Universally, the most requested accommodation for test situations is extra time. There is little literature to support this request for most visual disabilities. In fact, extra time is actually counterproductive for many visual disabilities. There is an unfortunate dearth of literature to support any type of accommodation for most visual disabilities, with the exception of large print or magnification devices for those with poor central visual acuity, increased lighting for those with decreased contrast sensitivity, line guides for those with left hemianopsia, or occlusion (patching) of one eye for those with **diplopia.**

Acuity Loss

The most time-honored accommodation for decreased visual acuity is enlarged print and, if necessary, enlarged illustrations. This is a very useful accommodation, although it should be noted that, as in all things, moderation is key. The print size should be large enough to be easily identified, but if the print is too large, reading efficiency clearly suffers (Lovie-Kitchin, Oliver, Bruce, Leighton & Leighton, 1994). This is because the span of recognition (the number of characters easily identified during a particular fixation) available with larger print sizes becomes proportionally smaller. Reading rates and efficiency are at a maximum when the available span of recognition is approximately 15–20 characters. As a general rule, if the print size needs enlargement to greater than 24 point, extra time is a reasonable additional accommodation to allow for the attendant decrease in reading rate.

Another valuable aid for readers with decreased visual acuity is a magnifier of some kind, often hand-held but usually a stand magnifier. Again, higher power magnification makes for a larger image of the print but fewer characters available per fixation, so the same caveats apply as for enlarged print.

In cases of severe loss of central visual acuity (poorer than 20/100), such as in some types of macular degeneration and late-stage retinitis pigmentosa, more comprehensive accommodations such as readers or audiotapes are appropriate. Of course, these accommodations are always appropriate for a student who has been classified as legally blind, no matter what the cause.

Visual Field Loss

As was mentioned previously, reading disability varies widely depending on the nature and size of the field loss. A right-field hemianopsia can be extremely disabling. Following the line with a finger to guide the eyes along the line is probably the best accommodation for keeping one's place. However, the reading process is extremely inefficient and frustrating for the examinee, and so this is one visual condition in which extra time is clearly indicated. A left-field hemianopsia is far less disabling on the whole and a line guide is typically sufficient. The examinee with this condition may also need an aid to transcribe the answers to the Scantron sheet. In some cases, the student's reading efficiency is so adversely affected that a reader or audiotapes may be necessary.

Other field losses are typically less disabling than hemianopsia for the reader, although they can be quite troublesome for orientation or mobility in other life activities. The accommodation provided should be determined by the nature of the visual field defect involved.

Visual Dysfunctions

Saccadic dysfunctions, although rare, can exist in adult populations. The best accommodation for this condition is probably using a line guide or the finger as a tracking guide. If the condition is very severe, as is often the case with nystagmus, extra time may also be in order. Because students suffering from saccadic disorders have inordinate difficulty keeping their place on computer-graded answer forms, they should be allowed to mark their answers on the test booklet in a testing situation. They might also be afforded extra time (or a proctor) to transcribe answers to the answer sheet after the allotted testing time is complete.

Focusing dysfunctions are among the most annoying of the visual dysfunctions, creating a host of symptoms, which include headaches above the brows, intermittent blurred vision, an intermittent period of poor comprehension while the reader is concentrating on keeping the print clear, and increased sensitivity to ambient lighting. These symptoms create a very inefficient reading situation. The accommodation provided can be as simple as over-the-counter reading glasses, or may require off-the-clock breaks, depending on the nature of the dysfunction.

Another accommodation that works fairly well for some with focusing problems is colored overlays. These seem to help by reducing the contrast on the page, thereby reducing the demand for precise accommodation. The questionable diagnosis of "scotopic sensitivity syndrome" probably manipulates this relationship (Solan, 1990). However, sunglasses often work just as well in these cases and may be a reasonable accommodation.

Binocular dysfunctions can also seriously compromise the efficiency of the reader, creating symptoms of intermittently blurred or double vision. One possible accommodation is elimination of the cause by occlusion of one eye. Many students have unconsciously discovered this accommodation already and read with their head resting on the left hand so that the left eye is occluded and no double vision can occur. Unfortunately, reading in a monocular condition is less efficient for readers who are typically binocular, so this accommodation is not universally applicable. It would certainly benefit the student if the examiner would ask the student to compare his or her reading efficiency in monocular and binocular conditions, to see if there is any advantage and then to report the findings in the request for accommodations. If this simple accommodation does not work, then off-the-clock breaks are appropriate.

Focusing and binocular dysfunctions generally worsen with the amount of time devoted to the near-point task. Therefore, extra time for test taking is probably only going to exacerbate the visual problem, unless the examinee spends most of the extra time looking at other places in the examination room. Unfortunately, such an accommodation would create difficulties for test security. Therefore, I would strongly recommend against extra test-exposure time for students with focusing and binocular dysfunctions except under unusual circumstances. Spending *more* time looking at the printed page will cause more harm than good. Therefore, only in rare circumstances would additional exposure time to the test be an appropriate accommodation for students with these visual conditions. When taking tests, off-the-clock breaks that give students an opportunity to remove themselves from the visual situation are far more effective.

SUMMARY

Typical symptomatology and findings are summarized for Accommodative (see Table 9.1), Vergence (see Table 9.2), and Oculomotor dysfunctions (see Table 9.3). No matter what the diagnosis, it is critical that the clinician provide more than just a narrative letter. Visual conditions can create a varied complex of reading problems in different individuals. Therefore, it is essential to provide a history of the

TABLE 9.1. Accommodative Dysfunctions

Condition	Typical symptomatology	Typical findings
Accommodative insufficiency	Near-point blur Headaches above the brow Intermittent distance vision blur	Reduced amplitude Reduced PRA Difficulty with minus lenses on facility testing Increased accommodative lag
Accommodative infacility	Intermittent distance vision blur (especially after near-vision tasks) Fatigue after a short period of reading Decreased reading comprehension and facility	Reduced accommodative facility (monocular and binocular) Reduced NRA and/or PRA
Accommodative hysteresis (excess)	Distance vision blur after near-point tasks Distance vision blur at end of the day Headaches above the brow Conjunctival injection after reading	Reduced NRA Difficulty with plus lenses on facility testing No apparent lag of accommodation

Note. PRA, positive relative accommodation; NRA, negative relative accommodation.

TABLE 9.2. Vergence Dysfunctions

Condition	Typical symptomatology	Typical findings
Convergence insufficiency	Words "run together" Intermittent distance vision blur after near-point tasks Headaches and/or nausea when reading in a moving vehicle Fatigue after 10–20 minutes of reading Declining reading comprehension and facility with time	Low AC/A ratio Higher exophoria at near Reduced NPC Reduced base-out ranges at near Difficulty with plus lenses on binocular accommodative testing Reduced NRA Reduced stereo-acuity (sometimes)
Convergence excess	Need to cover one eye when reading Intermittent near-vision blur Words "run together" Conjunctival injection of reading Declining reading facility with time	High AC/A ratio Higher esophoria at near Reduced base-in ranges at near Difficulty with minus lenses on binocular accommodative testing Reduced PRA Reduced stereoacuity (sometimes)
Functional vergence dysfunction (binocular instability)	Need to cover one eye when reading Words "run together" Declining reading comprehension and facility with time	Poor vergence ranges base-in and -out Reduced binocular accommodative facility Reduced NRA/PRA

Note. AC/A, accommodative convergence to accommodation ratio; NPC, near point of convergence; PRA, positive relative accommodation; NRA, negative relative accommodation.

condition, including the patient's subjective complaints specific to academic activities, results of all relevant tests, and the evaluator's impressions. This level of documentation is imperative to determining if the condition is truly disabling during reading, testing, and in other academic situations. This also allows determination of what, if any, accommodation would be *most* beneficial to the student.

TABLE 9.3. Oculomotor Dysfunctions

Condition	Typical symptomatology	Typrical findings
Fixational instability	Poor eye contact Loss of place errors	Slightly decreased visual acuity (~20/25) Difficulty on cover test
Saccadic dysfunction	Loss of place errors Difficulty filling in Scantrons	Poor saccades on gross observations Poor ratio and error scores on DEM
Pursuit dysfunctions	Few symptoms when reading	Poor pursuits on gross observations

Note. DEM, Developmental Eye Movement test.

SAMPLE REPORT

Visual Evaluation Report for John Q. Public

Date of birth: January 1, 1967
Evaluation date: October 1, 1997

History and Observations

Mr. Public was referred by his primary optometrist, Dr. Susan Everyperson, for a vision evaluation because of Mr. Public's continuing difficulties with near-point tasks. Mr. Public complains of burning sensations in his eyes at the end of the workday, difficulty with night driving, and fatigue when reading after 15 or 20 minutes. He feels he should be capable of reading more quickly than he does, although his comprehension is excellent.

Mr. Public has no major health problems. He is allergic to penicillin and ragweed, and takes Seldane as needed. His last eye examination was with Dr. Everyperson in June 1997. Mr. Public was diagnosed with convergence insufficiency (see below) and was advised that orthoptic/vision therapy could offer relief from his symptoms. Mr. Public had initially been diagnosed with myopia

Note. This fictional report is intended as a sample *only* and is not intended to suggest that the treatment recommended for this fictional character is appropriate for every case with similar findings.

(nearsightedness) when he was about 7 years old and the myopia has progressed fairly steadily right through adulthood.

Refraction and Ocular Health

Distance visual acuities with his current glasses were 20/15 (better than 20/20) with the right eye, 20/20 with the left, and 20/15 with both eyes. Mr. Public showed no increase in myopia during refraction.

Ocular health testing by Dr. Everyperson through dilated pupils revealed no visible ocular pathology or abnormality.

Eye Aiming and Eye Movements

Gross testing of Mr. Public's eye movements revealed pursuit fixations (ability to follow a moving object smoothly with the eyes) that were accurate, with full range of motion. Saccades (jumping eye movements, which are used in reading) were tested with the Developmental Eye Movement test. Mr. Public performed in the average range (standard score = 103). He showed average ability to read numbers quickly (standard score = 107).

Focusing

Mr. Public showed slow accommodative flexibility when asked to change focus rapidly from distance to near and back (standard score = 76). His ability to slowly and steadily relax focus with both eyes open was average (standard score = 100), and to stimulate focus in the same fashion with both eyes open was below average (standard score = 78).

Eye Teaming and Coordination

Mr. Public showed no manifest strabismus during the evaluation. Tests of his eye-coordination skills revealed a near point of convergence (ability to keep both eyes on an approaching target) of 1 cm (standard score = 109) with a recovery of single vision at 3 cm (standard score = 108). On more precise examination of this ability at near point with the prism vergence test, Mr. Public's ability to relax convergence was excellent (standard score = 145) and to stimulate convergence was poor (standard score = 23). His Keystone Visual Skills profile confirmed his difficulty converging his eyes and revealed a tendency to suppress his left eye. This suppression is the result of a longstanding difficulty aligning the eyes, and subsequent adaptation by suppressing, or ignoring, the signals from one eye to avoid double vision. Mr. Public's depth perception was slightly reduced at near and normal at distance.

Conclusions

Mr. Public has a convergence insufficiency with secondary focusing dysfunction and suppression. These conditions will tend to cause discomfort, eyestrain, headaches above the brows, and intermittently blurred or double vision. These symptoms can be quite disabling during reading.

Recommendations

It is recommended that Mr. Public enter a program of vision therapy to ameliorate his suppression and accommodative dysfunctions. This program would include office visits two times a week where each skill is isolated, developed, and then practiced until it becomes automatic. The skills are then integrated and techniques are used to make sure that he can use the skills in classroom, study, and testing situations. I estimate that five to six visits will be necessary to begin addressing the suppression and accommodative dysfunction, followed by 2 to 3 months of home techniques to address the convergence insufficiency directly.

Mr. Public will go through a period during the treatment program in which he may get headaches, and other symptoms will worsen. This is because the first phase of treatment is to break down the adaptations Mr. Public has made to work around his visual problem (suppression, for example). It will ease his difficulties before and during treatment if he is encouraged to take a 1- or 2-minute break for every 15 minutes of desk work. During tests of longer than 1 hour, he should be allowed off-the-clock breaks every 1/2 hour or hour. These strategies should no longer be necessary after treatment is concluded.

The prognosis for amelioration of Mr. Public's visual dysfunctions and abatement of his symptoms with the appropriate treatment is excellent.

GLOSSARY

accommodation   The ability of the human eye to change focus so as to make objects at different distances clear. After age 14, this function naturally decreases with age due to the hardening of the focusing lens material inside the eye, a process known as presbyopia. This process is the reason people over the age of 40 need glasses to help them focus on near-point objects.

acuity The resolution capability of the macula of the eye. This is typically expressed as a fraction, with the numerator denoting the testing distance and the denominator denoting the distance a person with average acuity would have to be from the target to see the same size letters. Since most eye examinations in this country are done at 20 feet, the numerator is most commonly 20. A person with 20/40 acuities therefore sees the same letters at twenty feet that the average person could see from forty. In contrast, a person with 20/15 acuity has better than average resolution capabilities, because they see at 20 feet letters that most people would have to be 5 feet closer to see. As you may have noticed by now, none of this has much relevance to the act of reading at a desk. Unfortunately, distance visual acuity testing is the most common screening given in educational settings, despite its poor validity.

amblyopia A decrease in the functional ability of one eye because of poor images obtained during the most sensitive period of visual development, which is from birth to age 6 or 7. The functions compromised in this condition are visual acuity, fixation, eye movements, focusing, and ability to coordinate with the fellow eye. The causes of amblyopia could be strabismus, a congenital cataract (clouding of the intraocular lens), or a large difference in the refractive error of the two eyes, typically with one being far more hyperopic than the other.

binocular coordination The ability to aim both eyes simultaneously at the object of regard. To look at a near-point object with both eyes requires convergence, and to look back at a distance object requires divergence. If both eyes are not aimed at the same object at the same time, double vision can result, or the patient may adapt by ignoring one eye (suppression).

contrast sensitivity The ability to distinguish gray objects on a slightly darker or lighter background. Most printed pages have high contrast, but such things as glare on a glossy page can markedly reduce print contrast.

convergence The ability to aim both eyes at a closer object. When you cross your eyes, you are demonstrating voluntary convergence. The human with normal convergence can maintain both eyes on an object that is as close as 5 cm (about 3 inches). People who have difficulty with this skill have a dysfunction known as convergence insufficiency. *Divergence* is the ability to aim both eyes at a far object.

diplopia A technical name for double vision. A person with this symptom will have great difficulty with reading because of overlapping images of the printed page.

divergence See *convergence*.

fixation   The ability to maintain the macula of the eye on a stationary object. A fixation is the visual period during which information is gathered.

hemianopsia   The loss of visual sensation from one side, that is, the patient with a right hemianopsia is essentially blind to objects that lie to the right of center. Because this is the area where determination of the next reading fixation is made, a person with a right hemianopsia makes poor judgments about where to gather the next chunk of information and as a consequence has very poor reading eye movements.

hyperopia   See *refractive error.*

macula   The portion of the retina that has the highest concentration of cone cells, and therefore the highest resolution capability. This area is a relatively small portion of the retina—approximately 2 degrees. All the rest of the retina is devoted to peripheral vision, with poor resolution capability but excellent sensitivity to motion and low contrast.

myopia   See *refractive error.*

near-point retinoscopy   A testing technique whereby the examiner can directly observe a patient's focusing response during a near-point visual task such as reading a passage from Gray's Oral Readings for comprehension (book retinoscopy) or isolated words (MEM retinoscopy).

nystagmus   A condition in which the eyes involuntarily shake, usually from side to side. This condition is typically congenital. If it first occurs later in life, it can be an indication of a serious neurological disorder.

phoria   How well the two eyes line up together when they are not allowed to look at the same target at the same time. Typically, the eyes are lined up very straight when this is tested at 20 feet, but the eyes drift out slightly when looking at a near-point target.

presbyopia   See *accommodation.*

refractive error   The condition by which the image of the object of regard is not seen clearly by the person. In myopia, the person needs a concave lens to bring images closer so they may be seen clearly. If a person is over-focusing, this condition can mimic myopia. In hyperopia, the person has to focus constantly to clear even the most distant objects, and has to focus very hard to make near-point objects appear clear. Hyperopia has been shown to have a detrimental effect on reading efficiency, but myopia has often been shown to be inversely proportional to academic achievement. Most school vision screenings rely entirely on distance visual acuity and can only detect myopia.

retinoscopy   An objective test of refractive error and focusing status.

saccades Eye movements that jump from one object to another, as opposed to pursuits, where the eyes follow a smoothly moving object. Saccadic eye movements are used in reading to jump from one information chunk (usually 1.5 to 2.0 words, in a college-level reader) to the next. The period of rest between saccadic eye movements is called a fixation.

strabismus The condition of having one eye in misalignment with the fixating eye. Typically, one eye turns in all the time (constant esotropia) or one eye turns out occasionally (intermittent exotropia). The eye that is misaligned is most commonly ignored (suppressed) so that people with strabismus actually function more efficiently in a reading situation than people with less severe binocular coordination problems, such as convergence insufficiency.

suppression The adaptation of the cortex of the brain where the person subconsciously ignores the image coming from one eye. This happens because of chronic difficulties using the two eyes together as a team, either from misalignment or from irresolvable differences between the two images that occurred during the very sensitive first 8 years of visual development.

visual field The extent of peripheral vision available to the viewer's perception. The normal extent of the visual field for each eye is typically described as 145° horizontally and 110° vertically.

REFERENCES

American Medical Association. (1995). *Guides to the evaluation of permanent impairment* (4th ed.). Chicago: Author.

Committee on Vision. (1994). *Measurement of visual field and visual acuity for disability determination.* Washington, DC: National Academy Press.

Equal Employment Opportunities Commission (EEOC). (1995). Compliance manual (Pub. No. 915.002). Washington, DC: Author.

Garzia, R. (Ed.). (1996). *Vision and reading.* St. Louis, MO: Mosby-Year Book.

Henderson, J. M., McClure, K. K., Pierce, S., & Schrock, G. (1997). Object identification without foveal vision: Evidence from an artificial scotoma paradigm. *Perception and Psychophysics, 59*(3), 323–346.

Lovie-Kitchin, J. E., Oliver, N. J., Bruce, A., Leighton, M. S., & Leighton, W. K. (1994). The effect of print size on reading rate for adults and children. *Clinical and Experimental Optometry, 77*(1), 2–7.

Physicians' Desk Reference. (1997). Oradell, NJ: Medical Economics.

Scheiman, M., & Rouse, M. (1994). *Optometric management of learning related vision problems.* St. Louis, MO: Mosby-Year Book.

Solan, H. A. (1990). An appraisal of the Irlen technique of correcting reading disorders using tinted overlays and tinted lenses. *Journal of Learning Disabilities, 23,* 621–623.

Sheedy, J. E., Bailey, I. L., Muri, M., & Bass, E. (1989). Binocular vs monocular task performance. *American Journal of Optometry and Physiological Optics, 63,* 839–846.

L ast Words

Michael Gordon, PhD
Shelby Keiser, MS

In many respects, this book serves as a testament to the Americans with Disabilities Act's (ADA; 1990, PL 101-336) broad impact upon American society. To cover just its application to higher education and professional testing, we had to assemble contributors from many disciplines to address a cornucopia of topics. Knowing the efforts we have expended to amass our panel of experts, we can empathize with those charged with ADA compliance at every college, university, and testing organization in the country. Each one must similarly wrestle with how to apply this law to the institution's unique goals, resources, and circumstances. That process inevitably entails bringing together, as we have for this project, advisors from many quarters.

We also have developed an even greater appreciation for how hard it is to avoid sliding into an "either/or" mentality. When decisions are complicated, as ADA-related decisions so often are, it is tempting to adopt either an "accommodations for all attitude" or the more conservative "accommodations for only the most unequivocal cases" approach. Neither pole insures a system that is fair both to individuals with disabilities and to the population at large.

While we have been continually impressed with the complexity of this subject, we have also come to see that certain fundamental concepts hold sway. As you know, we covered many of these principles in the first chapter because we wanted to provide a general framework for understanding the implications of the law for any particular topic.

But after traversing such an expansive field of clinical entities, administrative functions, and legal issues, we thought that some final review of the ADA's essence was in order. By way of summarizing the critical elements of the law, we present below a list of four questions. In many instances, answers to these questions will provide a basis for arriving at reasonable conclusions. For simplicity's sake, we refer consistently to a "student," understanding that in some circumstances the more appropriate label would be "examinee."

QUESTIONS AT THE HEART OF ADA DECISIONS FOR POSTSECONDARY EDUCATION

- Does this student meet accepted criteria for a diagnosis of a physical, psychiatric, or learning disorder?
- Relative to the average person, is the impact of this disorder so profound that it currently impairs the individual's ability to perform a major life activity?
- In what specific ways would the impact of the individual's disorder affect his or her ability to function within this specific educational program or testing situation?
- Within the context of this specific educational setting or testing situation, what accommodations would relieve the impact of this student's disability?

All the diagnostic and administrative particulars notwithstanding, resolving ADA-inspired problems rests on a sequential analysis of these questions. Even if an administrator is unclear, for example, about what constitutes standard criteria for manic–depressive illness, consideration of these four questions can point the way toward an informed use of professional consultation.

While exploration of clinical, administrative, and legal issues often follows the path outlined by these questions, many situations will prove enigmatic nonetheless. Quandaries can surface for many reasons: incomplete information, insufficient resources, and diagnostic characteristics that are ambiguous. Even if the relevant information is adequate, one can always count on human nature to throw out obstacles: university officials who keep tight reins on budgets, clinicians who are more concerned about advocacy than objectivity, faculty who are unwilling to be at all flexible, and students who chase psychiatric reasons for failure before considering explanations that reside closer to home.

One more source of confusion springs directly from serious limitations in general scientific knowledge about disabilities and how best to accommodate them. Too many of the decisions all of us have to make surrounding the ADA are based on uninformed opinion. To arrive at solid judgments, we should be able to rely on solid information about diagnostic criteria, metrics of impairment, and the impact of accommodations on certain disabilities.

Whether the topic is reading disabilities or neurofibromyalgia, too few sources of ADA-relevant scientific data are at the public's disposal. We should not have to guess, for example, what represents a valid and reliable measure of word decoding in adults, nor should we have to wonder whether that factor is at all relevant to adult learning and test taking. Currently, most decisions flow not from the relative clarity of empirical research, but from the fog of personal opinion, clinical experience, political orientation, unenlightened economic consideration, and, at times, old-fashioned prejudice.

While volumes such as this one are notorious for ending with clarion calls for more research, sounding that particular trumpet here seems completely justified. Weighty judgments that affect the quality of both individual and institutional life depend too heavily on guesswork. Our hope is that some of the energy directed toward advocating for one position or another can be invested in supporting or actually conducting research. While science will never make implementation of the ADA uncomplicated, it might at least make it less obscure.

Resources

ASSOCIATIONS

Health Resource Center
One DuPont Circle
Suite 800
Washington, DC 20036
Phone: 202-939-9320
E-mail: heath@ace.nche.edu
Internet: http://www.acenet.edu
A national clearing house for disabilities information.

AHEAD (Association on Higher Education and Disability)
P.O. Box 21192
Columbus, OH 43221
Phone: 614-488-4972
Fax: 614-488-1174
E-mail: ahead@postbox.acs.ohio-sate.edu
An organization of professionals promoting education, training, and dissemination of information.

JAN (Job Accommodation Network)
P.O. Box 6080
Morgantown, WV 26506-6080
Phone: 800-526-7234; 800-526-2262 (for Canada)
Consultations on legal and practical issues related to accomodations in the workplace.

FEDERAL AGENCIES

Department of Justice
Office of Americans with Disabilities Act Civil Rights Division
P.O. Box 66118
Washington, DC 20035
Phone: 202-514-0301

Equal Employment Opportunity Commission
1801 L Street, NW
Washington, DC 20507
Phone: 800-669-EEOC

Office of Special Education and Rehabilitative Services
330 C Street, SW
Switzer Building Room 3006
Washington, DC 20202-2500
Phone: 202-205-5507
Call this number for help with Section 504 of the Rehabilitation Act or with the Individuals with Disabilities Education Act (IDEA).

Office of Civil Rights
330 C Street, SW
Room 5000
Washington, DC 20202
Phone: 202-205-5413
Call this office for information about the Americans with Disabilities Act.

President's Committee on Employment of People with Disabilities
1331 F Street, NW
Washington, DC 20004-1107
Phone: 202-376-6200
Fax: 202-376-6219
E-mail: info@pcepd.gov

LEGAL RESOURCES

National Center for Law and Learning Disabilities
P.O. Box 368
Cabin John, MD 20818
Phone: 301-469-8308

National Employment Law Institute
444 Magnolia Avenue
Suite 200
Larkspur, CA 94939
Phone: 415-924-3844
Fax: 415-924-2908
E-mail: www.neli.org
A nonprofit organization that provides employment law services for attorneys and human resources personnel.

BOOKS ON THE ADA

Burgdorf, R., (1995). *Disability discrimination in employment law* (1st ed.). Washington DC: BNA Books.

Bruyere, S. M., & O'Keefe, J. (1994). *Implications of the Americans with Disabilities Act for psychology.* New York: Springer/American Psychological Association.

Frierson, J. (1995). *Employer's guide to the Americans with Disabilities* (2nd ed.). Washington, DC: BNA Books.

Latham, P. H.. & Latham, P. S. (1997). *Legal rights.* In S. Goldstein (Ed.), *Managing attention and learning disorders in late adolescence and adulthood: A guide for practitioners.* New York: Wiley.

National Employment Law Institute. (1997). *Resolving ADA workplace questions: How courts and agencies are dealing with evolving employment issues* (3rd ed.). Larkspur, CA: Author.

National Employment Law Institute. (1997). *Resolving ADA workplace questions: Checklists and suggested hints for human resources personnel.* Larkspur, CA: Author.

Rothstein, L. F. (1997). *Higher education and the ADA.* St. Paul, MN: Westgroup.

INTERNET RESOURCES

Americans with Disabilities Act Document Center
U.S. Department of Justice ADA Home Page
http://www.usdoj.gov/crt/ada/adahom1.htm

EDLAW Home Page
http://www.edlaw.net

Fedlaw-Disabilities
http://www.legal.gsa.gov/legal6a.htm
A listing of various disability-related laws and regulations.

FedWorld Home Page
http://www.fedworld.gov/
U.S. government web page with various government and disability links.

National Technical Information Service
http://www.ntis.gov/health/3he1142.htm
Annotated bibliography of ADA resources.

Evan Kemp Associates
Solutions@disability.com
Provides links to resources, products, and services.

EASI (Equal Access to Software and Information)
http://www.isc.rit.edu/~easi/

JAN Web Page
http://janweb.icdi.wvu.edu/kinder/
Many links to related sites including the Job Accommodation Network, which provides technical support and assistance with workplace disability issues.

U.S. Department of Education home page
http://www.ed.gov/

U.S. Department of Education Office of Civil Rights: Publications
http://www.ed.gov/offices/OCR/ocrpubs.html

American Bar Association Mental and Physical Disability Law Reporter
http://www.abanet.org/disability/reporter/home.html

ERIC Clearinghouse on Disabilities and Gifted Education
http://www.cec.sped.org/ericec.htm

Iowa State ADA and disability information
http://www.public.iastate.edu/~dus_info/steve.html

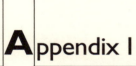

Appendix I

The AHEAD Guidelines for Documentation of a Learning Disability in Adolescents and Adults

The Association on Higher Education and Disability (AHEAD) is an international, multicultural organization of professionals committed to full participation in higher education for persons with disabilities. The Association is a vital resource, promoting excellence through education, communication and training.

The Board of Directors established an Ad Hoc Committee to study issues surrounding the documentation of a learning disability. The Board wishes to thank the members of the AHEAD Ad Hoc Committee on LD Guidelines for their efforts in laying the foundation of these Guidelines for use by the Association's members.

The Ad Hoc Committee members are:

Loring Brinckerhoff (Chairperson), Educational Testing Service, Recording for the Blind and Dyslexic

Joan McGuire (Liaison to the Board), University of Connecticut–Storrs

Kim Dempsey, Law School Admission Council

Cyndi Jordan, University of Tennessee–Memphis

Shelby Keiser, National Board of Medical Examiners

Catherine Nelson, Educational Testing Service

Nancy Pompian, Dartmouth College

Louise Russell, Harvard University

INTRODUCTION

In response to the expressed need for guidance related to the documentation of a learning disability in adolescents and adults, the Association on Higher Education and Disability (*AHEAD*) has developed the following guidelines. The primary intent of these guidelines is to provide students, professional diagnosticians, and service providers with a common understanding and knowledge base of those components of documentation which are necessary to validate a learning disability and the need for accommodation. The information and documentation that establish a learning disability should be comprehensive, in order to make it possible for a student to be served in a postsecondary setting.

The document presents guidelines in four important areas: (1) qualifications of the evaluator, (2) recency of documentation, (3) appropriate clinical documentation to substantiate the learning disability, and (4) evidence to establish a rationale supporting the need for accommodations.

Under the Americans with Disabilities Act (ADA) and Section 504 of the Rehabilitation Act of 1973, individuals with learning disabilities are guaranteed certain protections and rights of equal access to programs and services; thus the documentation should indicate that the disability substantially limits some major life activity. The following guidelines are provided in the interest of assuring that LD documentation is appropriate to verify eligibility and to support requests for accommodations, academic adjustments, and/or auxiliary aids. It is recommended that postsecondary institutions using these guidelines consult with their legal counsel before establishing a policy on documentation relating to individuals with disabilities. In countries not regulated by this legislation further modification may be appropriate.

These guidelines are designed to be a framework for institutions to work from in establishing criteria for eligibility. It is acknowledged that different educational settings with different student populations will need to modify and adapt these guidelines to meet the needs and backgrounds of their student populations.

Recommendations for consumers are presented in Appendix A to assist them in finding and working with a qualified professional in regard to documentation.

DOCUMENTATION GUIDELINES

I. Qualifications of the Evaluator

Professionals conducting assessments, rendering diagnoses of learning disabilities (LD), and making recommendations for appropriate accommodations must be qualified to do so. Comprehensive training and direct experience with an adolescent and adult LD population is essential.

The name, title, and professional credentials of the evaluator, including information about license or certification (e.g., licensed psychologist) as well as the area of specialization, employment, and state/province in which the individual practices should be clearly stated in the documentation. or example, the following professionals would generally be considered qualified to evaluate specific learning disabilities provided that they have additional training and experience in the assessment of learning problems in adolescents and adults: clinical or educational psychologists, school psychologists, neuropsychologists, learning disabilities specialists, medical doctors, and other professionals. Use of diagnostic terminology indicating a learning disability by someone whose training and experience are not in these fields is not acceptable. It is of utmost importance that evaluators are sensitive and respectful of cultural and linguistic differences in adolescents and adults during the assessment process. It is not considered appropriate for professionals to evaluate members of their families. All reports should be on letterhead, typed, dated, signed, and otherwise legible.

II. Documentation

The provision of all reasonable accommodations and services is based upon assessment of the impact of the student's disabilities on his or her academic performance at a given time in the student's life. Therefore, it is in the student's best interest to provide recent and appropriate documentation relevant to the student's learning environment.

Flexibility in accepting documentation is important, especially in settings with significant numbers of nontraditional students. In some instances, documentation may be outdated or inadequate in scope or content. It may not address the student's current level of functioning or need for accommodations because observed changes may have occurred in the student's performance since the previous assessment was conducted. In such cases, it may be appropriate to update the evaluation report. Since the purpose of the update is to determine the student's current need for accommodations, the update, conducted by a qualified professional, should include a rationale for ongoing services and accommodations.

III. Substantiation of the Learning Disability

Documentation should validate the need for services based on the individual's current level of functioning in the educational setting. A school plan such as an individualized education program (IEP) or a 504 plan is insufficient documentation, but it can be included as part of a more comprehensive assessment battery. A comprehensive assessment battery and the resulting diagnostic report should include a diagnostic interview, assessment of aptitude, academic achievement, information processing, and a diagnosis.

A. Diagnostic Interview

An evaluation report should include the summary of a comprehensive diagnostic interview. Learning disabilities are commonly manifested during childhood, but not always formally diagnosed. Relevant information regarding the student's academic history and learning processes in elementary, secondary, and postsecondary education should be investigated. The diagnostician, using professional judgment as to which areas are relevant, should conduct a diagnostic interview which may include: a description of the presenting problem(s); developmental, medical, psychosocial and employment histories; family history (including primary language of the home and the student's current level of English fluency); and a discussion of dual diagnosis where indicated.

B. Assessment

The neuropsychological or psychoeducational evaluation for the diagnosis of a specific learning disability must provide clear and specific evidence that a learning disability does or does not exist. Assessment, and any resulting diagnosis, should consist of and be based on a comprehensive assessment battery which does not rely on any one test or subtest.

Evidence of a substantial limitation to learning or other major life activity must be provided. A list of commonly used tests is included in Appendix B. Minimally, the domains to be addressed must include the following:

1. APTITUDE

A complete intellectual assessment with all subtests and standard scores reported.

2. ACADEMIC ACHIEVEMENT

A comprehensive academic achievement battery is essential with all subtests and standard scores reported for those subtests administered. The battery should include current levels of academic functioning in relevant areas such as reading (decoding and comprehension), mathematics, and oral and written language.

3. INFORMATION PROCESSING

Specific areas of information processing (e.g., short- and long-term memory, sequential memory, auditory and visual perception/processing, processing speed, executive functioning, and motor ability) should be assessed.

Other assessment measures such as nonstandard measures and informal assessment procedures or observations may be helpful in determining performance across a variety of domains. Other formal assessment measures may be integrated with the above instruments to help determine a learning disability and differentiate it from coexisting neurological and/or psychiatric disorders (i.e., to establish a differential diagnosis). In addition to standardized tests, it is also very useful to include informal observations of the student during the test administration.

C. Specific Diagnosis

Individual "learning styles," "learning differences," "academic problems," and "test difficulty or anxiety," in and of themselves, do not constitute a learning disability. It is important to rule out alternative explanations for problems in learning such as emotional, attentional, or motivational problems that may be interfering with learning but do not constitute a learning disability. The diagnostician is encouraged to use direct language in the diagnosis and documentation of a learning disability, avoiding the use of terms such as "suggests" or "is indicative of."

If the data indicate that a learning disability is not present, the evaluator should state that conclusion in the report.

D. Test Scores

Standard scores and/or percentiles should be provided for all normed measures. Grade equivalents are not useful unless standard scores and/or percentiles are also included. The data should logically reflect a substantial limitation to learning for which the student is requesting the accommodation. The particular profile of the student's strengths and weaknesses must be shown to relate to functional limitations that may necessitate accommodations.

The tests used should be reliable, valid, and standardized for use with an adolescent/adult population. The test findings should document both the nature and severity of the learning disability. Informal inventories, surveys, and direct observation by a qualified professional may be used in tandem with formal tests in order to further develop a clinical hypothesis.

E. Clinical Summary

A well-written diagnostic summary based on a comprehensive evaluation process is a necessary component of the report. Assessment instruments and the data they provide do not diagnose; rather, they provide important elements that must be integrated by the evaluator with background information, observations of the client during the testing situation, and the current context. It is essential, therefore, that professional judgment be utilized in the development of a clinical summary. The clinical summary should include:

1. Demonstration of the evaluator's having ruled out alternative explanations for academic problems as a result of poor education, poor motivation and/or study skills, emotional problems, attentional problems, and cultural/language differences.
2. Indication of how patterns in the student's cognitive ability, achievement, and information processing reflect the presence of a learning disability.
3. Indication of the substantial limitation to learning or other major life activity presented by the learning disability and the degree to which it impacts the individual in the learning context for which accommodations are being requested.
4. Indication as to why specific accommodations are needed and how the effects of the specific disability are accommodated.

The summary should also include any record of prior accommodation or auxiliary aids, including any information about specific conditions under which the accommodations were used (e.g., standardized testing, final exams, licensing or certification examinations).

IV. Recommendations for Accommodations

It is important to recognize that accommodation needs can change over time and are not always identified through the initial diagnostic process. Conversely, a prior history of accommodation does not, in and of itself, warrant the provision of a similar accommodation.

The diagnostic report should include specific recommendations for accommodations as well as an explanation as to why each accommodation is recommended. The evaluators should describe the impact the diagnosed learning disability has on a specific major life activity as well as the degree of significance of this impact on the individual. The evaluator should support recommendations with specific test results or clinical observations.

If accommodations are not clearly identified in a diagnostic report, the disability service provider should seek clarification and, if necessary, more information. The final determination for providing appropriate and reasonable accommodations rests with the institution.

In instances where a request for accommodations is denied in a postsecondary institution, a written grievance or appeal procedure should be in place.

V. Confidentiality

The receiving institution has a responsibility to maintain confidentiality of the evaluation and may not release any part of the documentation without the student's informed and written consent.

APPENDIX A:
RECOMMENDATIONS FOR CONSUMERS

1. For assistance in finding a qualified professional:
   • Contact the disability services coordinator at the institution you attend or plan to attend to discuss documentation needs.
   • Discuss your future plans with the disability services coordinator. If additional documentation is required, seek assistance in identifying a qualified professional.
2. In selecting a qualified professional:
   • Ask what his or her credentials are.
   • Ask what experience he or she has had working with adults with learning disabilities.

- Ask if he or she has ever worked with the service provider at your institution or with the agency to which you are sending material.
3. In working with the professional:
   - Take a copy of these guidelines to the professional.
   - Encourage him or her to clarify questions with the person who provided you with these guidelines.
   - Be prepared to be forthcoming, thorough, and honest with requested information.
   - Know that professionals must maintain confidentiality with respect to your records and testing information.
4. As follow-up to the assessment by the professional:
   - Request a written copy of the assessment report.
   - Request the opportunity to discuss the results and recommendations.
   - Request additional resources if you need them.
   - Maintain a personal file of your records and reports.

APPENDIX B:
TESTS FOR ASSESSING ADOLESCENTS AND ADULTS

When selecting a battery of tests, it is critical to consider the technical adequacy of instruments including their reliability, validity, and standardization on an appropriate norm group. The professional judgment of an evaluator in choosing tests is important.

The following list is provided as a helpful resource, but it is not intended to be definitive or exhaustive.

Aptitude

- Wechsler Adult Intelligence Scale—Revised (WAIS-R)
- Woodcock–Johnson Psychoeducational Battery—Revised: Tests of Cognitive Ability
- Kaufman Adolescent and Adult Intelligence Test
- Stanford–Binet Intelligence Scale (4th ed.)

The Slosson Intelligence Test—Revised and the Kaufman Brief Intelligence Test are primarily screening devices which are not comprehensive enough to provide the kinds of information necessary to make accommodation decisions.

Academic Achievement

- Scholastic Abilities Test for Adults (SATA)
- Stanford Test of Academic Skills
- Woodcock–Johnson Psychoeducational Battery—Revised: Tests of Achievement
- Wechsler Individual Achievement Test (WIAT)

Specific achievement tests such as:

- Nelson–Denny Reading Skills Test
- Stanford Diagnostic Mathematics Test
- Test of Written Language—3 (TOWL-3)
- Woodcock Reading Mastery Tests—Revised

Specific achievement tests are useful instruments when administered under standardized conditions and interpreted within the context of other diagnostic information. The Wide Range Achievement Test—3 (WRAT-3) is not a comprehensive measure of achievement and therefore is not useful if used as the sole measure of achievement.

Information Processing

Acceptable instruments include the Detroit Tests of Learning Aptitude—3 (DTLA-3), the Detroit Tests of Learning Aptitude—Adult (DTLA-A), information from subtests on WAIS-R, Woodcock–Johnson Psychoeducational Battery—Revised: Tests of Cognitive Ability, as well as other relevant instruments.

ppendix II

The Consortium Guidelines for Documentation of Attention-Deficit/Hyperactivity Disorder in Adolescents and Adults

The Consortium on ADHD Documentation consists of Loring C. Brinckerhoff (Chairperson), Educational Testing Service; Kim M. Dempsey, Law School Admission Council; Cyndi Jordan, University of Tennessee–Memphis; Shelby R. Keiser, National Board of Medical Examiners; Joan M. McGuire, University of Connecticut–Storrs; Nancy W. Pompian, Dartmouth College; Louise H. Russell, Harvard University.

INTRODUCTION

The Consortium's mission is to develop standard criteria for documenting attention deficit disorders, with or without hyperactivity (ADHD). These guidelines can be used by postsecondary personnel; examining, certifying, and licensing agencies; and consumers who require documentation to determine reasonable and appropriate accommodation(s) for individuals with ADHD. Although the more generic term, "Attention Deficit Disorder" (ADD), is frequently used, the official nomenclature in the *Diagnostic and Statistical Manual of Mental Disorders* (4th ed.) (DSM-IV; American Psychiatric Association, 1994) is "Attention-Deficit/Hyperactivity Disorder" (ADHD), which is used in these guidelines. The guidelines provide consumers, professional diagnosticians, and service providers with a common understanding and knowledge base of the components of documentation which are necessary to validate the existence of ADHD, its impact on the individual's educational performance, and the need for accommodation(s). The information and documentation to be submitted should be comprehensive in order to avoid or reduce unnecessary time delays in decision-making related to the provision of services.

In the main section of the document, the Consortium presents guidelines in four important areas: (1) qualifications of the evaluator, (2) recency of documentation, (3) comprehensiveness of the documentation to substantiate the ADHD, and (4) evidence to establish a rationale to support the need for accommodation(s). Attached to these guidelines are appendices giving diagnostic criteria for ADHD from DSM-IV and providing recommendations for consumers.

Under the Americans with Disabilities Act (ADA) and Section 504 of the Rehabilitation Act of 1973, individuals with disabilities are protected from discrimination and assured services. In order to establish that an individual is covered under the ADA, the documentation must indicate that the disability *substantially limits* some major life activity, including learning. The following documentation guidelines are provided in the interest of assuring that documentation of ADHD demonstrates an impact on a major life activity and supports the request for accommodations, academic adjustments, and/or auxiliary aids.

DOCUMENTATION GUIDELINES

I. A Qualified Professional Must Conduct the Evaluation

Professionals conducting assessments and rendering diagnoses of ADHD must have training in differential diagnosis and the full range of psychiatric disorders. The name, title, and professional credentials of the evaluator, including information about license or certification as well as the area of specialization, employment, and state or province in which the individual practices should be clearly stated in the documentation. The following professionals would generally be considered qualified to evaluate and diagnose ADHD provided they have comprehensive training in the differential diagnosis of ADHD and direct experience with an adolescent or adult ADHD population: clinical psychologists, neuropsychologists, psychiatrists, and other relevantly trained medical doctors. It may be appropriate to use a clinical-team approach consisting of a variety of educational, medical, and counseling professionals with training in the evaluation of ADHD in adolescents and adults.

Use of diagnostic terminology indicating an ADHD by someone whose training and experience are not in these fields is not acceptable. It is also not appropriate for professionals to evaluate members of their own families. All reports should be on letterhead, typed, dated, signed, and otherwise legible. The receiving institution or agency has the responsibility to maintain the confidentiality of the individual's records.

II. Documentation Should Be Current

Because the provision of all reasonable accommodations and services is based upon assessment of the *current* impact of the disability on academic performance, it is in an individual's best interest to provide recent and appropriate documentation. In most cases, this means that a diagnostic evaluation has been completed within the past 3 years. Flexibility in accepting documentation which exceeds a 3-year period may be important under certain conditions, if the previous assessment is applicable to the current or anticipated setting. If documentation is inadequate in scope or content, or does not address the individual's current level of functioning and need for accommodation(s), reevaluation may be warranted. Furthermore, observed changes may have occurred in the individual's performance since previous assessment, or new medication(s) may have been prescribed or discontinued since the previous assessment was conducted. In such cases, it may be necessary to update the evaluation report. The update should include a detailed assessment of the current impact of the ADHD and interpretive summary of relevant information (see Section III, G) and the previous diagnostic report.

III. Documentation Should Be Comprehensive

A. Evidence of Early Impairment

Because ADHD is, by definition, first exhibited in childhood (although it may not have been formally diagnosed) and manifests itself in more than one setting, relevant historical information is essential. The following should be included in a comprehensive assessment: clinical summary of objective, historical information establishing symptomology indicative of ADHD throughout childhood, adolescence, and adulthood as garnered from transcripts, report cards, teacher comments, tutoring evaluations, past psychoeducational testing, and third-party interviews when available.

B. Evidence of Current Impairment

In addition to providing evidence of a childhood history of an impairment, the following areas must be investigated:

1. STATEMENT OF PRESENTING PROBLEM

A history of the individual's presenting attentional symptoms should be provided, including evidence of ongoing impulsive/hyperactive or inattentive behaviors that significantly impair functioning in two or more settings.

2. DIAGNOSTIC INTERVIEW

The information collected for the summary of the diagnostic interview should consist of more than self-report, as information from third-party sources is critical in the diagnosis of ADHD. The diagnostic interview with information from a variety of sources should include, but not necessarily be limited to, the following:

- History of presenting attentional symptoms, including evidence of ongoing impulsive/hyperactive or inattentive behavior that has significantly impaired functioning over time.
- Developmental history.
- Family history for presence of ADHD and other educational, learning, physical, or psychological difficulties deemed relevant by the examiner.
- Relevant medical and medication history, including the absence of a medical basis for the symptoms being evaluated.
- Relevant psychosocial history and any relevant interventions.
- A thorough academic history of elementary, secondary, and postsecondary education.
- Review of prior psychoeducational test reports to determine whether a pattern of strengths or weaknesses is supportive of attention or learning problems.
- Relevant employment history.
- Description of current functional limitations pertaining to an educa-

tional setting that are presumably a direct result of problems with attention.

- Relevant history of prior therapy.

C. Rule Out of Alternative Diagnoses or Explanations

The evaluator must investigate and discuss the possibility of dual diagnoses, and alternative or coexisting mood, behavioral, neurological, and/or personality disorders which may confound the diagnosis of ADHD. This process should include exploration of possible alternative diagnoses and medical and psychiatric disorders as well as educational and cultural factors impacting the individual which may result in behaviors mimicking an Attention-Deficit/Hyperactivity Disorder.

D. Relevant Testing

Neuropsychological or psychoeducational assessment is important in determining the current impact of the disorder on the individual's ability to function in academically related settings. The evaluator should objectively review and include with the evaluation report relevant background information to support the diagnosis. If grade equivalents are reported, they must be accompanied by standard scores and/or percentiles. Test scores or subtest scores alone should not be used as a sole measure for the diagnostic decision regarding ADHD. Selected subtest scores from measures of intellectual ability, memory functions tests, attention or tracking tests, or continuous performance tests do not in and of themselves establish the presence or absence of ADHD. Checklists and/or surveys can serve to supplement the diagnostic profile but in and of themselves are not adequate for the diagnosis of ADHD and do not substitute for clinical observations and sound diagnostic judgment. All data must logically reflect a substantial limitation to learning for which the individual is requesting the accommodation.

E. Identification of DSM-IV Criteria

According to the DSM-IV, "the essential feature of ADHD is a persistent pattern of inattention and/or hyperactivity–impulsivity that is more frequent and severe than is typically observed in individuals at a comparable level of development" (p. 78). A diagnostic report should include a review and discussion of the DSM-IV criteria for ADHD both currently and retrospectively and specify which symptoms are present (these are reprinted in Chapter 5 of this volume).

In diagnosing ADHD, it is particularly important to address the following criteria:

- symptoms of hyperactivity–impulsivity or inattention that cause impairment which must have been present in childhood;
- current symptoms that have been present for at least the past 6 months;
- impairment from the symptoms present in two or more settings (for example, school, work, and home);
- clear evidence of significant impairment in social, academic, or occupational functioning; and
- symptoms which do not occur exclusively during the course of a Pervasive Developmental Disorder, Schizophrenia, or other Psychotic Disorder and are not better accounted for by another mental disorder (e.g., Mood Disorder, Anxiety Disorder, Dissociative Disorder, or a Personality Disorder).

F. Documentation Must Include a Specific Diagnosis

The report must include a specific diagnosis of ADHD based on the DSM-IV diagnostic criteria. The diagnostician should use direct language in the diagnosis of ADHD, avoiding the use of terms such as "suggests," "is indicative of," or "attention problems."

Individuals who report only problems with organization, test anxiety, memory, and concentration in selective situations do not fit the proscribed diagnostic criteria for ADHD. Given that many individuals benefit from prescribed medications and therapies, a positive response to medication by itself does not confirm a diagnosis, nor does the use of medication in and of itself either support or negate the need for accommodation(s).

G. An Interpretative Summary Should Be Provided

A well-written interpretative summary based on a comprehensive evaluative process is a necessary component of the documentation. Because ADHD is in many ways a diagnosis which is based upon the interpretation of historical data and observation, as well as other diagnostic information, it is essential that professional judgment be utilized in the development of a summary, which should include:

1. Demonstration of the evaluator's having ruled out alternative explanations for inattentiveness, impulsivity, and/or hyperactivity as a result of psychological or medical disorders or non-cognitive factors.

2. Indication of how patterns of inattentiveness, impulsivity, and/or hyperactivity across the life span and across settings are used to determine the presence of ADHD.

3. Indication of whether or not the student was evaluated while on medication, and whether or not there is a positive response to the prescribed treatment.

4. Indication and discussion of the substantial limitation to learning presented by the ADHD and the degree to which it impacts the individual in the learning context for which accommodations are being requested.

5. Indication as to why specific accommodations are needed and how the effects of ADHD symptoms, as designated by the DSM-IV, are mediated by the accommodation(s).

IV. Each Accommodation Recommended By the Evaluator Should Include a Rationale

The evaluator(s) should describe the impact, if any, of the diagnosed ADHD on a specific major life activity as well as the degree of impact on the individual. The diagnostic report should include specific recommendations for accommodations that are realistic and that postsecondary institutions, examining, certifying, and licensing agencies can reasonably provide. A detailed explanation should be provided as to why each accommodation is recommended and should be correlated with specific functional limitations determined through interview, observation, and/or testing. Although prior documentation may have been useful in determining appropriate services in the past, current documentation should validate the need for services based on the individual's *present* level of functioning in the educational setting. A school plan such as an Individualized Education Program (IEP) or a 504 plan is insufficient documentation in and of itself but can be included as part of a more comprehensive evaluative report. The documentation should include any record of prior accommodations or auxiliary aids, including information about specific conditions under which the accommodations were used (e.g., standardized testing, final exams, licensing or certification examinations) and whether or not they benefitted the individual. However, a prior history of accommodations, without demonstration of a current need, does not in itself warrant the provision of a like accommodation. If no prior accommodations were provided, the qualified professional and/or the individual should include a detailed explanation as to why no accommodations were used in the past and why accommodations are needed at this time.

Because of the challenge of distinguishing normal behaviors and developmental patterns of adolescents and adults (e.g., procrastination, disorganization, distractibility, restlessness, boredom, academic underachievement or failure, low self-esteem, and chronic tardiness or inattendance) from clinically significant impairment, a multifaceted evaluation should address the intensity and frequency of the symptoms and whether these behaviors constitute an impairment in a major life activity.

Reasonable accommodation(s) may help to ameliorate the disability and to minimize its impact on the student's attention, impulsivity, and distractibility. The determination for reasonable accommodation(s) rests with the designated disability contact person working in collaboration with the individual with the disability and when appropriate, college faculty. The receiving institution or agency has a responsibility to maintain confidentiality of the evaluation and may not release any part of the documentation without the individual's informed consent.

ACKNOWLEDGMENTS

The Consortium wishes to acknowledge the contributions of the following individuals and expresses its appreciation and gratitude for their time invested in reviewing these Guidelines and for their insightful comments: Russell Barkley, PhD, Director of Psychology, University of Massachusetts Medical Center; Michael Gordon, PhD, Professor, Department of Psychiatry, Director, ADHD Program, State University of New York Health Science Center; Mark S. Greenberg, PhD, Neuropsychologist, Department of Psychiatry, Harvard Medical School; Leighton Y. Huey, MD, Department of Psychiatry, Dartmouth Hitchcock Medical Center; Peter S. Jensen, MD, Chief, Developmental Psychopathology Research Branch, National Institute of Mental Health; Lynda Katz, PhD, President, Landmark College; Kevin R. Murphy, PhD, Assistant Professor of Psychiatry, Chief, Adult Attention Deficit Hyperactivity Disorder Clinic, Department of Psychiatry, University of Massachusetts Medical Center; Laura F. Rothstein, JD, Law Foundation Professor of Law, Law Center, University of Houston; Larry B. Silver, MD, Diplomat: General Psychiatry; Child/Adolescent Psychiatry; Marc Wilchesky, PhD, CPsych, Coordinator, Learning Disabilities Program, Counselling and Development Centre, York University; Joan Wolforth, MA, Coordinator, Office for Students with Disabilities, McGill University.

APPENDIX A:
RECOMMENDATIONS FOR CONSUMERS

1. For assistance in finding a qualified professional:
   a. Contact the disability services coordinator at a college or university for possible referral sources.
   b. Contact a physician who may be able to refer you to a qualified professional with demonstrated expertise in ADHD.
2. In selecting a qualified professional:
   a. Ask what experience and training he or she has had diagnosing adolescents and adults.
   b. Ask whether he or she has training in differential diagnosis and the full range of psychiatric disorders. Clinicians typically qualified to diagnose ADHD may include clinical psychologists, physicians, including psychiatrists, and neuropsychologists.
   c. Ask whether he or she has ever worked with a postsecondary disability service provider or with the agency to whom you are providing documentation.
   d. Ask whether you will receive a comprehensive written report.
3. In working with the professional:
   a. Take a copy of these guidelines to the professional.
   b. Be prepared to be forthcoming, thorough, and honest with requested information.
4. As follow-up to the assessment by the professional:
   a. Schedule a meeting to discuss the results, recommendations, and possible treatment.
   b. Request additional resources, support group information, and publications if you need them.
   c. Maintain a personal file of your records and reports.
   d. Be aware that any receiving institution or agency has a responsiblity to maintain confidentiality.

Index